THE
EMPEROR'S
LAST VICTORY

Gunther Rothenberg was the world's leading authority on the Napoleonic Wars. He served with the British, Israeli and US Military, was Professor of History at Purdue University in the US and was also the leading English-speaking historian of warfare in the German-speaking lands. His many distinguished works include *The Army of Francis Joseph*, *The Hapsburg Military Frontier* and *The Napoleonic Wars*.

THE
EMPEROR'S
LAST VICTORY

NAPOLEON AND THE BATTLE OF WAGRAM

Gunther E. Rothenberg

CASSELL

Cassell Military Paperbacks

Cassell
Wellington House, 125 Strand
London WC2R 0BB

1 3 5 7 9 10 8 6 4 2

First published in 2004
by Weidenfeld & Nicolson
This Cassell Military Paperbacks edition 2005

British Library Cataloguing-in-Publication Data.
A catalogue record for this book is available
from the British Library.

ISBN 0 304 36711 7

Printed and bound in Great Britain by
Cox & Wyman Ltd, Reading, Berkshire

www.orionbooks.co.uk

Contents

List of illustrations

List of Maps

Introduction

The Emperor's Last Victory does fitting justice to what is increasingly recognized as a fundamental turning point in the wars of 1792–1815, when Napoleon, although indeed victorious, encountered an army which was not only singularly persistent, but the first to bring divisions and corps into battle in a way which had been a monopoly of the French. The present study is a work of impeccable formal scholarship, as will be recognized by its supporting apparatus of references; it is also the product of a life and of sympathies which were as varied as any to be found in the author's generation.

Gunther Rothenberg's own experience of contrasting active service and contrasting military cultures was crucial to his formation as a military historian. He knew that both the fighting and what lay behind the fighting deserved serious consideration, and he had learned that military operations did not lend themselves to formulae: 'you just do the best you can with the forces at hand'.

His list of published works, his talk and his travels show him to have been a man thoroughly at home in the wider culture of central and eastern Europe, and more specifically the former territories of the Habsburg Empire. Indeed he was once described as 'the Emperor Franz

Joseph's most loyal subject'. He set himself against history as 'an exercise in nostalgia', yet there is affection as well as understanding in what he could write of the cities and little towns where 'still stands the barracks painted in the characteristic Habsburg faded yellow'.

Gunther was an enemy of academic careerism and bureaucracy, and he wrote in a clear and elegant English which is not always to be found among other professional historians on either side of the Atlantic. He was on the editorial board of the leading British historical journal, *War in History*, and lived to see military history accepted into the mainstream of British academic life. He was a frequent contributor to its transatlantic counterpart, the *Journal of Military History*, and his achievement remains a standing reproach to those circles which have sought to deny military history comparable status in America.

It is fair to adapt and apply to Gunther Rothenberg some phrases which are to be found in *The Army of Francis Joseph*, his favourite among his own writings: he 'carried out his mission, did his duty, and remained faithful'.

Christopher Duffy
London, June 2004

Author's preface

WAGRAM IN HISTORY

Other than the Battle of the Nations of October 1813, the Battle of Wagram, fought on 5–6 July 1809, was the largest engagement of the Napoleonic Wars, indeed of the early nineteenth century. Along a front of 14 miles, 300,000 French and Austrian troops supported by almost 1,500 guns clashed for two days. Combined casualties reached 72,000. If perhaps not as brilliant a victory as Austerlitz four years earlier – the Austrian army retired in good order and still combat capable – it was none the less a decisive victory for the French, the last Napoleonic victory to break the enemy's will to continue fighting.

As so often during these wars, promised British support was too little and much too late. None the less, Britain profited from the campaign of 1809 after Napoleon had been compelled to leave Spain hurriedly to take command in Germany. Had he been able to remain on the Peninsula, it is probable the campaign in Spain would have turned out very differently. The emperor might well have broken Spanish resistance and driven Wellington into the sea. Further, had he been able to transfer to central Europe the close-on 300,000 troops he was forced to keep in Spain, it may well have made the difference between victory and defeat in the Russian campaign of 1812.

The 1809 campaign has been called not just a turning point of the Napoleonic Wars but of warfare in general. Robert Epstein has described it as demonstrating the revival of 'symmetry' in European warfare, with the recent introduction of a corps system in the Habsburg Army narrowing, if not eliminating, the gap between the French and Austrians. In turn, this reduced Napoleon's capacity to deliver a decisive stroke and turned Wagram, the climactic battle of the campaign, into a two-day attritional engagement, foreshadowing the emergence of modern war. That said, the degree to which the Austrians had fully absorbed French operational methods by 1809, especially staff organization, remains in doubt.

James R. Arnold, on the other hand, has judged that the principal importance of the campaign was tactical. For him, the decisive factors were the increased weight of artillery fire – at Wagram the artillery of each side fired approximately 95,000 rounds – and the decrease in the effectiveness of battle cavalry, even if it was still useful in screening off breakthroughs and covering withdrawals. Epstein also disputes the notion that the quality of Napoleonic infantry had declined by 1809, and here their grim stand against great odds in an earlier battle of the campaign, at Aspern–Essling, must be added to their performance at Wagram. On both occasions the French and their allied troops alike fought extremely well, the German Confederation of the Rhine forces apparently immune to Austrian appeals to German nationalism.

These arguments, of course, are not mutually contradictory and with some reservations I accept both. There can be little doubt, for example, that Wagram was a forerunner of the operational and tactical developments of the American Civil War and, with modifications, of the Prussian victories in the wars of German unification. However, I place greater emphasis on the personalities and the generalship of the commanders on the two sides. I accept that as head of state and supreme commander Napoleon enjoyed greater flexibility while the Austrian commander, Archduke Charles, was often hampered by the ambivalence and mistrust of his elder brother, the Emperor Francis I, as well as by the interests of the senior officers and military bureaucracy. But Wagram was not simply a case of the Austrians losing the battle: Napoleon definitely won it. At Wagram, Napoleon's genius, his ability to combine detail in his preparations and then his superb battle handling of his corps, themselves led by enterprising commanders, was decisive. On the other hand, while a capable general, Archduke Charles lacked the hunger for victory. He did not use the weeks before the battle to good purpose and he was hesitant and slow in command, a style mirrored by his chief subordinates. As both in earlier and in later wars, with roughly equal numbers and quality of troops, generalship and leadership remained the decisive elements contributing to victory.

A NOTE ON RANKS AND NAMES

The highest rank in the Austrian Army in 1809 was generalissimus (or generalissimo), an ancient title resurrected specifically for Archduke Charles. Otherwise the highest rank was feldmarschall (FM), followed by feldmarschalleutnant, abbreviated as FML, or general der cavallerie (GdC). Below this was general major (GM) or major general, usually the commander of a brigade.

In the French Army the highest rank was marshal, actually an aristocratic title rather than just a military rank, followed by général de division (GD). Both ranks commanded corps, though the generals could also command smaller formations. The lowest general officer was général de brigade (GB). The Confederation of the Rhine ranks were similar with a general leutnant (GL) the equal of a général de division and brigade general (BG) the equivalent of its French counterpart.

Senior officers on both sides were usually members of the nobility, especially in the Confederation of the Rhine; in France, Napoleon had reintroduced noble titles in 1807. However, such titles, though used by Napoleon in addressing his corps commanders, have been largely omitted in the text. Also in the interest of brevity the often extremely long first names have been omitted or shortened in the text but are cited in full in the biographies. Thus, for instance, FML Josef Count Radetzky von Radetz becomes simply FML Josef Radetzky, while GD Count Claude Juste Alexandre Legrand is abbreviated to GD Claude Legrand.

Acknowledgements

My husband, Gunther E. Rothenberg, died after the manuscript had been edited but while the book was still in press. I want to thank Angus MacKinnon, the commissioning editor, and his successor, Ian Drury, for their support of the project, and – above all – Penny Gardiner for her friendship, enthusiasm and understanding. I am grateful to Dr Christopher Duffy for his Introduction, and to all concerned at Weidenfeld and Nicolson for their help. Above all, I wish to thank Professor Frederick C. Schneid of High Point University, Gunther's friend and former student, for his considerable commitment of time and expertise to oversee the completion of the book as a fitting tribute to Gunther as a scholar.

Eleanor Hancock

Author's Acknowledgements

The writing of this book was facilitated by the hospitality and support of the School of History, University College of the University of New South Wales, Australian Defence Force Academy, Canberra. I want to acknowledge the help provided by several of my former students at the University of New Mexico and Purdue University. These include Professors Robert M. Epstein, Frederick C. Schneid, and Lee W. Eysturlid who provided me with encouragement as well as specific data and documentation unavailable in Australia.

Also I wish to acknowledge the patience of the editors at Weidenfeld & Nicolson for their patience in extending the deadline for delivery of the manuscript. Specifically I want to thank Penny Gardiner, my personal editor and friend, whose encouragement made me continue to work when I had reached a dead end and for her painstaking editorial skills that have greatly improved the readability of the book. Finally, last but not least I wish to express my gratitude to my wife, Dr Eleanor Hancock, Senior Lecturer in the School of History at ADFA, who provided the all important daily support. It only remains to say that I remain personally responsible for any errors in the book.

Gunther E. Rothenberg VISITING PROFESSOR UNSW@ADFA

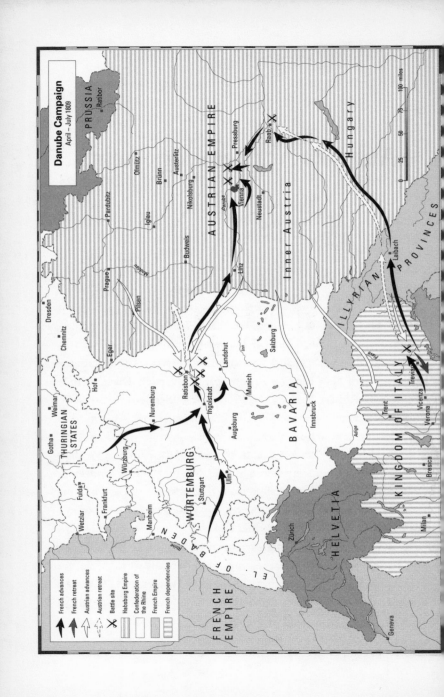

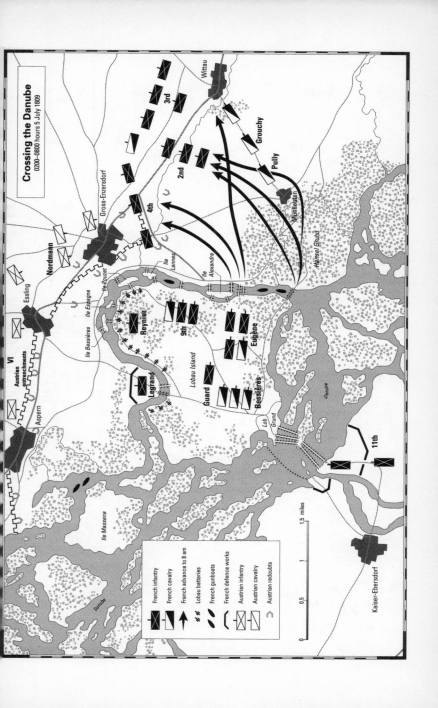

Crossing the Danube
0200–0800 hours 5 July 1809

Wittau

3rd

Grouchy

Pully

2nd

Gross-Enzersdorf

4th

Nordmann

Mühlleiten

Hansel Grund

Essling

Ile Lannes

Ile Bouzet

Ile Alexandre

Ile Espagne

Ile Bessières

Reynier

Austrian entrenchments

9th

VI

Legrand

Lobau Island

Eugène

Guard

Bessières

Aspern

Lob Grund

Danube

11th

Ile Massena

Kaiser-Ebersdorf

Danube

French infantry
French cavalry
French advance to 8 am
Lobau batteries
French gunboats
French defence works
Austrian infantry
Austrian cavalry
Austrian redoubts

0   0.5   1   1.5 miles

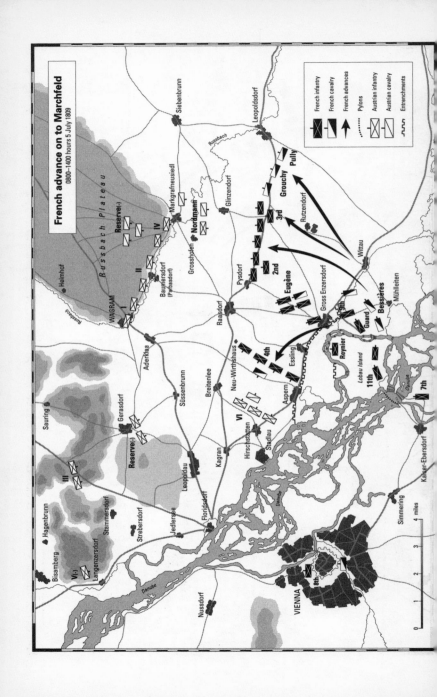

French advance on to Marchfeld
0800–1400 hours 5 July 1809

Key (legend):
- French infantry
- French cavalry
- French advances
- Pylons
- Austrian infantry
- Austrian cavalry
- Entrenchments

Labels on map:

Helmhof

Russbach Plateau

Russbach

Reserve(-)

IV

Markgrafneusiedl

Nordmann

Siebenbrunn

Glinzendorf

Leopoldsdorf

II

Baumersdorf
(Parbasdorf)

Grosshofen

Pysdorf

Pully

Grouchy

3rd

Rutzendorf

WAGRAM

I

Raabdorf

2nd

Eugène

Wittau

Aderklaa

Neu-Wirthshaus

4th

Gross Enzersdorf

5th

Bessières

Mühlleiten

Sauring

Gerasdorf

Süssenbrunn

Breitenlee

Aspern

Essling

Guard

Reynier

Lobau Island

11th

Reserve(-)

Hirschstätten

Shadlau

Kagran

Danube

7th

Kaiser-Ebersdorf

III

Leopoldau

Floridsdorf

VI

Nussdorf

Simmering

Jedlersee

Strebersdorf

Stammersdorf

Hagenbrunn

Bisamberg

V(-)

Langenzersdorf

VIENNA

8th

Danube

4 miles

3   2   1

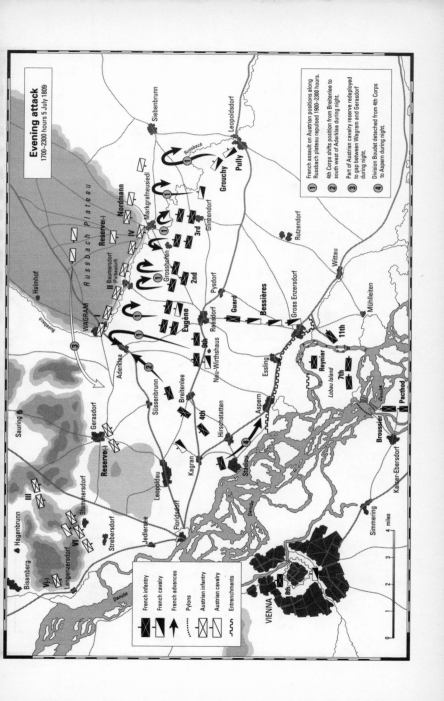

Evening attack
1700–2300 hours 5 July 1809

1. French assault on Austrian positions along Russbach plateau repulsed 1900–2300 hours.

2. 4th Corps shifts position from Breitenlee to south west of Aderklaa during night.

3. Part of Austrian cavalry reserve redeployed to gap between Wagram and Gerasdorf during night.

4. Division Boudet detached from 4th Corps to Aspern during night.

French infantry
French cavalry
French advances
Pylons
Austrian infantry
Austrian cavalry
Entrenchments

Siebenbrunn

Leopoldsdorf

Russbach

Pully

Grouchy

Glinzendorf

Nordmann

Reserve(-)

Markgrafneusiedl

IV

3rd

Rutzendorf

Wittau

II Baumersdorf
(Pfeilsdorf)

Grosshofen

2nd

Pysdorf

Mühlleiten

Russbach

WAGRAM

Eugène

Rössdorf

Guard

Gross Enzersdorf

Bessières

Helmhof

Aderklaa

9th

Neu-Wirthshaus

Essling

Reynier

11th

Sauring

Süssenbrunn

Breitenlee

4th

Hirschstätten

Aspern

Lobau Island

7th

Danube

Pacthod

Gerasdorf

Kagran

Broussier

III

Hagenbrunn

Stammersdorf

Reserve(-)

Leopoldau

Kaiser-Ebersdorf

Bisamberg

VI

Strebersdorf

Jedlersee

Floridsdorf

Stadlau

Simmering

Langenzersdorf

V(-)

Danube

VIENNA

8th

0   1   2   3   4 miles

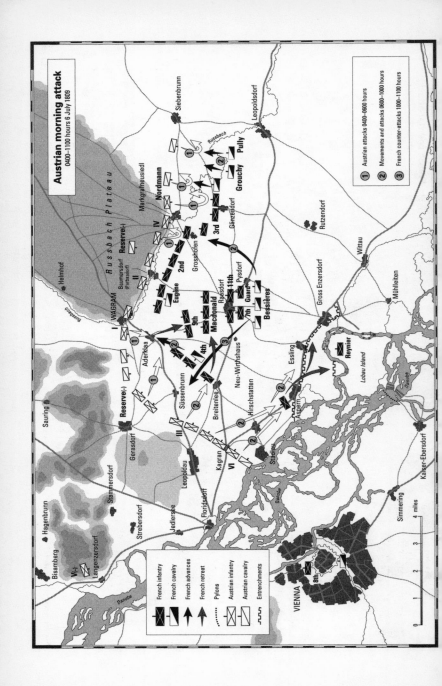

Austrian morning attack
0400–1100 hours 6 July 1809

① Austrian attacks 0400–0600 hours
② Movements and attacks 0600–1000 hours
③ French counter-attacks 1000–1100 hours

French infantry
French cavalry
French advances
French retreat
Pylons
Austrian infantry
Austrian cavalry
Entrenchments

Russbach Plateau

Siebenbrunn
Leopoldsdorf
Russbach
Pully
Grouchy
Nordmann
Markgrafneusiedl
Reserve(-)
IV
3rd
Glinzendorf
Rutzendorf
Wittau
Grosshofen
2nd
Eugène
Baumersdorf (Pebaslin)
II
WAGRAM
I
Macdonald
9th
Raasdorf
11th Pysdorf
7th Guard
Bessières
Mühlleiten
Gross Enzersdorf
AderKlaa
4th
Reserve(-)
Süssenbrunn
Neu-Wirthshaus
Reynier
Heinilof
Breitenlee
Essling
Lobau Island
Sauring
Gerasdorf
III
Kagran
VI
Hirschstatten
Aspern
Stadlau
Kaiser-Ebersdorf
Stammersdorf
Strebersdorf
Leopoldau
Floridsdorf
Jedlersee
Simmering
Danube
Hagenbrunn
Bisamberg
Langenzersdorf
V(-)
Danube
VIENNA
8th

0   1   2   3   4 miles

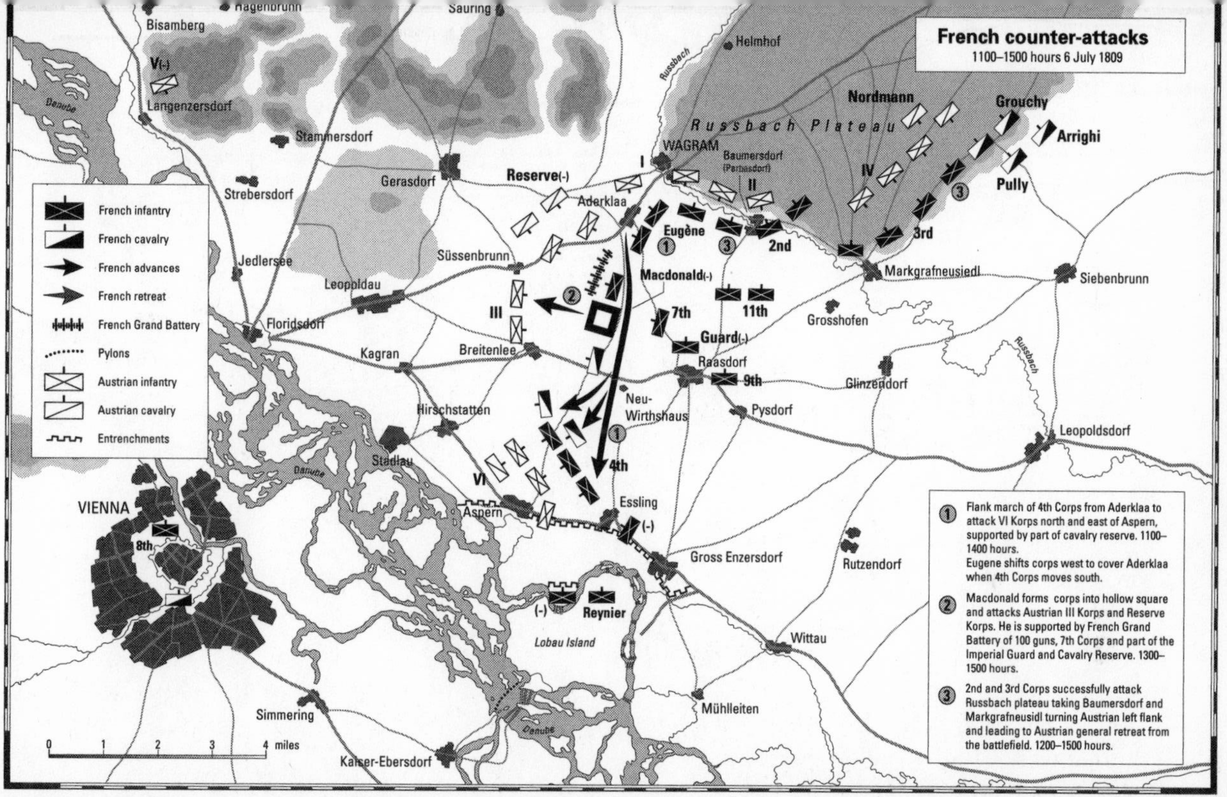
French counter-attacks
1100–1500 hours 6 July 1809
French infantry
French cavalry
French advances
French retreat
French Grand Battery
Pylons
Austrian infantry
Austrian cavalry
Entrenchments
Bisamberg
Sauring
Helmhof
Russbach
V(-)
Langenzersdorf
Danube
Stammersdorf
Gerasdorf
Strebersdorf
Reserve(-)
WAGRAM
I
Baumersdorf
(Parbasdorf)
II
Russbach Plateau
Nordmann
IV
Grouchy
Arrighi
Pully
3rd
2nd
Eugène
Aderklaa
Süssenbrunn
Jedlersee
Leopoldau
Floridsdorf
III
Macdonald(-)
7th
11th
Markgrafneusiedl
Siebenbrunn
Grosshofen
Guard(-)
Kagran
Breitenlee
Raasdorf
9th
Glinzendorf
Hirschstatten
Neu-Wirthshaus
Pysdorf
Leopoldsdorf
Stadlau
VI
4th
VIENNA
8th
Aspern
Essling
(-)
Gross Enzersdorf
Rutzendorf
Reynier
Lobau Island
Wittau
Simmering
Mühlleiten
0 1 2 3 4 miles
Kaiser-Ebersdorf
1 Flank march of 4th Corps from Aderklaa to attack VI Korps north and east of Aspern, supported by part of cavalry reserve. 1100–1400 hours.
Eugene shifts corps west to cover Aderklaa when 4th Corps moves south.
2 Macdonald forms corps into hollow square and attacks Austrian III Korps and Reserve Korps. He is supported by French Grand Battery of 100 guns, 7th Corps and part of the Imperial Guard and Cavalry Reserve. 1300–1500 hours.
3 2nd and 3rd Corps successfully attack Russbach plateau taking Baumersdorf and Markgrafneusidl turning Austrian left flank and leading to Austrian general retreat from the battlefield. 1200–1500 hours.

GUNTHER ERICH ROTHENBERG

11 July 1923 – 26 April 2004

Gunther Erich Rothenberg was born in Berlin on 11 July 1923, the second son of Erich and Lotte Rothenberg, née Cohn. His father was an export merchant and a German Army officer. Gunther inherited Prussian values of duty and service to the state from his family, which was highly educated and assimilated, with links to the civil and military service for over a century. With the coming to power of National Socialism when he was almost 10 Gunther's life changed from one of affluence to one of insecurity. Because of the worsening conditions for German Jews after 1933, Gunther and his mother left for the Netherlands in 1936–7, where they were later joined by his father. Gunther attended boarding school in England in 1937–8, before leaving for Palestine in 1939. He joined Haschomer Hazair and was active after his arrival in Palestine in several youth groups and in the Haganah.

In 1941 Gunther Rothenberg joined the British Army, rising to the rank of sergeant. Determined to play his part in the defeat of Nazism, he transferred from the Royal Army Service Corps to the Infantry and finally the Intelligence Corps and fought with the Eighth Army in Egypt, Italy, and Austria. Gunther saw action behind German lines in the desert and undertook a number of missions to link up with partisan groups in the Adriatic. His decorations by war's end included the Distinguished Conduct Medal and the Medal of Merit.

After serving in the British occupation of Austria, he was employed by US Intelligence as a civilian in Austria from 1946 to 1948, before returning to Palestine. There he joined the Palmach and fought in the War of Independence, rising to the rank of Captain in the Haganah, later the Israeli Defence Force.

In 1948–9 he migrated via Canada to the United States, to join his widowed mother. (His parents emigrated from the Netherlands to the United States in 1941.) Gunther enlisted in the US Army and then the US Air Force, fighting in the Korean War, and serving until 1955.

As a child Gunther had the ambition of becoming a professor of military history. Though he never finished high school, he graduated with a BA from the University of Illinois in 1954 while still in the USAF. He completed his MA at the University of Chicago in 1956 and his PhD in 1958 from the University of Illinois, and began what was to become an illustrious career. After four years teaching at Southern Illinois University, Carbondale, he was a member of the faculty of the University of New Mexico, Albuquerque, for ten years, rising to full professor. In 1973 he moved to Purdue University, where he spent the rest of his American academic career until May 1999. In 1985 Gunther was a Visiting Fulbright Fellow in the Department of History in the Faculty of Military Studies at RMC Duntroon. In 1999 Gunther retired from Purdue to settle permanently in Australia. From 1995 to 2001 he was a Visiting Fellow at the School of Historical Studies, Monash University. From July 2001 until his death, he was Visiting Professorial Fellow in the School of History at the University of New South Wales at the Australian Defence Force Academy. Gunther died in Canberra on Monday 26 April 2004, aged 80.

As a teacher and mentor Gunther excelled. In lectures – whether to undergraduates, graduates, or at the many staff colleges where he taught – Gunther was the consummate showman. He loved to talk, with the result that his classes were animated theatrical performances, entertaining, but suffused with a deep understanding of and love for history. He also loved his students, and for those whom he supervised as graduate students he had a special and enduring regard. They were 'his boys': a stern taskmaster, Gunther guided and nurtured them in their studies and subsequent careers, and in return they held him in a mixture of awe and deep affection. This was demonstrated in February this year, when Gunther was Guest of Honour at a meeting of the Consortium on Revolutionary Europe held in High Point, North Carolina. It was a very public way for many of his former graduate students to show the great esteem in which they held him. One of them wrote on hearing of Gunther's death: 'He was tough on the outside, and yet we, "his boys", knew the gentleness and kindness within. Our standard joke was, to paraphrase Kipling, "We'd rather be kicked by him than knighted by the Queen of England".' As a mentor, he transcended the role of professor by setting an example of what a historian can be, and providing the guidance for students to get there.

In addition to a full and extensive teaching load, and continuing participation in military education, Gunther quickly became one of the world's leading authorities on Austrian and Napoleonic military history. He was 'the father of the modern history of the Austrian military border' in Croatia, publishing *The Austrian Military Border in Croatia, 1522–1747* (1960) and *The Military Border in Croatia, 1740–1882* (1966). Then he turned to the study of the Austrian Army itself: *The Army of Francis Joseph, 1815–1918*, which he himself considered to be his best book, appeared in 1976. His article 'Moltke the Elder, Schlieffen and the Theory and Practice of Strategic Envelopment', which appeared in *Makers of Modern Strategy* in 1986, is one of the best analyses of the two commanders, and is read in universities and in armed forces' schools and colleges throughout the world.

In the 1970s he also established himself as an international Napoleonic scholar with *The Art of Warfare in the Age of Napoleon* in 1977. This is one of the authoritative works in the field, and regularly appears on course reading lists worldwide. It was followed by *Napoleon's Great Adversaries: the Archduke Charles and the Austrian Army, 1792–1814* (1982) and *The Napoleonic Wars* (1999). At the time of his death he was putting the finishing touches to this study of the Battle of Wagram.

Gunther was an extremely vital personality, with a wry sense of humour, who impressed all who met him. An adventurous and varied life gave him a deep understanding of human nature. Yet at the same time he was a very private person. He was guided by a deep sense of duty, which arose from his Prussian background. He had a strong sense of American patriotism, fuelled in part by his gratitude to the United States for having provided him a home and unlimited opportunity. He was also guided by devotion to Judaism, to the future of Israel and the survival of the Jewish people. Gunther died on the anniversary in the Jewish calendar of Israel's Day of Independence, the day for which he had fought as a soldier.

Gunther was married to Eugenia (Jean) Jaeger from 1952 to 1967. After their divorce, he married Ruth Gillah (Joy May) Smith in 1969, and brought up her children from her first marriage, Judith Goris (née Herron), Laura Allman (née Herron) and Georgia Jones (née Herron), as his own. Ruth died tragically in 1992. Gunther married Eleanor Hancock in Melbourne in April 1995.

CHAPTER ONE

The War of 1809

THE COMING OF THE WAR

Although the Austrian Habsburg rulers had always been reluctant to entrust the fate of their monarchy to the fortunes of war, from 1792 onward their army provided the largest force in the three coalitions raised against the armies of the French Revolution and Napoleon, carrying the main burden of fighting on land. Yet though defeated three times in a row – in 1797, 1802 and 1805 – on each occasion Austria was able to recover and fight again.[1] Each war cost the Habsburg monarchy territory and population and further damaged its weak treasury, but its defeat in 1805, above all its rout at Austerlitz in December that year, following a campaign of only three months during which its military establishment, as well as that of its Russian ally, was revealed as incompetent, was the most galling. Under the subsequent Treaty of Pressburg of 26 December 1805, the monarchy forfeited its last possessions in Italy – Venetia, Istria and Dalmatia – to Napoleon's Kingdom of Italy, and was forced to accord royal status to Napoleon's south German allies, the rulers of Bavaria and Württemberg. In addition Bavaria was awarded the Tyrol and Vorarlberg. Altogether the Emperor

Francis lost over 2.5 million of his 24 million subjects and one-sixth of his revenues. Austria also had to pay a war indemnity of 40 million francs.

To reinforce his control of Germany, Napoleon turned it into a puppet state, the sixteen-member Confederation of the Rhine, the Rheinbund. It consisted of the major French satellites in Germany – Bavaria, Württemberg and Baden – as well as most of the lesser German principalities in west and south Germany. Napoleon took the title of Protector of the Confederation. In 1807, Saxony was also made a member of the Confederation, and its ruler elevated to royal status. All members of the Confederation were obliged to introduce conscription and reorganize their forces on the French pattern as well as to furnish substantial contingents – 70,000 men in all – for Napoleon's armies when required. Its creation also marked the effective end of the Holy Roman Empire. Under pressure from Napoleon, on 6 August 1806 the last Holy Roman Emperor, Francis II, from 1804 also the self-proclaimed Emperor Francis I of Austria, resigned the venerable crown of the Holy Roman Empire.

Hardly surprisingly, the Treaty of Pressburg was bitterly resented in Vienna's governing circles. By 1808 a war faction had formed, determined to avenge the defeats of Ulm and Austerlitz at the earliest opportunity. It included the beautiful young empress, Maria Ludovica, the foreign minister, Philip von Stadion, Archdukes Ferdinand and John and a substantial number of senior officers and officials. They were supported by a cheering section of German exiles in Austria – Heinrich von Stein, Friedrich von Gentz and others – who loudly claimed that if Austria struck at France, the Germans would rise in large numbers to regain their freedom. Even Archduke Charles, the emperor's brother, otherwise deeply cautious about Austria's military potential, recognized the necessity of renewing the war, though only once a major overhaul of the Austrian military establishment had been put in hand. Yet even Charles drew the line at the kind of parallel reforms of state and society that would be needed if Austria were to match France militarily. Popular mobilization and the creation of an offensive strategic culture on the French model, which aimed at the rapid annihilation of the enemy, were anathema to all Austrians, not just the most obviously reactionary. This was not merely a matter of instinct, ingrained though it was. The complex political system of the multi-national Austrian empire required the kind of delicate balancing that discouraged fundamental change. To the extent that Charles was a reformer at all, it was in the spirit of the Enlightenment rather than that of the aggressively modernizing Napoleon. As has been observed by Peter Paret, 'A service whose most influential reformer was a conservative contending against soundly entrenched reactionaries could never become fully reconciled to the techniques and activity demanded of modern war'.[2]

EMPEROR FRANCIS AND ARCHDUKE CHARLES

Archduke Charles's cautious strategic concepts, as well as his differences with his imperial brother, dated back to the War of the First Coalition of 1792–7. Having rapidly risen to command in south Germany, in 1796 the young Charles had managed to divide and then defeat two French armies, Jourdan's and Moreau's, which had penetrated deep into Germany, driving them back across the Rhine.

Widely acclaimed as the 'saviour of Germany', the following year he was hastily appointed to stabilize the southern front where the army of General Bonaparte was moving into Styria to menace Vienna. After visiting Vienna, where much to the emperor's annoyance he urged peace, Charles arrived at the front in early March 1797. Here he found that his troops had lost the will to fight. 'Neither pleas, nor rewards, nor threats,' Charles wrote to Francis, 'were of any use to halt the fleeing rabble.' He warned that he could not hold even the best positions with such 'infamous troops' and that 'if this army is defeated, there is no salvation'.[3] Only peace, he concluded, could save the Habsburg monarchy. Neither then nor later would Charles stake everything on a decisive battle. As Carl von Clausewitz, the great Prussian commentator on war, observed, the archduke lacked 'enterprise and the hunger for victory'.[4] As always, his objective was to preserve the army, for Charles the ultimate guarantor of the Habsburg dynasty.

On 8 April 1797 French forward elements entered Leoben in Styria, only three days' march from Vienna. The day before, Vienna had proposed a five-day truce. This was agreed on the 18th. Peace negotiations duly followed. Charles, however, was ordered to return to his command in Germany and not to leave his headquarters without express permission. Like all Habsburg emperors since the days of Wallenstein, Francis was suspicious of the political ambitions of his senior commanders; further, after the 1797 campaign he resented the archduke's fame. Charles may have been a cautious strategist, haunted, even overawed by Bonaparte, but, subjected to constant political interference, his efforts to reform the Austrian Army, just as much as his command in the field, were hampered from the start.[5] The emperor remained determined to deny Charles political influence and was frequently swayed by advisors averse to the fundamental reforms proposed by the archduke. In 1797, he therefore sent his personal representative, MG Merveldt, to negotiate with the French. Under the subsequent Treaty of Campo Formio, agreed in October, Austria ceded the Austrian Netherlands and Lombardy to France, accepted French rule on the left bank of the Rhine and recognized the French satellite republics in Italy. In return, Austria received Venice and its mainland territory.

The Treaty of Campo Formio lasted only eighteen months. Great Britain had never been party to it and in the spring of 1799, managed to form a Second Coalition comprising itself, the Ottoman Empire, Naples, Russia and Austria. But it was a tenuous alliance at best. The war aims of the participants were at odds, and the Russian Army, the only considerable land force, was geographically remote. Furthermore there were justified doubts about the stability of Tsar Paul I. Austria hesitated to declare itself openly. In the end, worried by intelligence about the alliances and disturbed by Austrian and Russian troop movements, France moved first. French troops crossed the Rhine on 1 March 1799 and a formal declaration of war followed on the 17th.

Initially, with Napoleon absent in Egypt, the Second Coalition was victorious. Austrian and Russian armies were successful in Italy and Germany. In Germany, where Charles had been given command, the French were driven back to the Rhine. Once again, however, he was troubled by political interference from Vienna. After a short leave to restore his always precarious health – the archduke was epileptic – intriguing in Vienna saw him replaced by Archduke Joseph, the palatine of Hungary, but before this could be done Charles recovered and requested to retain his position.[6] On 4 May, Francis replied that he had decided to retain him as commander, but also ordered that his chief-of-staff should make a daily report, 'of all events, troop movements, etc.' to Vienna.[7] Clearly, relations between the brothers had not improved. Equally clearly, this tension was again among the major causes of the Austrian military failures that followed.

Charles, always sensitive and suspicious and now not consulted on major troop dispositions and grand strategy, achieved little in the summer and autumn of that year, failing to destroy the weaker French armies facing him, his attempts to cooperate with the Russian corps continually hampered by interference from Vienna. In the end, the offended Russians withdrew from the war, while in October Charles, at the end of his nervous energy, requested his brother to relieve him, claiming that, 'I shall be sick if I am forced to continue soldiering'.[8] But Francis delayed naming a successor until March 1800, by which point the strategic situation had changed drastically. Napoleon had returned from Egypt and in November had led the overthrow of a weak and corrupt French government. In December 1799, with the title of first consul, he had become the head of a new regime. Under his direction, the French crossed the Alps in May the following year and defeated the Austrian army in Italy at Marengo, forcing it to retreat into Venetia. In December, a second French offensive under Moreau defeated the Austrians in southern Germany. Vienna was compelled to accept an armistice and in February 1801 to agree peace terms at Lunéville, confirming the Treaty of Campo Formio.

Defeat again demonstrated the shortcomings of the Austrian military system. Charles, his reputation intact, was entrusted with extensive powers to implement reform.[9] Again, he at once ran up against opposition. By necessity his plans involved political as well as military matters, precisely what the emperor and his advisors had long sought to prevent.

Therefore, at the very moment Napoleon was creating an even more efficient military establishment in France – his authority clearly enhanced by his self-coronation as emperor in 1804 – Charles's attempts to do the same in Austria were being persistently undermined. In 1804, after the Emperor Francis had concluded alliances with Russia and Great Britain, both of which Charles opposed, the archduke's position was further weakened with the appointment of the incompetent General Mack as the *de facto* commander of the main Austrian army, now poised to invade Bavaria. Charles was left in command only of a weak and ill-supplied army in Italy.

The War of the Third Coalition proved another disaster for Austria. Mack's advance into Bavaria in September 1805 ended with his army being surrounded and cut off from the slowly moving Russians at Ulm in October. Before the month was over, he was forced to capitulate. Napoleon entered Vienna and pursued the combined Austro-Russians into Moravia where, on 2 December 1805, he destroyed them at Austerlitz. The battle ended the war and forced the emperor into the humiliations of the Treaty of Pressburg (see above).

In 1806, with Mack disgraced, the Emperor Francis reluctantly authorized Charles, who had escaped involvement in the debacle of Austerlitz, to resume his military reforms. Once again, there were differences between the Austrian emperor, egged on by advisors anxious to renew the fight with France, and his brother.[10] Charles was convinced that a long period of peace was required to repair the damages of repeated defeat and to reform the army; he also maintained that little trust could be placed in an alliance with Great Britain. As early as 1804 he had submitted a memorandum pointing out that Britain was unlikely to commit a powerful land force on the continent and that, 'Apart from

Marlborough no Englishman has ever believed that control of the seas could be achieved by fighting on the Danube'.[11]

But by 1808 it was clear that the war party in Vienna would prevail. In 1806 Napoleon had further extended his conquests in central Europe, destroying the Prussians at Jena and Auerstädt. The following summer, he had met Tsar Alexander I at Tilsit on the Baltic. Between them, they redrew the political map of central and eastern Europe. Prussia was stripped of its western lands, which passed to Napoleon's Confederation of the Rhine, while its holdings in Poland were re-created as a further French client state, the Grand Duchy of Warsaw. Russia gained a small area of Poland, around Belostok. The Tsar also reluctantly (and secretly) agreed to join Napoleon's attempted economic blockade of Great Britain, the Continental System, an attempt to shut down all continental commerce with Britain. Napoleon now stood at the zenith of his power, dominating Europe from the Pyrenees to the Russian frontier. Only Britain remained defiant.

Implementing the Continental System taxed even Napoleon, however. In the end, Russia's refusal to agree to it would prove his downfall. But for now, the problem was Portugal, a long-standing ally and trading partner of Britain. In October 1807 Napoleon had bullied the weak and divided Spanish government into allowing a French army to cross its territory to occupy Lisbon. With French troops already in Spain, the temptation to add the country to his burgeoning list of conquests was irresistible. As further French troops poured into Spain, in May 1808 Napoleon installed his brother Joseph on the Spanish throne, unceremoniously deposing King Carlos IV. Spain may have been backward in most respects, but it remained a land of fierce if quixotic patriotism. By the summer much of the country had broken into active revolt against the French invaders. Almost at once, Britain intervened, seeing the Spanish uprising as the opportunity it had long sought to deploy its land forces against Napoleon.

The dismay which the fall of yet another of Europe's monarchs generated in Austria naturally strengthened the demands of the war faction. Even Charles, though conscious that his reforms of the army were far from complete, accepted that war was inevitable, not least as the cost to Austria of maintaining its enlarged army was becoming unsustainable. In June 1808, he reluctantly agreed to the establishment of the *Landwehr*, a militia organization championed by Archduke John, this despite initially dismissing it as politically unreliable and militarily useless. It would, he argued, create the illusion that Austria disposed '... of large forces and [would] induce a false sense of security'. None the less, the *Landwehr* was to enrol all males between the ages of 18 and 45 in Bohemia and the hereditary Habsburg lands, in essence the German-speaking areas. Hungary, however, refused to participate, while in Galicia, where the Poles were suspected of sympathy with Napoleon, the measure was not introduced at all. In theory, 250,000 men would be raised, though in the event this number was never reached. The *Landwehr* was to be divided into 'normal' and volunteer units, administered by three directorates each headed by a member of the imperial family. Bohemia was assigned to Archduke Ferdinand d'Este; Upper and Lower Austria to Maximilian d'Este; and Inner Austria to Archduke John. Its combat capabilities were dubious. Described as 'sedentary troops' and originally limited to the defence of its home province, their equipment and training remained indifferent and their arms constituted a mix of outdated muskets. Commanded and trained by officers recalled from the retired list, the *Landwehr* was to train on Sundays and attend an annual three-week camp. Except for picked 'volunteer' units the bulk of the force showed little fighting spirit.

THE DECISION FOR WAR

Despite the growing risk of further war with Austria, evident among much else from the overtures it was making to Prussia and Britain to form a further coalition, Napoleon determined to deal first with Spain. After meeting Tsar Alexander at Erfurt in September, where he was promised that Russia would keep Austria in check, he transferred 200,000 men of his Grande Armée from Germany to Spain, where in

November he assumed personal command. The Imperial Guard, three corps from Germany, together with two Italian, one Polish and one German division, raised the Army of Spain to 305,0000 men. These rapidly defeated the remaining Spanish regulars and scattered the irregulars. In December, Napoleon entered Madrid. But on 17 January 1809, worried about reports from Paris and Vienna, Napoleon left Spain and returned to Paris on the 23rd to take command of the French and allied forces in Germany to meet the Austrian threat.

In fact the Austrians had now already formally decided to commit themselves to a further war at a conference held on the night of 23 December (and reaffirmed by a Crown Council on 8 February 1809). In part, the decision stemmed from the recommendations of Prince Metternich, the Austrian ambassador in Paris. Napoleon, claimed Metternich, had lost the support of the French population, was overstretched in Spain and would be able to muster no more than 206,000 men for a further Austrian campaign, 78,000 of them unreliable German troops from the Confederation of the Rhine and 21,000 of them equally unreliable Polish troops from the Duchy of Warsaw. He also asserted that Russia, a nominal French ally, would remain neutral. With Austria able to call on an army 400,000 strong, its position seemed unassailable. As events would show, he was right only about Russia.

The initial preparations for the war did little to inspire confidence. For one thing, despite accepting the position of supreme commander of all Austria's field armies on 12 February, Archduke Charles was a great deal less than sanguine about Austria's prospects of defeating Napoleon. Later, he would claim that he had not supported the decision to go to war.[12] Preparations on the diplomatic front were equally discouraging. Though reports of Russian troop concentrations on the Galician frontiers were rightly discounted, in March, thoroughly cowed by Napoleon, Prussia repudiated a provisional undertaking for an alliance with Austria. Only Britain, which had promised financial support and a diversionary effort in north Germany, held out much prospect of genuine help.

None the less, in February the field army, 283,000 strong, was activated. At the same time a corps structure was hastily introduced and the eight-corps strong main force assembled in north-west Bohemia to strike into the Main region. Charles, however, hesitated, concerned that his army was not combat ready and that logistics would be difficult to maintain. In mid March, he switched his main axis of advance from Bohemia to the Danube in order to protect Vienna. It was a change that improved neither the condition of the army nor its strategic position. It created wastage of men and horses, while the delay proved costly, perhaps fatal, allowing the French and their German allies to reinforce and consolidate their forces. When the Austrian army finally opened hostilities by crossing the Bavarian frontier on 10 April, Charles had very little confidence in a successful outcome.[13] It was scarcely an ideal frame of mind in which to launch a war against the greatest military power in Europe.

CHAPTER TWO

The contending armies

THE ANATOMY OF THE HABSBURG ARMY

Embroidered by patriotic legend, the war of 1809 occupies an honoured place in Austrian military history. Yet it was undertaken on the basis of false strategic assumptions and with an army still far from fully combat capable. Soon after the final decision for war had been made on 8 February, its commander, Generalissimus Archduke Charles, had lost what little confidence he had in the campaign, telling General von Heldenfeld, his chief-of-staff, that, 'I did not vote for war; let those who did assume responsibility'.[1] The archduke had good reason to worry about the state of his army. He had made substantial reforms, but despite promises made in 1806 when he had been appointed the emperor's chief military advisor for a second time as well as generalissimus, he rarely had a free hand to implement his reforms. His brother, the Emperor Francis, and his faction at court – as well as the various other archdukes, the military bureaucracy embodied in the Hofkriegsrat and a number of reactionary senior officers – had constantly interfered with his plans, frequently obstructing them. Disliking his brother, easily taken in and always suspicious, in March 1808 the emperor had gone so far as to set a number of officials to spy on the archduke. In this climate of intrigue and suspicion, it was hardly to be wondered at that the Austrian army should have entered the campaign in disarray.

CHARLES'S THEORIES ON
STRATEGY AND GRAND TACTICS

It was the absence of a common up-to-date strategic doctrine, so Archduke Charles believed, that had largely contributed to the dismal performance of Austria's senior commanders in the catastrophic campaign against Napoleon in 1805. In an attempt to put right these shortcomings, in 1806 he published a manual, *The Fundamentals of the Higher Art of War for the Generals of the Austrian Army.*[2] Though it contained some new ideas, overall it remained faithful to the formal traditions of eighteenth-century warfare. In essence, the manual continued the essentially defensive strategic culture of the Habsburg army, which was concerned above all with preserving the army intact so as not to risk the collapse of the state. The manual opened with the statement that 'war was the greatest calamity that can befall a state', and continued with the assertion that there existed permanent strategic laws based on 'irrefutable mathematical verities'. Above all these included calculation of 'the means to achieve a desired objective'. The manual declared that 'equal forces can never achieve a decisive result', and, breaking with the cordon system, claimed that 'the real art of war is how to concentrate superior numbers at the decisive point'. On the other hand, it also warned commanders against exposing their lines of communications, stating that, 'Security of the lines of communications remains a basic necessity'. The old Austrian fighting system, the *Generalsreglement*, dating back to Maria Theresa in 1769, held that each general had his assigned place in battle, his duties rigidly circumscribed by precise orders. The archduke's manual did not change this. It said nothing about the responsibilities and the initiative expected of senior commanders; similarly, the emphasis on careful planning and supply and the alignment of large formations in battle tended to check individual enterprise. On the other hand, as Charles admitted later, Austria's senior commanders, who had grown up with the old system, were in any case not inclined or even able to adapt to a new style of warfare. Writing a remarkably honest account of his activities before and during the 1809 campaign, the archduke noted that there had been too little time for reforms to be completed and that most senior commanders favoured delaying the start of the campaign.[3] In addition, the disastrous financial position of the state had prohibited any large-scale manoeuvres during the period 1806–9. When, with war now inevitable, corps formations were hastily introduced in February 1809, their commanders had no experience in handling large combined arms formations and were largely reliant on staff officers who themselves lacked training and experience.

Charles also oversaw the publication of a series of teaching manuals elaborating tactical doctrines, entitled *Contributions for the Practical Instructions of Officers of the Austrian Army*. In all there would be eight, the first appearing in 1806 and the fifth in 1808. The remaining four were published after 1809. The series reflected the pronounced formalism of his strategic thinking, stressing linear closed-order formations. But again, two years of reform were too short to change the fighting culture of an army. Charles realized that while the Austrian Army of 1809 was much improved, it was still not equal to the French.[4] As he wrote in a memorandum after the war: 'Just before the outbreak of hostilities there were three important innovations in the army: the establishment of the *Landwehr*, the formation of independent all-arms corps, and the reorganization of the field artillery. But there was not enough time for these innovations to become firmly established and they had to be used before they had been tested.'[5]

To add to these shortcomings, there were question marks over Archduke Charles himself. Delbrück, the great Prussian historian, observed that the Austrian leadership in 1809, 'overestimated the capabilities of the man whom they placed in command'.[6] If this sounds a harsh judgment on the man who was clearly the most able Austrian general of the period, it was none the less borne out by the initial phases of the war of 1809. Furthermore, conscious of his dynastic standing and dignity, he was aloof not only from his troops but even from his senior commanders, sharing his proposed strategic moves only with his chief-of-staff and more often with his confidant, the first adjutant general, Friedrich Grünne. In fact, the adjutant general came to control access to the commander-in-chief, much to the annoyance of his corps commanders, themselves still selected by seniority and birth rather than by experience and merit.[7] As Charles realized, almost of these men were products of the Theresian army and the wars against the Turks and had neither the intellectual capacity nor the imagination to break the bonds of their own experience and assume their new responsibilities under the corps system.[8]

In March 1809 GdC Archduke John, 29 years old and with very little experience, commanded the two-corps Army of Inner Austria. Archduke Ferdinand d'Este, the emperor's 29-year-old brother-in-law and a competent officer, commanded VII Corps in Galicia, and Archduke Ludwig led V Corps but was relieved after Aspern–Essling though he returned 'at the general disposition' before Wagram. I Corps was under GdC Count Bellegarde, 53 years old and a learned soldier, if lacking enterprise, who had served with Charles in 1796. A Bohemian aristocrat, FZM Count Kolowrat-Krakowsky, 61 years old, commanded II Corps; FML Prince Hohenzollern-Hechingen, aged 52 and considered a competent soldier, led III Corps. FML Prince Rosenberg-Orsini was in charge of IV Corps, while GdC Prince Liechtenstein, highly regarded by Charles, commanded the Reserve Cavalry, and FML Baron Kienmayer, another steady officer, led II Reserve Corps. The only corps commander not of noble birth was FML Johann Baron Hiller of VI Corps, an able soldier but given to temperamental excesses. His relations with Archduke Charles were already tense. When commander of the Karlstadt Militär Grenze (Military Border), one of the several districts along the Austro-Turkish frontier, where all men were liable to military service in return for land grants, he had clashed with

Charles over the extent of the reforms necessary. Matters did not improve during the 1809 campaign itself. Relations between Charles and Hiller became so bad that the general, claiming illness, would leave his command on the eve of the Battle of Wagram.

Compounding the difficulties facing the Austrians, the army's staff system remained defective. Archduke Charles did not possess a chief-of-staff comparable to Berthier, Napoleon's able chief-of-staff, while the staff manuals dated back to the last decades of the previous century. In February 1809, with the army already mobilizing, Charles dismissed his chief-of-staff, FML von Heldenfeld, an unstable character, given to drinking in dives and keeping low company, long at odds with Grünne. His replacement, GM von Prochaska, was a man of modest talents and widely believed to be under the influence of the second adjutant, GM Wimpffen. Neither Grünne nor Wimpffen favoured an aggressive strategy. Moreover, army headquarters divided into four major and several minor departments, with the all-important Operations Chancery, which issued campaign and battle orders, becoming ever larger and more cumbersome. The hasty and belated introduction of corps formations complicated matters further. With only a small permanent staff available, untrained officers had to be assigned when the corps system was activated. Functions and composition of corps staffs mirrored that of the army staff and, in the field, administrative duties consumed too much valuable time. The Austrian staff was competent in administration and map making, but lacked experience in operational matters. In consequence, Austrian operational staff work was slow, often inefficient and on several occasions caused critical delays that compromised operations.

The corps themselves varied slightly in composition. Each line corps had three divisions, one designated as the advance guard composed of light troops including some light horse and two light 3-pounder batteries, each with eight pieces. The two line divisions comprised two or three line brigades each. There was no divisional cavalry, but each division had a 6-pounder support battery, normally placed in the corps artillery reserve. Average strength of the line corps stood at 29,000 to 32,000 men and between 64 to 84 guns. The Austrian Army lacked elite guard formations. The two reserve corps were regarded as elites, combining heavy cavalry with grenadier battalions drawn from the line infantry. The large I Reserve Corps fielded twelve grenadier battalions and six regiments, three brigades, of heavy horse; the weaker II Reserve Corps had one five-battalion grenadier brigade and two heavy cavalry brigades.

Perhaps the most important of the reforms carried out by Archduke Charles was the new *Dienst-Reglement* for the infantry, which consisted of forty-six 'German' and fifteen 'Hungarian' line regiments, the former conscripts, the latter nominally volunteers raised by the Hungarian Diet. The *Reglement* aimed to humanize discipline and raise troop morale by better treatment. It sharply condemned brutality as destructive to the concept of military honour and instead appealed to the soldiers' military virtues. 'Love of his monarch and an honest life ... obedience, loyalty, resolution: these are the soldierly virtues.'[9]

The introduction of the code was accompanied by a shortened term of conscription, a move under discussion since 1802. Charles, who considered life-long service detrimental to morale, had wanted to reduce the term of service to a uniform eight years in all branches. The resistance to this among the military hierarchy was such that in the end, and as specified by decree in May 1808, service would be for ten years in the infantry, twelve in the cavalry and fourteen in the artillery, with discharges staggered to prevent a sudden exodus of trained men. The decree also established two reserve battalions for each of the German infantry regiments, with officers provided by each unit, and the rank and file consisting of men subject to conscription who had received four weeks of training in their first year and three weeks each year thereafter. The youngest reservists and recently discharged soldiers were to form a third battalion in each regiment, and if this did not provide sufficient numbers for active service, the shortages were to be made good by recruits chosen by lot from the fourth garrison battalion. The reserve provisions did not apply to the Hungarian regiments or to the *Grenzer* of the Military Border.

These small reductions of the service obligation for the professional army should not be considered a step towards the creation of a popular force. Charles and most senior generals always opposed militias as unreliable and of dubious value in battle, but agreed in the end, in June 1808, to their formation because the state finances did not permit a larger regular force to be maintained. Original estimates proposed that Austria would raise 180,000 men and Hungary 50,000, but the Hungarian Diet, never cooperative in military matters, refused. However, it did promise to call out its ancient levy, the *insurrectio*, if needed, and after a bitter debate promised to levy an extra 20,000 recruits the next year. In any case, except for some volunteer formations, the combat value of the nominal 170 *Landwehr* battalions, most poorly trained and equipped, with only seventy units actually mustered, remained problematic. During the war they failed as a home defence, but when their best units were brigaded with the regulars or used as individual fillers for the line, they did good service. For instance, seventeen *Landwehr* battalions would fight at Wagram. Also of potential importance were the ancient shooting guilds of the Tyrol, the *Landes Schützen*, volunteers who, resentful of having been placed under Bavarian rule after 1805, were planning to rise in support of Austria.

REFORMS OF THE MAIN COMBAT ARMS

The mainstay of the army remained the regular line infantry. When mobilized, each of the German regiments, meaning all units raised outside the Kingdom of Hungary, were composed of three battalions and two grenadier companies, which on campaign were usually detached to form converged elite battalions and brigades. In the German regiments companies numbered 220 men, while the traditionally stronger Hungarian units had 238 men in each company. Few companies, however, ever reached full strength. The light infantry was composed of seventeen *Grenzer* infantry regiments, each formed in three battalions of six companies of varying sizes. Finally, in 1808, nine *Jäger* battalions, each of six companies, were raised. The most common infantry weapon was the M 1798 17.56mm-calibre musket, 150cm long and weighing about 4.8kg. The first two ranks of the *Jäger* were equipped with carbines, the third rank and all non-commissioned officers with short rifles. Ammunition issue was sixty pre-assembled cartridges, while rifle-armed men carried the makings of 100 rounds.

Charles considered infantry 'able to fight in every type of terrain' as the single most important arm of the army. New infantry regulations were issued in 1807. Although sometimes described as innovative, they retained the battalion as the basic combat unit and the three-deep line as the ideal formation, with columns used for movement and attacks against fortified places. Movement was to be carried out at the 'ordinary' or the 'manoeuvre' step, 90 to 95 steps per minute for the first and 105 steps for the second. A third tempo, the double or charging pace, 120 steps per minute, existed but was rarely used because it tended to disrupt alignment.

The best-known innovation was the 'mass', a formation one company wide and six companies deep. Replacing the square, a mass could manoeuvre, if slowly, either in closed or open order. In closed order, with the files touching the pack of the men in front, such masses could stand against cavalry charges and also manoeuvre on flat ground. While vulnerable to artillery, the mass formations performed well, repelling cavalry charges on the flat terrain of Aspern–Essling and Wagram.

If Austrian line infantry was generally sound, its main shortcoming was that in broken terrain and in skirmishing it was rarely equal to that of the French. The regulations provided that the third rank of each battalion could be detached as skirmishers, deployed some 300 paces from the main body with formed support platoons making up two-thirds of the skirmish line. As Radetzky, probably the best young Austrian general of the Napoleonic wars, observed ruefully, fighting in skirmish or open order could be undertaken only in a very limited manner because 'we do not understand this type of fighting'. The *Jäger*, who operated without many formal instructions, did rather better, but the *Grenzer*, Austria's original light infantry, had been converted to line tactics in the 1770s and no longer excelled as skirmishers.

As for uniforms, all line regiments wore a short single-breasted white jacket (brown in the case of the *Grenzer*), with a high collar, small cuffs and short turnbacks in the regimental colours. German regiments wore white breeches with knee-length black gaiters, while the Hungarians and *Grenzer* sported tight light-blue pants and half-boots. Hair was cut short, and a crested leather helmet covered the head, though a cheaper light cloth shako, tapering towards the bottom, was introduced in the Hungarian regiments. The Grenadiers retained their traditional bearskins, while the *Jäger* wore a pike-grey uniform and a black Corsican hat. The *Landwehr*, by contrast, generally had little more than a grey smock and a black hat.

The Austrian horse comprised thirty-five regiments: eight of cuirassiers, six of dragoons, six chevaulegers, twelve hussars and three uhlans. Cuirassiers, wearing only a breastplate, which put them at a disadvantage in a melée, and dragoons were designated as heavy cavalry, the remainder as light. The heavy regiments had six squadrons of 135 men; the light cavalry was larger, with eight squadrons of 150 troopers in each regiment. All troopers carried a cut-and-thrust weapon. The heavy cavalry also had straight and heavy swords while the hussars and uhlans carried curved sabres. The uhlans, of course, were equipped with lances. There was a liberal allocation of firearms. Each trooper had two pistols, and each squadron had at least eight carbines and eight short rifles, a carryover from the wars against the Turks when Austrian horse had made considerable use of mounted fire. By 1809, however, shock action with the *armes blanches* was regarded as the primary tactic.

Cavalry regulations, the last issued in 1806, continued the two-squadron division as the main tactical formation with the two-deep line the standard combat formation, the thin fighting line proving a distinct disadvantage against French cavalry utilizing compact columns. An even greater disadvantage was the lack of instructions and training for multi-regiment charges, which led to the use of single regiments, even squadrons, for futile attacks. The tendency to splinter cavalry strength, though opposed by Charles, was further reinforced by corps commanders demanding cavalry flank cover during movements in column, often receiving it in the form of small detachments. As a result, instead of being able to act on the battlefield as an independent strike force, the Austrian mounted arm was becoming a support element. Its combat capabilities were further weakened when its horse artillery, only partly mounted and not trained to support charges, were increasingly used as field artillery in 1809. Finally, the cavalry was seriously short of mounts and its effective field force, on paper around 36,000, numbered only 22,000 troopers.

Charles reorganized and strengthened the artillery, making it more effective, though still not equal to that of the French. He withdrew the regimental 3-pounders and combined them into eight-gun brigade batteries; the relatively few 6-pounders were sent to the corps artillery reserve and, usually combined with two 7-pound howitzers, were classified as support batteries. To augment the heavy 12-pounders, usually two or three batteries to each corps, some 6-pounder batteries were assigned as position batteries to the corps and army reserve artillery, the latter forming the Haupt-Dispositions-Reserve. Austrian artillery was well designed and Napoleon did not hesitate to incorporate captured pieces in his artillery park.

Normally support and position batteries were employed under the direction of the corps *Artilleriechef*, a feasible arrangement because, fighting in compact units, frontages seldom exceeded 2,500 yards. To replace the infantrymen providing the brute force to assist the gun crews, a new body, the *Artillerie-Handlanger* Corps, was established. Artillery transports were militarized and cadres assigned to the batteries. Though the new artillery organization, 742 field pieces in 108 batteries, aimed to provide massed fire, this was not often realized in practice. Few senior commanders appreciated the potential – and limitations – of artillery, while individual battery commanders, often over-aged because of exceedingly slow promotions in this branch, still tended to regard each individual piece as a discrete fire element. As a result, the archduke's instructions that artillery always should act as part of a combined arm were often disregarded. None the less, if never as flexible an instrument as the French artillery, by the end of 1809 campaign the Austrian artillery was capable of delivering heavy massed fire.

THE NATIONALITY PROBLEM

Throughout its history the Habsburg army had to face its unique nationality problem. On the highest level there was the question of the Kingdom of Hungary, whose 'ruling nation', nobility and clergy, repeatedly at odds with the ruling monarch in Vienna, had extracted a special military status that by 1792 had resolved itself into an uneasy truce between equals. Hungary's contribution to the army remained disproportionately small compared with that of the other lands of the monarchy and, even in time of crisis, the crown had to negotiate and cajole for manpower and supplies rather than to command. There was also the problem of emerging nationalism. While still in a nascent stage, except perhaps among the Magyars, command of an army whose regiments variously spoke German, Czech, Flemish, Serbo-Croat, Italian, Magyar, Romanian and Polish could, one officer observed, 'cause a singular confusion'. To overcome this, German had been introduced as the language of drill manuals, regulations and formal commands, though most officers had at least a smattering of other languages. Still, by the last decade of the eighteenth century, one officer questioned whether an army of 'Hungarians, Croats, Transylvanians, Italians, Bohemians, Moravians, Poles, Wallachs, Slavonians, Austrians, Styrians, Tyroleans, Carnioleans, and gypsies could march under one flag and fight for a cause it knows nothing about'. But in the end it fought and, as far as the rank-and-file was concerned, fought well enough.[10]

NAPOLEON AT WAR

In contrast to Archduke Charles, Napoleon enjoyed supreme authority as ruler of France and commander-in-chief and was able to formulate and execute his own strategy.[11] Unlike the archduke, Napoleon was prepared to take risks and, though he paid respect to the great captains of the past and recent military theorists, his strategy was always pragmatic. The destruction of the enemy's main field force in a decisive battle rather than the occupation of enemy territory or the capture of the enemy's capital was his main objective. The main instruments he used to achieve this were a superb staff, and the corps system he developed after 1800.

Command and control required a substantial staff apparatus, but his all-important personal staff – the Maison – remained quite small. It included Marshal Berthier, Prince of Neuchâtel, the chief-of-staff; General d'Albe, his chief topographical officer; and a small number of staff officers. In addition, there was a pool of trusted senior aides who would be sent on special missions, acting 'in the name of the Emperor'. The emperor, however, remained his own operations officer, and Berthier did not participate in planning. Napoleon's main combat formations were the army corps, the smallest force of all arms. Primarily infantry organizations, each consisted of two to four infantry divisions, a brigade of light cavalry and several batteries of artillery. The exact size and composition of forces allocated to each corps varied, reflecting its assignment and the talents of its commander, normally one of his marshals. As a group, Napoleon's marshals had all seen considerable active service and displayed personal bravery in combat. That said, few were capable of independent command at the highest formation level, a fact that Napoleon, accordingly never likely to be challenged by his marshals, was more than content to accept.

There was also an independent cavalry corps. And above all there was the Imperial Guard, established in 1804. An all-arms *corps d'élite*, it enjoyed special privileges and, expanding steadily, it numbered about 12,000 by 1809. Though regarded as the ultimate reserve, in fact Napoleon rarely committed the Guard to combat, especially the grenadiers of the Old Guard.

To execute his desired strategic objective – a major, decisive battle – the various corps adopted a loosely quadrilateral formation, the *bataillon carrée*, with the self-contained corps marching within one day's distance of each other. The first corps to come into contact with the enemy was to engage him at once, while the other corps, showing an extraordinary marching capability, would hurry to its support. When concentration had been achieved, Napoleon's forces frequently outnumbered those of his adversaries. In battle, Napoleon would try to divide an enemy by gaining the 'central position' and then defeat one part of the enemy first. Alternatively, he would attempt to pin the enemy's front and turn his flank. On the rare occasions he used frontal attacks, the results were not always satisfactory.

Napoleon generally left tactics at unit level in the hands of subordinates. The corps, and even more the divisional formations, as his basic manoeuvre elements, fought as a whole according to its training level, while the problems of communication during a large battle made personal intervention in tactical detail impractical. Generally, however, the French Army continued the skirmisher, line and column tactics introduced just before and during the Revolution, though now supplemented by Napoleon's own innovations of great cavalry charges and the aggressive use of artillery. Underpinning the whole, however, was the remarkably effective system of conscription introduced at the start of the French revolution. Napoleon was always able to count on at least adequate levels of manpower.

NAPOLEON PREPARES FOR A NEW WAR

In early 1809, as Austria's belligerent intentions became clear to the French emperor, a substantial proportion of the French Army, 200,000 men in all, comprising line regiments, the Imperial Guard and contingents from the minor states of the Confederation of the Rhine, were engaged in Spain. Napoleon's principal forces in Germany, the Army of the Rhine, brought into being after the old Grande Armée had been disbanded in October 1808, were widely dispersed and numerically weak, their main remaining combat element Marshal Davout's 3 Corps. Clearly, substantial reinforcements were needed, but transferring them from Spain would take far too long. Realizing the need to reconstitute an army in Germany as rapidly as possible, Napoleon issued a number of important orders even before he left Spain for Paris on 17 January 1809. The Old Guard was returned to Germany, though even travelling for part of the way by requisitioned wagons and forced marches, its main elements could not arrive before the end of May. In Germany, it was to join the newly formed regiments of the Young Guard, 3,200 men raised from picked recruits.

At the same time, Napoleon recalled Marshals Lannes, Lefebvre, Bessières, and Masséna, General of Division Oudinot and other senior officers from Spain to assume new commands in Germany. He also instructed the princes of the Confederation of the Rhine to prepare their contingents. These ranged from small units combined into a single regiment to substantial forces such as the 32,000 men provided by Bavaria. The same message went to Prince Poniatowski of the Grand Duchy of Warsaw, and Eugène de Beauharnais, Napoleon's able stepson and viceroy of the Kingdom of Italy.

Napoleon also made considerable efforts to raise additional troops in France to reinforce his forces in Germany. As early as September 1808, previously deferred men from the 1806–9 classes had been called up. On 15 January 1809 instructions for an advance call-up of additional recruits from the 1810 class were also issued. These men, a total of 80,000, were to provide the 3rd and 4th battalions for the infantry. At the same time, the military academies were emptied and Saint-Cyr cadets, due to graduate in May, as well as some senior sergeants, were commissioned at once. Substantial forward ammunition depots were established at Strasbourg, Augsburg and Ulm; ration stocks, biscuits and hardtack at Passau and Munich. Finally, General of Division Bertrand, inspector general of engineers, was ordered to build up large stocks of tools for all corps, repair bridgeheads along the Bavarian river and transfer 1,100 sailors to assist the engineers. By the time Napoleon reached Paris on 23 January, additional manpower, *matériel*, rations and other supplies were becoming available.[12]

On 4 March the emperor hurriedly issued orders to assemble a new army, designated *La Grande Armée de l'Allemagne*, by 30 March. A hastily formed organization, it necessarily showed signs of improvisation. To be sure, the main operational framework and the combat-proven leaders remained. Imperial Headquarters controlled an army cavalry reserve under Marshal Bessières, with three divisions of heavy cavalry, as well as the not yet completed army artillery reserve and the Old Guard, itself still marching east. Immediately available north of the Danube valley and now concentrating around Nuremberg, was the 60,000-strong 3 Corps, nicknamed the 'Emperor's X Legion', and commanded by Davout, the Duke of Auerstädt. It consisted of four veteran French infantry divisions with its right flank covered by its two attached cavalry divisions: General Montbrun's light cavalry and Saint-Sulpice's heavy cavalry. A further reserve was provided by Saint-Hilaire's infantry division, which had arrived from the shores of the Baltic in forced marches (and was assigned to 2 Corps within a week). Facing the river Inn was Lefebvre's 7 Corps with three Bavarian divisions, while south of the Danube, with headquarters at Augsburg, Masséna was collecting his 4 Corps, including a competent Hessian brigade. Pending the arrival of Lannes, Duke of Montebello, the hastily constituted 2 Corps under General Charles, Duke of Reggio, was assembled around Ulm. Marshal Bernadotte, Prince of Ponte Corvo, was to take command of the Saxon army supported by a weak French division under General Dupas. Overall, while containing a larger proportion of raw recruits than usual and critically short of artillery, the new Army of Germany was rapidly reaching the numbers, commanders and organization to withstand an Austrian offensive.

THE CONTRIBUTION OF
THE CONFEDERATION OF THE RHINE

Troops from the Confederation of the Rhine, the satellite Kingdom of Italy and the Grand Duchy of Warsaw constituted an important part of Napoleon's forces during the campaign of 1809. While some German units had participated in sieges between 1805 and 1807, in 1809 nearly

100,000 men, some incorporated in French divisions and corps, others organized in their own corps and divisions, took part for the first time in major combat operations. Their divisional structures differed slightly from the French, and usually included all three combat arms: two infantry brigades, a cavalry brigade and divisional artillery. Though often resented, Napoleon stuck to his policy that all major formations would be commanded by French officers.[13]

Bavaria, Württemberg, Baden, Hesse and Saxony furnished the most important contingents. The newly established Westphalian Kingdom had substantial forces, 25,000 men, but its best troops were engaged in Spain and its remaining troops, reinforced by Dutch regiments, saw no major combat. They were primarily engaged putting down revolts and insurrections in north Germany and forming a reserve to deal with the expected British landings. By contrast, the Bavarian army had undergone a major reform under Maximilian I Joseph (raised by Napoleon from elector to king in 1806), and saw substantial action. Bavaria had introduced conscription in 1804 with the result that by 1809 it was able to provide the largest German contingent to Napoleon's army, 32,000 men and all trained on the French model. Its infantry component numbered thirteen line regiments and seven light infantry battalions, while the mounted arm had six regiments of horse. Its artillery regiment, reformed after 1801 by emigrant French gunners, was twenty companies strong, with twelve assigned to 7 Corps under Marshal Lefebvre, Duke of Danzig, an Alsatian by birth, German speaking and popular with his men and his Bavarian divisional commanders alike. Lefebvre's corps was organized into three divisions, each composed of two infantry and one cavalry brigade, supported by four artillery batteries, 3-pounder light, 6-pounder line and 12-pounder reserve. Alerted initially in the summer of 1808, then placed on standby before being fully mobilized in February 1809, by 20 March, 7 Corps held a line along the Isar to the Bohemian border. As the forward element of Napoleon's gathering army, it would take the brunt of the initial Austrian offensive.

King Friedrich of Württemberg, an absolute and domineering ruler, so fat he had to use a special cut-out table to eat, was an unlikely figure as a soldier. Under the Rheinbund treaty he was obliged to provide Napoleon with 12,000 men, which he raised by selective conscription. His officers for the most part were German and promoted by merit rather than birth. Mounted troops consisted of four light regiments, including one guard unit, while the foot consisted of seven line infantry battalions, a guard infantry battalion, four light infantry battalions, partly rifle armed, and a garrison battalion. The twenty-two guns of the artillery formed three batteries, two horse and one foot, all fielding 6-pounder guns and 7-pounder howitzers. Until February 1809 the army used Prussian drill; then it was hastily, but successfully, converted to the French combat system. Originally the Württembergers, who had gained a fine fighting record in 1807, were to be joined with some French formations and a combined force of troops from the minor states of the Rheinbund. In the end, however, they became 8 Corps, commanded by General of Division Vandamme, an efficient tactician but a crude and difficult man, detested by his German subordinates. Even so, his corps contained some of the best infantry of the Confederation troops.

Baden and Hesse troops contributed smaller numbers. Though Baden troops had not done well in earlier campaigns, the state had been compelled to send one infantry regiment to Spain. As a result there were many new conscripts among the 6,300 men incorporated into Legrand's division of Masséna's 4 Corps. Yet throughout the 1809 campaign, they performed all the missions assigned to them and earned extravagant praise from their French superiors. In contrast to Baden, Hesse's small army had done well in 1806–7 – 'brave and good soldiers', Napoleon called them – and their small all-arms contingent, 4,300 in all, was a welcome accession to 4 Corps, joining Saint-Cyr's division. Their performance was excellent and praised by French commanders from Napoleon down.

By contrast, the conduct of the Saxon 9 Corps has provided the greatest controversy. Although a French ally since late 1806, its ruler had resisted all modernization. Recruitment and tactics remained based on the outdated Prussian model of the Seven Years' War. Serfdom continued in the kingdom and entry into the officer corps was based on birth. Tactics remained linear, centralized control was paramount and initiative stifled. Even so, Saxon infantry had done well during the siege of Danzig and the cavalry had distinguished itself at the battle of Friedland.

In 1809 the Saxon army numbered twelve infantry line regiments, dressed in white uniforms, each of two battalions of five companies, including one grenadier company. In practice, the grenadiers were detached to form battalions of four companies each. Mobilization was slow and found all regiments below strength, with the shortage made good by hastily impressed recruits. Its cavalry, four heavy and five light regiments, enjoyed an excellent reputation, even though the French had confiscated most of its horses, as a result of which only twenty squadrons could be mounted and put in the field in 1809. The Saxon artillery was the weakest branch of its army. It was poorly trained and the four hastily formed batteries, each with four 8-pounder guns and two 8-pounder howitzers, were slow to manoeuvre and fire. In keeping with his principle that all major formations were to have French commanders, Napoleon appointed Bernadotte, perhaps his least reliable marshal, to head the 12,500 men of 9 Corps.

Finally, there were close to thirty small states in the Rheinbund whose populations were too small to provide viable individual units. Moreover, many of these states had already made troop contributions to the war in Spain. But Napoleon could not afford to lose the remaining manpower they represented and their individual military forces, all with different uniforms, weapons and training standards, were combined into seven, later reduced to six, Rheinbund regiments. Originally destined to join Masséna, four regiments were formed around Würzburg as a division under General of Division Rouyer and initially attached to Davout's corps. Displaying considerable professionalism, they participated in no major battles but fought many skirmishes. They took part in the opening campaigns in Bavaria, provided a small contingent to assist in crossing the Danube at Wagram and fought well against the Tyrolean insurgents. In all, the total contribution of the Rheinbund troops was a significant addition to Napoleon's Army of Germany, which by early April, with reinforcements arriving daily, numbered 175,000 men.

THE ARMY OF GERMANY

The forces that Napoleon assembled in Germany in 1809 were no longer the well-trained army of 1805. They necessarily contained a great many new recruits as well as newly commissioned junior officers and substantial numbers of foreign troops. Even some French regiments from the recently incorporated *départements* in France itself were composed of foreigners. Moreover, given the relentless pace of Napoleon's campaigning, training standards had inevitably declined.

There were no changes in corps or divisional organization. Since 1808, French infantry battalions had been organized into six instead of nine companies: one of grenadiers, one of *voltigeurs* and four of fusiliers. In theory, each company should have had 140 men; in practice, this target was never reached and battalions rarely had over 600 men. Their main weapon was the modified 1777 musket, 175cm long, weighing 4.375kg with a calibre of 17.5mm. Although regiments still were designated as line of light, in reality all could be deployed as skirmishers. On the battlefield, French infantry usually operated in columns of divisions, a formation two companies wide and three deep, firing in three ranks and forming squares to repel cavalry charges. Finally, except for the Imperial Guard, especially the grenadiers of the Old Guard who always fought in their regulation dress complete with bearskins, French infantry uniforms no longer conformed to the official pattern. French industry was unable to keep up with campaign wastage. Many soldiers lacked basic items of clothing and departed on campaign in a great variety of gear, even in captured uniforms.

Cavalry consisted of heavy and light regiments, the heavy normally in four squadrons 250 strong, formed in two ranks, while light cavalry regiments tended to be larger. The heavy cavalry consisted of cuirassiers, carabiniers and dragoons designed as the main strike force in battle. The first two carried breast armour and back-plates and were armed with a heavy straight sword and two pistols; the dragoons also had a short musket. *Chasseurs à cheval*, lancers and hussars formed the light cavalry, used mainly for reconnaissance though sometimes also in battle. French cavalry was well mounted and trained, and their most useful capability was that they could fight in large, division-sized formations.

Artillery was in the process of transformation, replacing its 4- and 8-pounders with the newly introduced light 6-pounders, the so-called 'System of the Year XI'. But the transition was far from complete in 1809 and contributed to the initial shortage of artillery in Germany. The organization of the French artillery remained much the same throughout the army, with all batteries having guns as well as howitzers. Foot as well as horse batteries normally fielded six guns and two howitzers. A variable number of batteries were allocated to each division, while reserve artillery, including the heavy 12-pounders, was kept in corps and army reserve parks. From 1807 on Napoleon used massed artillery to pave the way for the assault. 'Fire', he asserted, 'is everything; the rest does not matter.' For all that, his artillery always remained quite small. His Grande Armée of 1805 had only two pieces for every 1,000 men. The ratio thereafter rose only slowly. Between 1807 and 1809 it stood at three per 1,000 men. Napoleon never reached his target of five guns per 1,000 soldiers, though the ratio was partially increased by using captured Austrian guns. Once it had arrived in Germany, the artillery of the Old Guard, sixty guns strong, constituted the army's artillery reserve.

As always, a strong point of the French Army was its combat leadership. In 1809, with the French facing not just a larger army but one that had adapted many French methods, this was particularly important. Not only was Napoleon clearly superior to Archduke Charles, his staff and senior commanders were unequalled by the Austrians. All were personally brave and experienced in leading and controlling corps and, when necessary, using their own initiative in tactical situations. If out of his depth in independent command, Berthier was the most able chief-of-staff in Europe, while Davout, Masséna and Lannes were, after Napoleon, the best commanders in the French Army. Lefebvre and Oudinot were adequate in corps command. Bernadotte, on the other hand, despite a highly inflated opinion of himself, was the least reliable of the marshals. Below this level, French divisional commanders and staffs, as well as regimental commanders and specialist officers, all remained far superior to their Austrian counterparts. But perhaps the most important factor was that Napoleon was adored by his troops, French as well as foreign, and that his presence, and the hope of his approval, spurred them on to great efforts.

FIRST MANOEUVRES: AUSTRIA

In March 1809 Austrian army headquarters and six corps (five line and one reserve) had deployed in north-west Bohemia but were then shifted south to the Inn, joining one line and one reserve corps already there. This force formed the main Austrian army, the *Hauptarmee*. Operating on its southern flank in Italy was the two-corps Army of Inner Austria, while in Galicia there was one strong corps. In addition, a small corps was mustering in Croatia to recover the lost territory in Dalmatia, and another was deployed facing Saxony. Altogether the eight corps of the main army numbered about 200,000 men, the Army of Inner Austria had 60,000, the Galician corps 30,000 and the Croatian corps about 10,000. Another 8,000 or so were placed in brigades along the Saxon border as a core for expected popular anti-French insurrections. Finally, reserves to fill the third battalions and form *Landwehr* units were becoming available slowly. While far short of its projected paper strength of 470,000, the main army was considered adequate to defeat the still-dispersed French and its related allied forces in Germany.

The reason for the main army's original concentration in Bohemia was that when war had been planned it was correctly assumed that the principal theatre of operations would be in Germany, and that victory here required an early offensive. There remained the question of choosing a major line of operations. On 25 December 1808, when Prussian cooperation of 80,000 men was still expected, Charles instructed chief-of-staff Mayer to prepare plans for a strike with the major part of the field army from north-west Bohemia into the Main valley. The troops were ordered into their assembly areas in January 1808. Early the next month, however, the archduke changed his mind. Intelligence reports of increased French and Confederation of the Rhine activities and news that the Prussians were not now coming unnerved Charles. Worried about poor communications across the Bohemian mountains and concerned that his forces were vulnerable to a French offensive from Bavaria, on 19 March the archduke decided to shift his main operational axis from the Main to the Danube, 'in keeping with the rules of the art of war, while defending the heart of the monarchy'. An Austrian offensive here, he claimed, would not only protect Vienna but would place the army in a better position to support an uprising in the Tyrol, and improve cooperation with the campaign in Italy. Leaving I and II Corps behind in Bohemia, Charles began to redeploy the bulk of his army to the south bank of the Danube.[14] When Mayer demurred, he was dismissed, on 13 March.

The change was a mistake. If the concentrated Austrian army had struck from Bohemia in late March it would have caught the French army still mustering and might have thrown the enemy off balance. Given the Austrians' temporary numerical superiority, it should then have been possible to retain the initiative. But with Charles congenitally averse to risk-taking, this fleeting opportunity was lost. Further, not only did the move back to the Danube and the Inn give the French a crucial extra month to coordinate their forces, it did nothing to improve strategic cooperation with John's army in Italy. Further, the two corps left behind in Bohemia now operated to no good purpose, while the main army arrived at its new point of departure, Braunau-

Schärding on the river Inn, with its troops fatigued, its equipment ruined and its supply arrangements strained.[15] None the less, it was from here, on the night of 9–10 April, that the Austrians crossed the river Inn into Bavaria to open their campaign in earnest.

FIRST MANOEUVRES: FRANCE

Detained by domestic matters and in any case not expecting the Austrians to move before the end of April, Napoleon remained in Paris, from where he issued a stream of letters, orders and decrees to his forces assembling in Germany. That they did not always arrive in sequence was inevitable in a time of improved but still uncertain communication. That said, in good visibility, messages sent by the optical Chappe telegraph could reach Strasbourg from Paris in ten minutes; couriers needed three days. Napoleon had already formed the major outlines of his campaign plan. Italy was to be a secondary theatre of war, while Vienna was his principal objective and he intended to use the Danube as his main line of operations. 'Nothing', he wrote, 'can be of greater advantage than following the course of the Danube.'[16] On 30 March he sent his chief-of-staff, Berthier, and his operational staff ahead to Germany. Here, they were not to command, but to transmit and execute the emperor's voluminous orders.

With his army not yet fully operational, the emperor decided to cede the initiative to the Austrians, though he wanted to prevent the Austrians from getting between Davout and the Danube. 'If the Austrians attacked before 10 April the army should concentrate behind the Lech, its right at Augsburg and its left at Ingolstadt or if need be Donauwörth.' As his army strengthened, Napoleon became more confident and decided to make Ratisbon his focal point, with 15 April set as the date for this concentration. If Charles invaded Franconia, the Army of Germany could then attack his rear; if, having divided his forces, he operated along the Danube the emperor would crush the separated Austrian wings singly. Concentration at Ratisbon by 15 April was the key point of this plan.

The immediate consequence of the Austrians opening their campaign earlier than Napoleon expected was that command in Germany was left in the hands of Berthier. Moving forward to Donauwörth, his difficulties were compounded when a critical order sent by telegraph to Strasbourg on 10 April was delayed by fog until 16 April. In the meantime, it was overtaken by a subsequent order, carried by courier and containing a crucial elaboration of the first, which arrived on the 13th. As ever striving manfully to execute Napoleon's orders, in accordance with this second order Berthier repositioned his corps. When eventually the original order arrived, Berthier had hastily to reposition them again. In this confusion of order and counter-order, Berthier's plaintive message to Napoleon of 15 April – 'In the present circumstances,' he wrote, 'I should very much welcome the arrival of Your Majesty' – seems a considerable understatement. The consequence of this muddle was that when Napoleon arrived in Donauwörth early on the morning of 17 April, having left Paris on the 13th, he found his two major bodies 80 miles apart. Davout was at Ratisbon, Masséna at Augsburg. Between them, there were only three Bavarian divisions.[17]

Ever since, Berthier has been derided as an incompetent and indecisive strategist, a bungler who placed the army in great danger. In the same way, Napoleon has won wide praise for his swift and decisive remedial actions. But this overlooks the fact that Napoleon should have been aware that the telegraph to Strasbourg was down and that he could easily have added a copy of the first order to the second, clarifying his intentions. In any case, Napoleon's orders, often dictated in haste, were far from clear. It also overrates the danger presented by the Austrian advance, which seldom exceeded 6 miles a day. With the enemy moving at a snail's pace, Napoleon had time to place his corps in his preferred strategic formation, the *bataillon carrée*, in which the various corps moved independently but in supporting distance, able to come together rapidly when the main enemy body was sighted. Within a few days the situation in Bavaria was totally reversed.

CHAPTER THREE

The initial Austrian offensive into Bavaria

AUSTRIAN WAR PLANS

The Austrians advanced into Bavaria on a broad front, three columns crossing the river Inn on 9–10 April. Their first objective was the river Isar, some 50 miles distant. Crossing at Schärding were IV Corps and I Reserve Corps, at Mühlheim III Corps, while the main force, V Corps, VI Corps and II Reserve Corps, moved through Braunau. Further south, Jellacic's division marched from Salzburg to take Munich. Finally, a rebellion in the Tyrol that would threaten Napoleon's line of communications and consolidate the link between the main army and that of Inner Austria was an integral part of the Austrian war plan. To support the revolt a combined division from VIII Corps under FML de Chasteler, Belgian born, crossed the frontier from Carinthia into East Tyrol on 9 April, the signal for the pre-planned rising.

Although encountering no resistance except for fleeting contact with Bavarian light horse, Austrian forward movement was slow. To sunder the enemy before he could concentrate – and Archduke Charles was confident that the French could not do so before 18 April – it was necessary to reach the Danube, a distance of 85 miles, in eight march days. However, encumbered by a large artillery train and massive supply columns, and hampered by the absence of reliable maps and torrential spring rains that turned roads to mud, the advance fell behind schedule.

Austrian sources frequently blamed the bad roads and weather for the slow pace of advance, though conditions were no better for the French. The basic reasons were more complex. Fearful of provoking popular resentment and concerned about troop discipline, at no point was Charles willing to accept the requisitioning system practised by the French. Requisitioning was restricted to replenishing magazines, and each corps was followed at one day's distance by its supply column, carrying among other requisites the heavy field ovens to bake the bread rations. The most important cause of the slow advance, however, was that the corps commanders had not been trained to march troops in corps formations and so continued the old march system. Their infantry columns were too wide for the available secondary roads, while the inclusion of the brigade batteries in the march column led to frequent traffic stoppages. After only two days, Archduke Charles discovered that his army needed a day of rest for recuperation and maintenance and to allow supplies to catch up. That night, with light drizzle falling and with formations badly mixed up, the troops bivouacked, their mood not improved by a general order to issue a half-litre of wine to all. 'Unfortunately,' the official history records, 'there was no wine to be issued.'[1]

Matters went little better to the north where I and II Corps also made slow progress. Though they forced Davout to move south towards Ratisbon on secondary roads, Bellegarde and Kolowrat failed to bring him to battle. While good enough old-fashioned soldiers, they were clearly out of their depth in an independent role, their problems compounded by the failure of their light cavalry to provide intelligence. In fact, throughout the campaign the Austrian light horse, and for that matter the French, failed to provide good intelligence.

On 16 April Jellacic reported that he had taken Munich, and the same day V Corps made its first serious contact with the Bavarians, at Landshut, where there was a major wooden pile-bridge across the Isar. Charles had expected to encounter the three divisions of Lefebvre's 7 Corps there, though in fact only Deroy's division opposed him. In command of V Corps's advance guard, the enterprising FML Josef Radetzky had occupied the town the night before and discovered that Bavarian efforts to demolish the bridge had been only partially successful. During the morning, V Corps engineers, covered by an artillery barrage, repaired the damage and after a short skirmish light infantry crossed the structure and cleared the Bavarians from the left bank. That morning, after IV and VI corps had also crossed the river, and with his single division threatened by envelopment, Deroy, whose task had been to observe and delay the Austrians, fell back on Abensberg near the Danube to link up with the other divisions of 7 (Bavarian) Corps.

Having secured crossings over the Isar at Landshut and Moosburg, Charles now planned to exploit his advantage. He decided that while V and VI Corps, supported by I Reserve Corps, would guard his left flank, the bulk of his army, some 90,000 men strong, would march to cross the Danube near Kehlheim west of Ratisbon. He intended to link up there with Bellegarde and attack the outnumbered Davout, whom he believed to be still north of Ratisbon. He reported to Francis that 'My operations will most probably move to the Danube, where it appears that the enemy is concentrating'.[2] On 17 April he advanced his main army 6 miles on the main road linking Landshut with Ratisbon towards Pfaffenhausen, and was now only two marches away from Kehllheim and Ratisbon. He issued orders to Bellegarde on the right and Kolowrat on the left to move towards Amberg. However, he did little more during the days of 17–19 April, even though he was in a most favourable situation, having seized the central position against two widely separated and individually outnumbered enemy corps.

In this fashion he let his opportunity slip away. Some authors claim that he suffered an epileptic seizure, others hint that he lacked strategic vision and resolve. In any case, the two main French bodies under

Davout and Masséna were still separated by several days' marches and could not have linked up, and even if the Austrians had advanced at only a moderate rate they would have reached the Danube and their strategic objective. But for three days Charles failed to make any major strategic movements.[3] Meanwhile, time was running out. On the morning of 17 April Napoleon arrived in Donauwörth. The emperor soon realized the danger facing his army and took energetic measures to save the situation.

NAPOLEON'S COUNTERSTROKE

When Napoleon's travelling coach clattered into Donauwörth before dawn, Berthier was absent. The chief-of-staff had ridden out towards Augsburg looking for his emperor. In the absence of his chief-of-staff, Napoleon studied the available reports, maps open and dividers in hand. He found that instead of being concentrated on the Lech in supporting distance of each other, his corps were widely scattered. Discounting smaller formations, Davout's large corps was spread out on both banks of the Danube around Ratisbon, Lefebvre was assembling at Abensberg and Masséna and Oudinot were encamped around Augsburg. Neither Charles nor Napoleon had a precise knowledge of the other's dispositions. The emperor, of course, knew about the slowly moving Austrian main force, which he designated the Landshut column. He was also aware of the approach of the considerable Austrian forces north of the Danube threatening Davout, whom Charles still assumed was retiring towards Ratisbon. Clearly, the most urgent task facing Napoleon was bring his exposed and dispersed corps into supporting distance.

Even before a much-relieved Berthier had returned before noon, Napoleon had formed the outlines of a plan of operations and issued a stream of orders. Discarding his initial intent to stand on the defensive behind the Lech, he now intended to wrest the initiative from Charles and then destroy him, using part of his army to pin the Austrians frontally, while another part would turn the Austrian left. To this end he planned to link up Davout and Lefebvre near Abensberg to constitute the pinning force, while he would use Masséna and Oudinot to move forward to Pfaffenhausen, ready to fall on the Austrian left. Additional formations such as Vandamme's Württemberg 8 Corps, Pajol's small French division, Rouyer's unattached Rheinbund division and Nansouty's heavy cavalry division were, if needed, to reinforce the Bavarians. About 1.30 p.m., a scant twelve hours after his arrival, Napoleon's orders went out to Davout, Masséna and Oudinot. Davout was to march on Ingolstadt, but given the distance, nearly 60 miles, could not arrive there before late the next day. But Davout, a marshal with an acute strategic sense, was already prepared. He had reached Ratisbon on the 18th and had deployed his infantry divisions – Morand, Gudin, augmented by Saint-Hilaire's division, which had arrived from its Baltic garrison in forced march – around the town. Friant, retreating from an encounter with Bellegarde at Amberg, was still on the other side of the Danube but was approaching rapidly. In addition, 3 Corps disposed of Saint-Sulpice's 2nd heavy and Montbrun's light cavalry divisions. A strong Corps Reserve Artillery with two 12-pounder batteries, four heavy guns each, four battalions of sappers, one of *pontonniers*, some miners and substantial equipment and provision trains, rounded out a large, experienced and well-led fighting force ready to move on short notice. Anticipating Napoleon's order, Davout had already scouted the roads to the south-west, and during the night of 18–19 April had dispatched a battalion to secure the vital Saal defile where the main road along the Danube could be easily blocked. During the night of 19 April he marched out from Ratisbon. To shorten his march columns he moved his corps along four roughly parallel routes. While his trains took the main road along the river, his artillery, infantry, and cavalry stiffened by some infantry, took the secondary roads, little more than farm tracks. He left one regiment behind, the 65th Line under Colonel Coutard, to defend Ratisbon and especially the bridge across the Danube with orders to destroy it rather than to allow it to fall into Austrian hands.

Meanwhile, at about 7 in the evening both Masséna and Oudinot had received their orders, repeated in more explicit form during the night. They were to march from the vicinity of Augsburg and make with all speed for Pfaffenhausen, but despite Napoleon's personal post-script to Masséna on his last set of orders – 'Action! Speed! I greet you'[4] – the marshal had not moved during the night and arrived at Pfaffenhofen only on 19 April, linking up with Oudinot, whose corps passed under Masséna's operational control for a grand sweep on Landshut. Also on 18 April Lannes, a great offensive commander and one of Napoleon's few personal friends, had arrived from Spain. The next day he assumed command of a task force drawn largely from 3 Corps, Morand and Gudin's infantry and Jacquinot's brigade of light cavalry, further reinforced by the heavy cavalry divisions of Nansouty and Saint-Sulpice, for a total of 25,000 men. By the evening of 19 April Napoleon's corps were within supporting distance and ready to take the offensive the next day. Even so, the emperor was mistaken about the actual Austrian dispositions.

LANDSHUT AND THE BATTLE OF ECKMÜHL

Until the morning of 18 April, the Archduke Charles still assumed that Davout was north of the Danube, but was then informed that 3 Corps had already entered Ratisbon. He cancelled his intended crossing of the Danube upstream from Ratisbon and decided to employ his main force, III, IV, and I Reserve Corps, together with Kolowrat's corps coming from the north, to trap Davout. By evening these corps, having marched north-east, reached the vicinity of Rohr, only 15 miles from Ratisbon, while Kolowrat was closing in on the opposite bank of the Danube. His left wing, V, VI and II Reserve Corps, was ordered to cross the Gross Laber river to attack the Bavarians.

On 19 April, Davout led his corps south-west to close up with Lefebvre, now aligned with Demont's reserve division on his right upstream and Vandamme's corps to his left. The terrain between the Danube and the Laber west of Ratisbon is complicated, covered with forests, broken by ridges and cut by valleys and streams. As Davout marched west, his flank and rearguard encountered elements of the Austrian III and IV Corps, but the terrain here favoured the French open-order tactics. With whole infantry regiments in skirmish order, Generals Saint-Hilaire, Friant and Montbrun checked the Austrians and then drove them out of the villages of Tengen and Thann to gain manoeuvre room. Meanwhile, Lefebvre with two divisions, Crown Prince and Deroy, had driven the Austrians back. Throughout the day Austrian commanders moved slowly and carefully, leaving behind units to secure their immediate line of communications but undermining their numerical superiority. Then, too, Charles, though only a few miles from the fighting, but always mindful of the need for a reserve to cover a possible retreat, had refused to commit his II Reserve Corps grenadiers.[5]

By nightfall, Davout had linked up with Lefebvre's Corps and Vandamme's 8 Corps and was approaching Abensberg from the east. During the night of 19 April the two armies faced each other along a 50-mile front, from Ratisbon to Pfaffenhofen. From left to right, Charles had a brigade near Pfaffenhofen, VI Corps at Augsburg, V, VI and II Reserve Corps to the south of Abensberg, III, IV and I Reserve Corps between Thann and Eckmühl, and II Corps advancing on Ratisbon from the north. Napoleon had Masséna and Oudinot pushing towards Pfaffenhofen, Lefebvre and Vandamme before Abensberg, and Davout placed from Abensberg to Abbach, with the 65th still holding Ratisbon. With his corps now in effective supporting distance, Napoleon disposed of nearly approximate numbers. He planned for Davout and Lefebvre to anchor his offensive. Lannes's task force was to attack the Austrian centre while Masséna and Oudinot, supported by Vandamme and the cavalry, were to move on Moosburg and Landshut to cut off the Isar crossings and destroy the Austrian left, believed by Napoleon to be the main body of the Austrian army. In other words, while Napoleon was shifting his forces to the south, Charles was concentrating to the north.

The combats of 20 April are collectively referred as the battle of Abensberg, though they were not a single action. The French offensive began around 9 in the morning, and after numerous engagements by evening had achieved some of its objectives and destroyed the combat cohesion of V and II Reserve Corps, which fell back in disorder on Hiller's VI Corps. However, the Austrians were not destroyed. With Masséna not having reached Landshut, Hiller stubbornly managed to contest the Landshut crossing. Still, by evening the Austrian army had been cut in two, with losses totalling over 6,000 men and twelve guns.[6] Napoleon now assumed that he had destroyed the main body of the Austrian army. In fact, two-thirds of that army were still combat capable. In the north, Charles had managed to maintain a fairly orderly front against Davout and Lefebvre on the line from Tengen to Peising. Meanwhile on the Danube, Liechtenstein's I Reserve Corps and Kolowrat's II Corps had forced Coutard's out-of-ammunition regiment to bury its flag and surrender Ratisbon in the afternoon. More important was that Coutard had not been able to destroy the massive bridge over the Danube, thus giving Charles control over a vital river crossing and contact with his previously isolated right wing. Now Kolowrat could support the Austrian centre, which Charles had withdrawn to a 9-mile line from Abbach on the Danube to Eckmühl on the Gross Laber, pitting Davout's and Lefebvre's diminished corps against almost three corps: some 70,000 Austrians against 36,000 French.

On the morning of 21 April Napoleon still assumed that he had eliminated the main strength of Archduke Charles's army. In reality, however, only two corps had been hurt and Hiller, leaving behind a strong rearguard to defend the bridgehead and the town of Landshut, was retreating east with three corps. Napoleon also did not know that the vital bridge at Ratisbon was now securely in Austrian hands. He was aware that Davout was under pressure and sent Wrede's Bavarian division and Oudinot with two divisions to reinforce him with up to six divisions, while ordering Vandamme to position himself to contact Davout's right flank and be ready to assist him in case of an emergency. Meanwhile, the emperor and his staff rode to Landshut. Although by this time Masséna had crossed the Isar at Moosburg and was moving up to Landshut, the emperor detailed one of his senior aides, General Georges Mouton, to lead a converged grenadier force of the 17th Line across the pile bridge, already set alight by Hiller's rearguard. It was a notable feat of arms, typical of the personal combat leadership shown by senior Napoleonic commanders and their aides.

It was also perhaps unnecessary. With Masséna's main force across the Isar at Moosburg, Hiller could not afford to be cut off. He tried to bring out as much of his ammunition train as he could, but eventually had to abandon some 600 ammunition wagons, 60 pontoons and 14 flags. By evening he was retreating on the road towards Vienna pursued at a distance by Bessières and all available light cavalry. To the north, however, Davout faced a build-up of the Austrian central column. Kolowrat's II Corps, Liechtenstein's Hohenzollern's III Corps, Rosenberg's IV Corps, a total of 75,000 men, along with I Reserve Corps, faced Davout and Wrede, who had but 36,000 men deployed in an arc from the Danube to Eckmühl. About mid morning Davout reported the growing threat to Napoleon. 'Sire,' Davout wrote, 'I have the whole army in front of me,' adding, 'I will hold my position – I hope, but the troops are worn out and the enemy artillery is three times larger than mine.'[7] During the day Friant and Saint-Hilaire, supported by Montbrun's and Piré's light horse, fought against greatly superior numbers, and it was not until General Piré, sent as Davout's personal emissary, arrived at 2 a.m. on 22 April that Napoleon realized that in the north Davout faced the bulk of Charles's army.

Acting on this intelligence, Napoleon ordered an immediate concentration on Eckmühl and with his battle staff rode towards the battle. On the way he issued a proclamation to his French and allied troops. 'Soldiers: The territory of the Confederation of the Rhine has been violated. The Austrian general supposes that we are to flee at the sight of his banners and abandon our allies to his mercy. I arrive with the speed of lightning among you.' There was considerable truth in this statement. Napoleon's army was coming and it was coming fast.

During the morning of 22 April French troops, with Lannes's provisional corps leading, marched between 17 and 20 miles. Shortly after 4 p.m. Davout, alerted by ten pre-arranged cannon salvoes from Gudin's batteries, ordered a counter-attack to fix the Austrians and by mid afternoon Lannes struck against the Austrian left from the south and east. Attacked from two directions, although only Rosenberg was heavily engaged, the Austrian commanders did not understand that the corps system meant that the forward units would soon be supported and did not hold long enough to be reinforced. When Rosenberg's troops began to retreat in disorder, leaving behind most of their guns and ammunition carts, they carried Hohenzollern and Liechtenstein's corps with them. Charles now ordered a withdrawal north to the river.

To protect their withdrawal, at about 7 p.m. on 22 April, he committed part of his mounted reserve, twenty-nine half squadrons, near Alt Eglolffsheim. Fighting as separate regiments, and without the support of their cavalry batteries, which had already been pulled back, the Austrians were worsted by sixty-six French and allied squadrons supported by eighteen guns. Even so, the unequal combat had gained time and at about 10 that night the exhausted French broke off pursuit. During the night and the following morning, using both the stone bridge and a hastily built pontoon bridge some 5 miles east, Charles extricated the bulk of his troops to the north of the Danube leaving behind 6,000 men to defend the medieval fortress and stone bridge. After the dense morning mist lifted on 23 April, the emperor was frustrated when a series of assaults delivered against Ratisbon failed. Napoleon could neither afford to leave the place behind in Austrian hands nor mount a regular siege. The immediate capture of Ratisbon was vital. He was still worried how any setback would affect the loyalty of the Rheinbund princes. He was anxious, too, that failure might after all encourage the Prussians to intervene on the Austrian side. With reports of setbacks in Italy, he could also not afford to give Archduke John time to bring his estimated 75,000 men north. Therefore he believed that he had no choice but to renew the assault regardless of cost. The task was entrusted to Lannes. While supervising preparations, the emperor was hit by a spent cannon ball and slightly wounded on his right foot. While the wound was dressed, the news that he had been wounded spread like wildfire through the French ranks. Losing no time, Napoleon, though in considerable pain, at once mounted his horse and, riding down the ranks, stopping to bestow decorations and promotions to deserving soldiers, immediately restored the morale of his troops.

After two assaults by volunteers from Morand's division had been beaten back with heavy losses, Lannes in person stepped forward. Grasping a scaling ladder he shouted, 'Before I was a marshal I was a grenadier – and so I am still'. As he started to carry the ladder forward his aides tried to deter him. Exclaiming that they all would be dishonoured if the marshal were wounded before all his aides were killed, they wrestled the ladder from him. The sight of a marshal of the empire tussling with his aides as to who should lead the assault inspired a cry of enthusiasm from the entire division. Officers and men rushed forward to scale the walls, and when the assault troops entered the town the Austrian garrison capitulated. Yet beyond delaying Napoleon for some hours and again demonstrating the inspiring style of Napoleonic combat leadership, the affair did little to change the overall situation.

CHARLES RETREATS TOWARDS VIENNA

To the end of his life Napoleon was proud of the way he had handled his command in the six days following his arrival at the front. In exile on Saint Helena he said: 'The battle of Abensberg, the Landshut manoeuvres and the battle of Eckmühl were my most brilliant and most skilful actions.'[8] Still, though he had hurt the Austrian army, he had not destroyed it. But having suffered heavy casualties, 10,700 on 22 April alone, Archduke Charles had turned despondent. Even while combat continued at Ratisbon, on 23 April he sent a message to his brother advising him to make peace: 'With half the army in dissolution, I have no option but to cross the Danube at Ratisbon and make for Bohemia.' The army, he continued, had to be saved at any price and no reliance could be placed on either the *Landwehr* or the *insurrectio*. On the contrary, the army might 'well be needed to deal with events in the interior of the Monarchy'. An end to hostilities, he told the emperor, was imperative and the sooner the better, 'because once the enemy has entered the lands of Your Majesty they will be ruined and like Prussia occupied for many years'.[9]

After the fall of Ratisbon a vigorous pursuit with several French corps might have brought disaster to Charles, and it was one of Napoleon's maxims always to destroy the main enemy army before moving on his capital. But considering that the archduke was two days ahead and worried about developments in Italy and news of insurrections in Germany, Napoleon decided to end the war quickly by conquering the enemy capital. Initially sending Davout after Charles, he countermanded the order once the archduke had entered Bohemia. 3 corps recrossed the Danube on 29 April as Napoleon turned against Hiller This decision violated his basic strategic principle and has been considered by some historians as a mistake. Perhaps so. For even as the Austrian army marched east towards Bohemia, for once matching the French marching speeds, an average of 14 miles a day, the archduke, acting on his own, tried to come to an accommodation with Napoleon. 'Your Majesty', he wrote, in a letter allegedly composed by Grünne and dated 28 April, 'has announced your arrival by cannon shots without leaving me time to compliment you. I had hardly heard of your presence when the losses I sustained caused me to realize it painfully.' He continued with the suggestion that 'perhaps Fortune has chosen me to assure my country a durable peace', and closed the letter assuring Napoleon that, 'I feel flattered Sire to have crossed swords with the greatest captain of the age ... I beg Your Majesty to believe that my ambition always leads me towards you and that I shall be equally honoured, Sire, to meet you either with the sword or the olive branch.'[10]

Though Napoleon ignored this abject communication, it did much damage to Charles's reputation in Vienna, where there were renewed efforts to remove him from command. But there was no one to replace him. Meanwhile, making his way through Bohemia into Austria, he arrived on 16–17 May on the historic Marchfeld, east of Vienna on the left bank of the Danube. Together with Bellegarde, who had joined him during the retreat, and Hiller, who had crossed over to the right bank at Krems, the archduke now disposed of some 130,000 men. But he had arrived too late. Despite this rapid march, the capital had already been surrendered to Napoleon.

HILLER'S RETREAT AND
THE CAPITULATION OF VIENNA

Following the French breakthrough south of Abensberg on 20 April, Hiller, with his own and elements of two other corps, found himself cut off from the main body of the army. He retreated south-east and on 24 April at Neumarkt, 20 miles from Landshut, he turned against Bessières's Franco-Bavarian pursuers. In a brief engagement, 23,000 foot and 4,000 horse inflicted 2,500 casualties on a weaker French enemy numbering but 16,000 foot and 2,000 horse. But it was not possible to exploit this success. Now aware that Charles was retreating and that Masséna and Lannes were across the Isar, Hiller continued to retreat, making good use of the several tributaries flowing north to the Danube. He crossed into Austrian territory at Braunau on the Inn on 26 April. The same day Legrand's division of 4 Corps stormed Schärding, compromising Hiller's next defence line and compelling him to fall back to the line of the Traun.

After receiving numerous and conflicting instructions from Archduke Charles as well as from Vienna, where the court was beginning to interfere with operations, Hiller, much to the anger of the archduke, chose to obey the imperial instructions.[11] After first moving to Linz, where a fortified camp was alleged to have been prepared and *Landwehr* units mobilized, and finding neither fortifications nor *Landwehr* battalions, a few volunteer units excepted, willing to fight, he took up positions at the market village of Ebelsberg, 5 miles south-east of Linz. This small place, with only eighty-two houses, provided an excellent defensive position located east of the Traun, which was spanned by a 400-yard wide bridge. The streets were narrow and there was a castle overlooking bridge and market. Although Lannes had already crossed the river upstream at Wels, Masséna decided to make a frontal assault across the fortified bridge which the Austrians, hoping to save some transport, had failed to blow. As Claparède's and Legrand's divisions, spearheaded across the bridge by the Tirailleurs du Po and the Tirailleurs de Corse, entered the town, heavy and bloody fighting developed. Here the 4th, 5th, and 6th battalions of the Vienna *Landwehr* volunteers, an exception to the previously poor performance of the *Landwehr*, distinguished themselves. Hiller, who spent the decisive hours calmly lunching on the castle terrace, concerned above all to preserve his corps, refused to commit his ample reserves after he realized that his rear was menaced by Lannes. About 2.30 in the afternoon he ordered his troops to retire from the town. The last Austrian defenders were the 6th Company of the 4th Vienna Volunteer Battalion, the 1st Battalion of the Mittrowsky Infantry No. 40 and an anonymous gunner who continued to serve his cannon to fire canister at the charging French. Casualties had been heavy on both sides: some 8,300 Austrians and 3,500 French were dead, wounded and captured. About 1,000 of the wounded died in the fire that subsequently swept through the wooden shingle buildings in the main street.[12]

The engagement, though costly to the Austrians, had improved morale, but the time bought at Ebelsberg proved insufficient to save Vienna. Evading a rather slow French pursuit, Hiller crossed to the north bank of the Danube, burning bridges and removing all boats along a substantial part of the river, arriving at Saint Pölten, 12 miles from the capital, on 10 May. Assured by Archduke Maximilian, the emperor's brother-in-law, that the capital would be stoutly defended, he detached five grenadier battalions to assist in its defence and then managed to get his corps across the Danube at Krems on 11 May, rejoining the main army at Florisdorf five days later.

THE CAPITULATION OF VIENNA

With over 200,000 inhabitants, Vienna in 1809 was the largest city in central Europe. It was located on the right bank of the Danube, with a small branch of the river separating the city from a large island with the Prater Park and the Leopoldstadt suburb. The city itself was divided into the walled Inner City, housing some 50,000 inhabitants, and a semi-circle of suburbs. Except for the excise walls, the suburbs were unfortified, while the fortifications of the city were outdated with only forty-eight guns mounted on its bastions. But there was a wide, if overgrown, glacis and several hundred guns were stored in the arsenal. From 5 May on, efforts were made to improve the works and 8,000 civilian labourers were employed to clear the glacis and dig hasty fieldworks.[13]

Vienna also had a substantial garrison: eight line battalions and the five grenadier battalions sent by Hiller, fourteen *Landwehr* battalions and 6,000 civic militia. In addition, an appeal for volunteers had received an enthusiastic response, though at the appearance of the French advance guard many of these patriotic defenders slunk away. The Viennese were not known for heroic steadfastness. None the less, while the works were clearly inadequate, an aroused population might have made Napoleon pay dearly for the conquest of the city. But neither Archduke Maximilian nor the citizenry were prepared to fight to the bitter end. The imperial court, library and other institutions were packed up and left Vienna, together with many of the leading citizens. When on 11–12 May French advance elements from Lannes's corps seized Prater island and threw a few howitzer shells into the streets, there was panic and Maximilian, informed that Charles would not arrive until 18 May, decided to evacuate the capital. Had he defended the city it might have put Napoleon in a difficult situation, caught with one part of his army fighting in the streets while the other would have had to turn against the relief army.

But Maximilian lost his nerve. Vienna capitulated on 12 May and late that evening he marched out accompanied by a disorderly column of soldiers, carriages, carts and horses. Encountering a disconcerted Hiller at the north end of the Tabor Bridge he declared, 'I hereby hand this entire mess and the command over to you'. In his haste to leave the city, Maximilian made no attempt to destroy the hundreds of guns in the arsenal or the stores in the magazines, and even abandoned a war chest of 4 million florins. Also left behind to surrender the city was General O'Reilly with seventeen senior and 163 junior officers and 2,000 men.[14]

French troops entered Vienna in force on May 13 and the populace quickly came to terms with its new masters. The great families, the Starhembergs, Czatoriskys, Batthyanys and others, freely opened their palaces to extend generous hospitality to French officers, and intimate relations soon developed between high-society ladies and French officers.[15] And at the lower social level, as one scandalized contemporary reported, 'soldiers and girls from the lower classes mingled on the bastions ... where scenes took place that made Vienna look like Sodom and Gomorrah'.[16] Napoleon had little to fear from the population even after his repulse at Aspern–Essling. He issued a proclamation taking 'its good citizens under my special protection' and ordered General Antoine Andréossy, appointed military governor of Vienna, to inspect the Civic Guard and retain an effective force of 6,000 men with 1,500 to 2,000 muskets in service.[17]

AN EVALUATION

Although the campaign in Bavaria had not achieved the early and decisive victory favoured by Napoleon, it had been an impressive performance. With an improvised and hastily assembled army, about one-third foreign troops and with many raw conscripts, Napoleon had first seized the initiative from the archduke and then driven him back into the Austrian heartland. If this was no longer the army of 1805, it had fought well. But despite reforms that had improved the Austrian Army, the official Austrian history noted sadly, the 'army still was not equal to the requirements of mobile warfare'. On the strategic level the staff had been unable to coordinate movements while corps commanders had shown little initiative and always kept back too many reserves. On the tactical level the French remained more mobile and were clearly superior in broken terrain.[18]

As was his unfortunate habit, Charles blamed his subordinates. He was right to assert that they had not been able to handle independent command, though he forgot that he had done nothing to prepare them for such a role. Moreover, Charles, always concerned with maintaining the dynastic prestige, had willingly accepted the appointment of his brothers and other senior members of the dynasty – Archdukes Ludwig, John, Maximilian and Ferdinand – as corps commanders, positions for which they were clearly unqualified. The other corps commanders, save Hiller, with whom his relations were acrimonious, were all aristocrats, albeit veterans, and all shared the archduke's predilection for caution. At the same time, as supreme commander, Charles rarely revealed his intentions to them while his instructions, issued by Grünne, were often obscure and ambiguous. To remedy this situation during the retreat to Bohemia, the corps system was abolished, though the designation was retained, and he resolved to return to the old and familiar system of fighting the entire army as one tightly controlled body. Chief-of-staff Prochaska, blamed for the staff shortcomings, was dismissed on 8 May and replaced by MG Franz Wimpffen despite his protests that he lacked the qualifications for the position.[19]

There also were administrative and command changes. Kolowrat and Hohenzollern exchanged corps, I and II Reserve Corps were combined in a single Army Reserve under Liechtenstein, and an Army Advance Guard was created and placed under Klenau. Finally, in mid May, Archduke Ludwig, another of the emperor's brothers-in-law, who had never commanded any troops or revealed any great military talent, reported himself sick, retired from his position in command of V Corps and was replaced by FML Heinrich, Prince of Reuss-Plauen.

As for the Austrian multi-national regular troops, regimental officers as well as the rank and file had fought with their usual stolid bravery. However, the legend that in 1809 Austria, or at least its German-speaking areas, was animated by strong patriotic feelings, a view still held by many historians, is at least questionable. The Austrian leadership distrusted the population, and, though there was much patriotic posturing, when challenged only a few *Landwehr* units fought well and, except for the Tyrol where resistance continued beyond the final armistice, there was no broad popular resistance. Still, in some respects the occupation of Vienna was hollow. While defeated, Charles had managed to escape total destruction. An essentially defensive-minded general who still hoped to come to an accommodation with the enemy, he now was positioned behind a wide river, prepared if necessary to resist any attempt by Napoleon to cross over. The war was not yet over.

CHAPTER FOUR

The subsidiary theatres

The Austrian war plans for 1809 called for offensives on several fronts. In addition to the main thrust against the French and their allied armies in Germany, there were to be complementary operations in north Italy, Dalmatia and Galicia, as well as support for a hoped-for popular rising in Saxony. It was felt that early success would enlist support from the Confederation of the Rhine, while major victories might cause the re-entry of Prussia and Russia in the war against Napoleon. In the Tyrol, in particular, careful plans were laid to provide support for a major insurrection against Bavarian rule. Finally, there was a belief that perhaps even in Italy there might be popular revolts against the French.

Among these potential and actual theatres of operations, the most important, though always clearly secondary for both Austria and France, was north Italy. Here, in addition to defeating the French–Italian forces, Austria hoped to regain the territories lost since 1796 – Lombardy, Venetia, Dalmatia as well as the Tyrol. Napoleon regarded his forces in Italy, the Army of Italy, led by his stepson Eugène de Beauharnais, viceroy of the Napoleonic Kingdom of Italy, as the right wing of his deployment, and was primarily concerned to defeat the invading

Austrians, Archduke John's Army of Inner Austria, so as to prevent them from reinforcing the main Austrian army along the Danube. Any minor insurrections against French rule, mainly in north Germany, were to be contained by the newly formed Westphalian 10 Corps, a Dutch division, and in the worst case by a reserve corps under Marshal Kellermann assembling at Frankfurt.

EUGÈNE'S ARMY AND
THE STRATEGIC SITUATION IN ITALY

Napoleon has frequently been blamed for not instructing his senior commanders in the higher art of war, but the case of his young stepson Eugène de Beauharnais is a clear exception. Only 27 years old in 1809, throughout 1808 and into 1809 Eugène received a series of detailed notes regarding the art of war and the defence of the kingdom from his stepfather. In addition, Napoleon provided Eugène with experienced advisors and commanders. These included Generals Charpentier, who had campaigned with Masséna in north Italy, as chief-of-staff, and Paul Grenier, a highly competent old soldier who was given a divisional and later corps command when the Army of Italy reorganized after its initial defeat. The most influential French corps commander was General Etienne Macdonald, who arrived in Italy after the fighting had begun. Having been under a cloud because of his association with General Moreau and partly because of his affair with Princess Pauline from 1800 to 1808, Macdonald was eager to re-establish his reputation and, though his memoirs tend to award himself more credit than was due, he was clearly an excellent fighting soldier. The third corps commander was the veteran General Baraguey d'Hilliers, while General Emmanuel de Grouchy was appointed to lead the army's cavalry reserve. Following his stepfather's example, Eugène kept his Royal Guard, commanded by Brigadier Giuseppe Lecchi, under his personal control. At the next level several division commanders had either fought in Italy in 1805 or in other parts of the empire and on the whole were better than their Austrian counterparts. Despite this talent around him and the emperor's constant personal interest and advice, Eugène was clearly in command of the Army of Italy and improved as the campaign progressed.

While the content of the imperial notes and instructions varied during the period 1808–9, Napoleon tended to emphasize strategic defence: in the end, it was the main French army on the Danube that would decide the fate of Italy during the course of a war. Even when in January 1809 the emperor became concerned with the growing evidence of Austria's belligerent intentions and sent a new set of notes with even more precise instructions, he still advocated a defensive strategy for Eugène's Army of Italy.[1] In any case, Napoleon did not regard war as imminent, and, perhaps relying too much on the Tsar's promises made at Erfurt, expected Vienna to have second thoughts. But even if war came, he held that an Austrian offensive could not open before the end of April, perhaps even May. He did make preparations to strengthen and concentrate his forces in Germany, though 15,000 new recruits were earmarked for Italy. In addition, in January he had warned his German allies of a possible threat and instructed them to mobilize, while Eugène levied some 9,000 new recruits in the kingdom. By March 1809, Eugène's army comprised nine infantry divisions – six French and three Italian – as well as three cavalry divisions: two dragoons and one light cavalry. The regiments of the Army of Italy were solid troops, if not all up to strength or fully trained, especially those units recalled from Spain and Naples and six battalions from Dalmatia. An initial drawback was that the Army of Italy was not organized in corps until several weeks after the beginning of war. Still, including the two veteran French divisions, about 7,000 men each, of General Auguste Marmont's Army of Dalmatia, the later 11 Corps, Eugène's forces – 56,700 infantry, 5,600 cavalry, 5,120 Royal Guard, a total of well over 70,000 with 132 guns – far outnumbered the Austrian Army of Inner Austria preparing to invade the kingdom.[2]

Even so, the size of the Army of Italy did not offset the shortcomings of its strategic dispositions. Napoleon's instructions to his stepson advocated that at least initially he remain on the strategic defence behind the natural barriers provided by the numerous rivers and mountains to the north. And though by the end of March the situation in Germany was becoming more threatening, the emperor, relying on Russian support and wishing to avoid provoking the Austrians by premature concentrations, did not revise his instructions. 'As for me,' he wrote to Eugène, 'I will remain stationary for all of April and I do not think that the Austrians will attack especially with the Russians moving on Hungary and Galicia.'[3] But after 1 April the situation had clearly changed and Napoleon's failure to alert Eugène was a serious miscalculation.

Napoleon had given Eugène a free hand to evacuate the forward area between the Isonzo and Piave rivers, in an extremity to fall back to the Adige or even the Piave, but he had not yet given him permission to form corps or appoint corps commanders. Therefore, though receiving numerous reports about Austrian concentrations, Eugène retained a false sense of security and left his army dispersed across the kingdom. In March he had only part of his army deployed forward: two divisions, General Serras's 1st (French) and Broussier's 2nd (French), supported by a cavalry brigade between the Isonzo and Tagliamento rivers. The rest of the army was deployed behind the successive river lines. Two additional French divisions, Grenier's 3rd and Lamarque's 4th, were between the Tagliamento and the Piave, while the Italian divisions were in front of the Adige river. The Italian Royal Guard and the cavalry divisions encamped behind the Adige and the Guard at Milan, while Barbou's 4th and Durutte's 6th (French) divisions were organizing in north central Italy around Bologna. Clearly these dispositions were compromised if the insurgents, reinforced by regular Austrian troops, took much of the Tyrol, though in the event the hardy mountaineers were neither willing nor able to provide a strategic threat in the Italian plain. In any case, Napoleon's instructions to remain on the strategic defensive explain Eugène's decision not to concentrate beyond the Piave or withdraw from the Isonzo.[4] Even clear warnings from agents in Trieste could not shake Eugène's conviction that war was not imminent, and on 10 April he wrote to his wife that he did not expect hostilities in the near future.[5]

THE AUSTRIANS INVADE ITALY

But the Austrian Army of Inner Austria was already marching. Its commander, Archduke John, had led an army at Hohenlinden in 1800 and a corps in 1805 and had been defeated on both occasions, but his dynastic status ensured him another command. A stubborn and uncooperative man, he held a greatly exaggerated opinion of his military talents and was unwilling to subordinate himself when needed to Archduke Charles. His command consisted of two corps: VIII (24,500 infantry and 2,600 cavalry, under FML Albert Gyulai, concentrating in Carinthia); and IX (22,000 infantry and 2,000 cavalry, under FML Ignaz Gyulai, who also held office as Ban of Croatia, concentrating in Carniola). In addition to its regular troops each corps had second-line components, *Landwehr* and *insurrectio*, which remained as a general reserve inside their province of origin, and deployed a division-sized task force. The first task force, originally assigned to VIII Corps, was under FML Johann de Chasteler, who with 10,000 foot and 370 horse, was to enter the Tyrol on 9 April to trigger a prearranged insurrection there and cut communications between the French armies in Germany and Italy. Detached from IX Corps was Major General Stojevich, who was assigned some 12,000 *Grenzer* to attack Marmont and recover lost Austrian territory in Croatia and Dalmatia.

When all these detached formations and units are subtracted, John had fewer than 46,000 men available to attack Eugène, though he had retained one major advantage: his troops were organized in corps. By 9 April both corps were deployed concentrated in their jump-off positions at Villach and Tarvis in Carithia, from where they were to surprise the two unsupported divisions of the Army of Italy between the Isonzo and the Piave. On 10 April the Austrians advanced in several columns through the valleys to Pordenone. The main force of VIII and IX Corps, heavy snowfalls and mist notwithstanding, moved via Caporetto to Cividale and on 13 April occupied Udine. Meanwhile, Eugène had originally decided to execute the defensive scheme prescribed by Napoleon calling for a delaying action falling back to the Adige, a scheme based on the assumption of an enemy offensive driving from the east. But if Eugène's previous thinking had disregarded intelligence reports about the coming Austrian offensive, he now swung to the other extreme and believed the exaggerated news coming from the Tyrol. Here the small Bavarian garrison, six battalions and a cavalry squadron distributed in small stations at Innsbruck, Prunecken, Brixen and Sterzing, had been overrun by the combined forces of Chasteler's division, which Eugène overestimated at 18,000, even 20,000 strong, supported by Tyrolean insurgents. Also two columns of French troops, 4,500 in all, marching north to join the Army of Germany, had been forced to surrender or driven back to Trent. These events seemed to compromise a defensive north–south front along the Piave, Brenta or Adige rivers and appeared to threaten the strategic left and rear of the Army of Italy.

But the apparent division of two enemy forces also presented an offensive opportunity if Eugène could use his central position to defeat one part of the enemy first and then turn against the second. On 11 April Eugène ordered d'Hilliers to take charge of all French and allied troops in the Tyrol. He allocated Fontanelli's division to Baraguey, while the 112th Infantry and the 7th Dragoons, together with the remnants of the French column at Trent, formed a provisional division under General Honore Vial. By 14 April Baraguey disposed of 10,300 foot and 1,100 horse, adequate to protect Eugène's exposed and vulnerable left flank. Greatly overestimating the strength of Chasteler's Austro-Tyrolean forces, however, by the end of the month Baraguey had retired to Rivoli, north of Verona. But with clear orders not to retreat further, here he held, protecting the strategic left of the Army of Italy.

Meanwhile Eugène concentrated his forces to deal with John's offensive. Broussier and Serras were ordered to fall back east to the Livenza river, where a total of five infantry divisions and one of light cavalry were assembling near Sacile, with two additional divisions, Lamarque's infantry and Pully's dragoons, expected to arrive by 15 April.

The day before, the viceroy had sent an over-confident letter to the emperor explaining that events in the Tyrol had forced him to abandon the defensive and attack John. He continued that reinforcements had already arrived, a lie, as Lamarque was still at Vicenza and Pully at Padua, and that he expected to defeat the Austrians within two days.[6] On 16 April, near Sacile, a small town 25 miles south-west of Udine, Eugène, with about 41,000 men, including 2,000 cavalry and 64 guns, prematurely attacked the Austrians, nearly equal in strength though with 4,000 horse and 148 guns. After severe fighting Eugène was repulsed and fell back with 3,000 killed and wounded, losing 3,500 prisoners, an eagle and 15 guns. Although John, who always tended to move slowly, still had fresh troops, he did not conduct an energetic pursuit and this gave Eugène time to make an orderly retreat to the Adige–Alpone line, the position originally recommended by the emperor, where he halted and reorganized. He now received permission for his army to adopt the corps formations and in consequence created an army artillery reserve under General Sorbier, an experienced gunner. Finally, pressure against Baraguey was slackening as Chasteler moved his troops north to hold a new Bavarian offensive. Eugène now gathered additional reinforcements and for the first time managed to concentrate almost his entire army.

But Eugène had been defeated at Sacile and though in his communications to Napoleon he tried to minimize the affair, the emperor was exasperated. On 30 April he sent an angry letter threatening his stepson with possible relief from command. 'War is a serious business,' Napoleon wrote, 'in which one can compromise one's reputation and country.' The letter continued that a serious mistake had been made in giving Eugène command of the army and that the emperor wished that he had sent Masséna to take charge. 'If circumstances become pressing, you should write to the king of Naples [Marshal Murat] asking him to join the army, you will give up command to him and place yourself under his orders.'[7] Clearly, the emperor was concerned about John's possible appearance on his right flank along the Danube.

However, much delayed by events in the Tyrol, the letter arrived only on 6 May, and by then the situation in Italy had changed radically. After Sacile, John had reverted to the customary Austrian rate of advance. Though the distance from Sacile to the new French positions at Caldiero, located in the fork between the Alpone and Adige, 10 miles east of Verona, was only 60 miles, he took eleven days and arrived there only on 27 April. If he had ordered an all-out pursuit after Sacile things might have turned out differently. But when John finally arrived at Caldiero he faced a reconstituted and fully concentrated Army of Italy, almost double his strength, and he also was aware of the Austrian defeat in Bavaria. On 29 April John had received orders from the Emperor Francis to withdraw his army north along the Inn valley to join the main army, a course of action that had become patently impossible.

Eugène, meanwhile, had developed a plan to destroy the Austrians once they closed up to the Adige–Alpone line. He would use the Adige line as a screen to mass his army and hurl it across the river, bringing superior forces to bear against a part of the Austrian front. Simultaneously, the division-sized garrison of Venice, commanded by General Auguste Cafarelli, some 8,000 strong, was to attack and threaten John's left. Thus the Army of Inner Austria would be caught between converging forces.

In the end there was no need for this ambitious plan. After repulsing a foolish sortie by Eugène on 27 April, John retreated north with FML Johann Frimont's division as his rearguard. On 8 May he attempted to slow the pursuing Army of Italy, further reinforced by the Venice garrison and Fontanelli's division, at the Piave. Using good tactical sense, showing that he had learned his lessons at Sacile, Eugène carefully concentrated most of his army, a divisional-size Advance Guard, six infantry and three cavalry divisions and the Royal Guard, a total of between 45,000 and 48,000 men. Despite being hampered by the swollen river that became too dangerous to ford in the afternoon, the Army of Italy broke Austrian resistance by evening. Although his actual casualties were small and the viceroy called off his pursuit prematurely, the Austrians were dispirited. Eugène had shown himself a competent battle captain and compensated for his defeat at Sacile. This time he sent a detailed report to the emperor boasting of his success.[8]

ARCHDUKE JOHN RETREATS INTO HUNGARY

John's army was now outmatched. When he rallied his troops after Sacile, he found but 24,000 men and ordered a general withdrawal from Italy. However, still hoping to rally local support, he split his army. Ignaz Gyulai, Ban of Croatia and authorized to call out the Croatian *insurrectio*, was ordered to Laibach in Slovenia with part of VIII Corps, there to join Stojevich's corps repelled from Dalmatia by Marmont. The remainder of his corps joined IX Corps moving on Villach in Carinthia. In turn, Eugène divided his army into two main columns, one under Eugène and the other under Macdonald. The Austrians could find some moral solace when, in the narrow valley passes towards Carinthia, Eugène's progress was impeded by the heroic defence of two reinforced blockhouses at Malborgeth and Predil, the 'Austrian Thermopylae'. Each of these works, a blockhouse with an additional redoubt and stockade, was manned by a few gunners and some 250 Croat *Grenzer* but could not hold out for long. None the less, their resistance bought three days, while Macdonald proceeded towards Laibach. Malborgeth was outflanked by a French division before being stormed on 17 May; Predil held out under heavy bombardment before its defenders were overwhelmed by a two-regiment assault on the next day, 18 May.[9]

On 19 May, John had received orders to march north and join with Kolowrat, then on the north bank of the Danube near Linz, in operations against Napoleon's rear. But John correctly judged this enterprise hopeless and indeed, on 18 May, Kolowrat's attempt to cross the Danube had been repelled with heavy losses. Instead, he marched to Graz in Styria where he hoped to unite with Jellacic's strong division, 8,000 men who had been forced out of Bavaria and would have provided a most useful reinforcement for the Army of Inner Austria.

While waiting at Graz, John missed an opportunity to fall on either Eugène or Macdonald, each of their columns weaker than his own force. Instead he waited for Jellacic to join him, but Jellacic, a remarkably unlucky and inept general, did not manage to bring many reinforcements. After making a successful retreat through the Tyrol and fighting off Wrede's pursuing Bavarian division, Jellacic blundered, while still in line of march, into Grenier's two divisions at Saint Michael near Leoben on 25 May, still some 30 miles north of Graz. Dispersed and defeated, only a remnant of 2,000 Austrians joined John the next day. Grenier lost but 600 men. Informed that John's army was in retreat, Marmont had taken the offensive on 14 May and, after demolishing Stojevic's forces on 16 May, reached Laibach on 3 June. Here instructions reached him to continue his advance to Graz which he took on 26 May, only to receive orders three days later to join Napoleon's army preparing for a second crossing of the Danube.

John remained at Graz for four days. Then, leaving Gyulai and several battalions of VIII Corps behind with orders to retard the French pursuit, he began his retreat to Körmend (Komorn) on the Hungarian frontier. On reaching this fortress the Army of Inner Austria, including the remnants of Jellacic's division, counted hardly 15,000 men. At Körmend John picked up supplies and reinforcements and now his forces numbered 14,000 regulars, 3,000 *Landwehr* and 4,000 horse, of which half were *insurrectio* cavalry. Ignaz Gyulai's IX Corps still was at Agram in Croatia, 100 miles to the south-west. At this point Napoleon, who on 21–22 May had been repulsed in his attempt to cross the Danube against Charles at Aspern–Essling, became perhaps overly concerned about the possible junction of John and the Austrian main army and now ordered deployments to prevent such an eventuality. Davout's 3 Corps was sent to Pressburg, the Army of Italy ordered to Neustadt, some 18 miles south of Vienna, and Macdonald's Corps, little more than Lamarque's division, was instructed to take Graz. This decided John to redirect his retreat, and he now attempted to concentrate whatever formations were still detached and in reach at Raab where

Archduke Joseph, the palatine of Hungary, had assembled some 20,000 *insurrectio* troops, predominantly cavalry, good riders but lacking combat skills. John arrived at Raab on 13 June.

One day later, the Army of Italy attacked the combined Austrian forces, numbering some 30,000 men, at Raab. On 6 June, Napoleon, still concerned about a possible recovery of the Army of Inner Austria, had instructed Eugène to attack the Austrians at Raab and attached two cavalry divisions, Colbert and Montbrun, to the Army of Italy.[10] The battle of Raab was the climax of the 1809 Italian campaign for Eugène. John had deployed his forces in an excellent defensive position, anchored on the marshy and steep-banked river Raab and with a ridge and a stone farmhouse dominating the centre. Marshy ground prevented any outflanking moves to the north, leaving only the southern approach open to a flank attack. Throughout the day there was bitter fighting in the centre, where John had tried to stiffen his troops by interspersing regular units with *insurrectio* troops. With only one Italian division, Severoli's, left, Eugène attacked across the river but was initially unable to bring artillery across. Suffering severe casualties, Severoli was at first forced back and General Durutte's French division was brought in to assault the farm position, which would change hands five times.

Eugène now sent Montbrun's and Grouchy's cavalry to seek a ford across the Pancsa creek to the south. One was found, though it was defended by a small three-gun Austrian battery. Bringing forward two horse artillery companies, twelve guns, the Austrian guns were silenced and Montbrun's and Grouchy's horsemen engaged the Austrian cavalry, mainly *insurrectio* squadrons. The Austrian cavalry was put to flight within a short time, while in the centre Pacthod's division and the Royal Italian Guards took the farmhouse. The battle was lost and John retreated. His forces divided, the Hungarians seeking refuge in the town and citadel of Raab, which fell on 23 June, the remainder moving north across the Danube to Komorn and eventually to Pressburg to be contained by a force under Baraguey. This was Eugène's second major victory, won, moreover, on the anniversary of Marengo, 14 June

1800. It renewed the emperor's confidence in the abilities of his step-son. On 28 June Napoleon told Eugène that the Army of Italy was no longer independent but was to be incorporated into his main army.[11] On 1 July it was ordered to join the great concentration at Vienna.

There remained one more dramatic episode. Broussier's weak division, fewer than 4,000, had been left at Graz where the citadel remained in Austrian hands. He was also supposed to be joined by Marmont's 11 Corps. But the Duke of Ragusa moved so slowly, despite a reprimand from Napoleon, that he arrived only on 27 June. As a result, between 25–27 June Broussier was engaged by almost 22,000 Austrians of IX Corps, albeit mainly *insurrectio*, and compelled to retreat. During the engagement the 84th Line of Broussier's division demonstrated the mettle of French infantry, withstanding repeated attacks by Austrian troops who outnumbered it ten to one. When news of the engagement and the splendid performance of the 84th reached Napoleon, he ordered that the regimental flag be embroidered with the phrase 'Un contre dix' ('one against ten'), making the regiment the equal of the famed 'terrible' 57th Line. If the often-stated asser-tion that the calibre of Napoleon's troops had deteriorated in 1809 had any currency, the 84th Line had not heard of it. On 29 June Marmont and Broussier were ordered to evacuate Graz and join the army near Vienna. Only one weak division, General Jean-Baptiste Rusca's, was to maintain a blockade at Graz, garrison Klagenfurth in Carinthia and guard communications with Italy.

THE TYROLEAN INSURRECTION

As has been repeatedly pointed out, the picture of a great national German uprising to support the Habsburgs in 1809 has been greatly overstated. Despite the introduction of the *Landwehr*, the ruling classes always remained reluctant to arm the populace at large, fearing they might get out of hand. For their part, though willing to make a fine show when the enemy was far away, the population as a whole was not really prepared to fight. In the words of an English historian,

'Popular resistance simply lacked the potential to justify the weight it has been given'.[12] With one exception, the various risings in the spring and summer in Germany at best had nuisance value for the French, who in any case promptly wiped them out, and had no influence on the main theatre of operations in the Danube valley.

The exception was the Tyrolean insurrection, which though short-lived at times approached the level of popular revolt on the Iberian Peninsula. It not only maintained itself in the face of serious reverses, but continued after Austria made peace with Napoleon in October. Most important, however, the insurrection, pre-planned in Vienna, played an integral role in Austrian strategy. Supported from the outset by a substantial detachment of regulars under FML Chasteler, the Tyrolean insurgency threatened the right flank of Napoleon's advance in Germany and at times appeared to menace Eugène's advance into Inner Austria.

Under Habsburg rule, the Tyrol had enjoyed a privileged status, with limited exemption from conscription – troops recruited here were genuine volunteers – the right to retain its own militia, the *Landes Schützen*, and the privilege to determine its own taxation in a provincial assembly largely drawn from the free peasantry and the burghers of the towns. When the centralizing Emperor Joseph II had tried to impose uniform government, conscription, taxation and church reform through-out his domains in 1789, he was confronted by resistance across the Tyrol and rapidly obliged to revoke his military and administrative reforms. In 1792 and again in 1799, sharpshooter levies had been called out but achieved little. But there was much resentment when, after the Tyrol was ceded to Bavaria in 1805, the new centralizing administration immediately began to demolish the ancient liberties of the Tyroleans. Interfering with the ecclesiastical affairs of a deeply Catholic popula-tion, changing the civil administration and even abolishing the name of Tyrol and dividing the country into three administrative districts caused serious resentment that was exploited by Archduke John and the war party in Vienna. The final cause for the Tyrolean revolt was the Bavarian attempt to introduce conscription in late 1808 and early 1809.

Secret meetings had taken place since as early as 1806 and plans were laid for any insurrection to be immediately supported by a substantial Austrian troop detachment and arms deliveries. It should also be noted that the indigenous sharpshooter guilds were well armed and highly competent in the use of their privately owned short carbines. None the less, the idea of a popular insurrection worried the reactionaries in Vienna. It was during one of these planning meetings that Andreas Hofer, an innkeeper and leader of the incipient revolt, was introduced to the Emperor Francis II as a 'genuine patriot', a statement that evoked Francis's famous observation: 'But is he a patriot for me?'

The Tyrolean insurrection did not come as a total surprise to Napoleon or the Bavarian authorities. But having taken the correct decision to concentrate on destroying the main Austrian army under Charles, they took a calculated risk. With the main body of the Bavarian army under Lefebvre fighting in the north, the total Bavarian force in the Tyrol amounted to fewer than 4,200 men, whose principal mission was to protect communications along the main road connecting the Army of Italy and the Army of Germany. This weak force, commanded by the incompetent General August Kinkel, was divided into penny packets around Innsbruck and Brixen, both towns divided by the Brenner Pass, with small detachments north along the Inn to Altbayern and south to the Kingdom of Italy. Only the fortress of Kufstein near Salzburg, lightly held by some depot companies but mounting sixty guns, provided a strong position.[13]

When on 9 April the promised Austrian troop aid, Chasteler's augmented division, had crossed the frontier at Lienz, the Tyrolean sharpshooter *Schützen* militia, alerted by church bells and signal fires on the mountains, assembled at once. On 10 April they drove out the small Bavarian garrison at Sterzing, two under-strength light-infantry battalions, which retreated south across the Brenner Pass. Three days later, now 15,000 combatants strong, commanded by Major Martin Teimer, a retired officer, and inspired by popular leaders like Hofer and the fanatic Capuchin monk Josef Speckbacher, they defeated a 4,000-

strong Bavarian–French force in the first battle of Mount Isel, 2 miles south of the capital Innsbruck. Continuing on to Innsbruck, on 16 April after a short siege the garrison, 3,860 Bavarians and 2,050 French, capitulated, providing the insurgents with a valuable booty of five cannons, two mortars, thousands of muskets and considerable stores. The same day Chasteler's leading brigade entered Innsbruck while a 2,000-strong French column marching on the main road from Italy to the Danube was attacked by the insurgents and forced to capitulate. Success spread the revolt west to adjoining Vorarlberg, ceded to Württemberg at Pressburg, where insurgents under Anton Schneider, a lawyer, drove the small garrison out of the country and occupied Bregenz. Encouraged, Tyrolean war parties even raided into south Bavaria, creating bitter hostility by their looting, brutality and occasional atrocities that would carry over into the guerrilla war in the home country. With almost no regular troops available, the Munich government was compelled to create ad hoc forces by the first week of May, notably a special 7,500-strong Mountain Sharpshooter (*Gebirgschützen*) Corps under Count Max von Arco.

After Ratisbon, Lefebvre was detached to deal with the insurrection. In the end, his intervention with Deroy's and Wrede's divisions from 7 Corps, assisted by small contingents of Confederation of the Rhine troops, decided the issue. On 12 May Deroy relieved Kufstein and the next day Wrede defeated Chasteler's main body at Wörgl, a village 10 miles south-east of Kufstein, driving the Austrians and Tyroleans back into Carinthia. The Austrians lost 200 dead and wounded, 2,000 prisoners of war, nine cannon and three flags. The victory, however, was marred by a level of atrocities that caused Lefebvre, a hard man, to issue an order-of-the-day stating that he was deeply offended by the conduct of the troops. 'Who', he demanded, has permitted 'the many cruelties, murders, looting?' He continued 'that soldiers had no right to killed unarmed civilians, plunder houses and huts, and torch villages. I ask you soldiers, where were your feelings of humanity?'[14]

On 19 May the Bavarians reoccupied Innsbruck and, convinced that he had broken the revolt, on 22 May Lefebvre took the bulk of his forces back to Salzburg, leaving behind only Deroy's division, little above 5,000 combatants, in the capital. But only three days later the Tyroleans, this time led by Hofer and Haspinger, rose again. The second battle of Mount Isel on 25 May remained undecided, but four days later the third battle of Mount Isel was a victory of 1,400 Austrian regulars and some 13,600 Tyrolean levies over the Bavarians under Deroy and enabled the Tyroleans to occupy Innsbruck again. For once optimistic following the success at Aspern–Essling, the Emperor Francis now gave his solemn assurance that Austria would retain the Tyrol in any peace treaty, an undertaking he would break after he was defeated.

The Battle of Wagram and the Armistice of Znaim released additional French and German troops, Rouyer's division, Bavarians and Saxons among them, which, conducting a concentric offensive, reoccupied Innsbruck by 30 July. Even so, by the next day, 1 August, the rebellion flared up again. Once more, the insurgents, now fighting without the support of regular Austrian troops and with the Austrian civilian administrator withdrawn from Innsbruck, were initially and surprisingly victorious. On 4 and 5 August the Tyroleans led by Speckbacher managed to ambush Saxon and Bavarian troops in a narrow valley, named the Sachsenklemme (Saxon clamp) ever since. Blocking the defile at its narrowest point with well-placed rocks and tree trunks, they inflicted about 500 casualties and forced the remaining 700 to surrender. On 13 August Lefebvre with 10,000 men was defeated in the fourth battle of Mount Isel, a success that enabled Hofer to enter Innsbruck again. Here he proclaimed a provisional government in the name of the Emperor Francis I, assuming the title of military governor (*Landeskommandant*). When the rebels also gained victories in the west and south of the country, a deeply despondent Lefebvre evacuated the Tyrol. But this was the last notable success of the insurgents. The defeat of Austria allowed Napoleon to employ overwhelming resources to crush the revolt. Mustering 50,000 Bavarian, Württemberg, Saxon and

Italian troops, he ordered a methodical offensive. On 28 October a Bavarian detachment once again occupied the capital. Hofer had managed to mobilize some 8,000 men south of Innsbruck, but these were the 'last levy', old men and boys, and their activities lacked cohesion and enterprise. When attacked by Wrede in the fifth battle of Mount Isel on 1 November, the Tyroleans broke and fled. Ultimately this engagement decided the fate of the country.

Though Hofer fought on, he rapidly lost support. Food was short, many were disillusioned and it became increasingly difficult to keep men fighting. Moreover, in the new offensive, a deliberate effort was made to curb troop brutalities and to gain the hearts and minds of the population. The Bavarians in particular had learned a good deal about pacification and mountain fighting. Now more disciplined, the French and allied troops committed fewer atrocities while, by occupying the valleys, they forced the Tyrolean insurgents to take refuge in the inhospitable mountains. With supplies short, resistance flagged and then ceased in the north of the country; within a month the south-west of the country was similarly pacified. Hofer himself took shelter in a mountain hut, but his hideout was betrayed and he was captured on 27 January 1810. Despite pleas for mercy from Prince Eugène and others, a French court-martial tried him as a rebel and he was executed by firing squad in the dry ditch of Fortress Mantua on 20 February. As Carl von Clausewitz, the great interpreter of war, pointed out, national insurrections 'thrive in mountains, but always need support from small regular units'.[15] In the campaign of 1809 these conditions prevailed initially in the Tyrol, but after the withdrawal of Chasteler's division, the Tyroleans stubbornly fought on, greatly aided by the terrain which provided them with tactical advantages. But they had to come down from their mountains for food and this proved their tactical Achilles heel. Strategically, once Napoleon was established near Vienna and given Charles's reluctance to cross the broad river to attack him, any temporary interruption of communications between Germany and Italy had little effect.

SPRING INSURRECTIONS IN NORTH GERMANY

Austrian hopes for a national uprising in north Germany were also to be disappointed. Neither the three insurrections in Westphalia nor the Duke of Brunswick's operations in central Germany inspired a national revolt. They were embarrassments only, easily dealt with by reserve and allied forces, including Dutch and Danish units.[16] They opened with insurrections in the Kingdom of Westphalia, a member of the Confederation of the Rhine since 1807, created by combining Hanover with the duchies of Brunswick and Hesse-Cassel and ruled by King Jerome, Napoleon's brother, from the capital, Kassel. Like all other members of the Rheinbund, Westphalia was to provide an army for field service. This was originally set at 25,000, but wanting a well-founded force Napoleon then decreed it should consist of only 12,500 men. But overly ambitious, Jerome raised a larger army with a disproportionately large Royal Guard and with his line regiments – four infantry regiments, one light battalion, two cavalry regiments and two foot artillery batteries – manned with volunteers and conscripts. In addition, various units of National Guard were formed. Officers were found from various sources, with at least 50 per cent of them Hessians, some 25 per cent Prussian, Brunswick and Hanoverian and the remainder French. Holding mainly senior and staff positions, the French officers, largely cronies of King Jerome, aroused a fair amount of dislike and compromised the emergence of a national Westphalian force. While conditions of service were enlightened, the army had not yet been fully formed or coalesced and in the spring of 1809 Westphalia was beset by three small uprisings, two led by former Prussian officers, one by an active-duty Prussian officer.

In late 1808 and early 1809 one regiment of chevaulegers and one infantry division had been ordered to Spain, leaving King Jerome with only his Royal Guard, one under-strength cuirassier regiment, one formed and three as yet still assembling infantry regiments, all widely dispersed, at his disposal. The first uprising came between 2 and 4 April, that is even before Austria opened hostilities.

Friedrich Karl von Katte, a pensioned former Prussian lieutenant, had been approached by German conspirators directed from Vienna and had agreed to raise a force to take Magdeburg fortress. Though he spent several months trying to recruit followers, he had only about 300 men when he attempted to march on Magdeburg. After crossing the Elbe from Prussia into Westphalia, he encountered a mounted patrol of Westphalian National Guards and fled back across the river. His force disbanded and Katte escaped into Bohemia to join the Duke of Brunswick's enterprise.

The collapse of Katte's enterprise should have been a warning. The next attempt at a revolt also only lasted three days, 22–24 April, and was led by a former Prussian officer, Wilhelm Freiherr von Dörnberg, who had been taken into the Royal Guard where he attempted to gain support for another revolt. Dörnberg was an experienced officer, though lacking judgment, but his associates, recruited in the various former states that been combined to form Westphalia, were self-important and confused enthusiasts. Acting on the news of the initially successful Austrian invasion of Bavaria and anticipating support from a Prussian military revolt, Dörnberg's scheme was apparently to seize Jerome and his French generals and capture the capital. Beyond this the plotters had no concrete plans.

On 22 April, while Napoleon was beating the Austrians at Eckmühl, Dörnberg raised the standard of revolt, assembling about 4,000 men. He had already given up his attempt to capture Jerome, but on the 23rd was marching at the head of his small column towards Kassel. While surprised by developments, Jerome did not panic. He was able to muster some loyal troops who managed to halt and then to disperse the disorderly rebels of the main body, while other insurgent groups met a similar fate. By the evening of the 23rd the insurrection had collapsed, its leader fleeing in disguise to Bohemia. Jerome, despite advice to the contrary, had remained in the capital and by reminding his officers to remember their oath, had kept waverers in line to lead their troops against the rebels.

Finally, there was the attempt by a Prussian major, Ferdinand von Schill, a cavalry officer who had gained a reputation leading raids against the French rear in 1807 and who hoped that his vision would inflame a national revolt in north Germany and lead Prussia to re-open the war against France. On 28 April he led his 2nd Brandenburg Hussars out of Berlin and, after informing them of his intent to invade Westphalia, rode on towards Magdeburg. But when he learned that this strong fortress was prepared for defence, he turned south towards Saxony to appear before Wittenberg. Though he asserted that he was but the vanguard of the Prussian Army, two energetic Saxon captains refused either to capitulate or to comply with his demand for a very substantial amount of money.

Frustrated, Schill turned north into Westphalia. After scoring some minor successes he found that the population, fearing that the enterprise was likely to degenerate into brigandage, was not about to rise against the French. By 4 May he received intelligence that Dörnberg had failed and that a French–Westphalian force from Magdeburg was marching to intercept his small force – which he had renamed the Freikorps Schill in order not to compromise Prussia – to block his onward march. On 5 May a small force consisting of two companies of the French 22nd Line, four Westphalian companies and two guns confronted Schill at Dodendorf south of Magdeburg. The ensuing encounter was a minor tactical victory for Schill but a costly one, with Schill increasingly disappointed that the Westphalians had not gone over to him and that his losses – twelve officers, seventy men and numerous horses – could not be replaced. Discouraged, he crossed into the duchy of Mecklenburg-Schwerin and then began his march north along the Elbe and east towards Stralsund in Swedish Pomerania, where he hoped to find support from the Royal Navy and from the Swedish troops. Schill reached Stralsund on 24 May and seized the dilapidated fortress, encountering negligible resistance. Here some Swedish soldiers and militia infantry from Rügen Island joined his force, bringing it up to 1,400 men with fifteen pieces of artillery.

In Kassel, meanwhile, Jerome's government, believing that Schill was but the vanguard of a Prussian invasion, had panicked and on 4 May had called on the minister of war in Paris and on Kellermann for support. Napoleon refused and told Jerome that his 10 Corps was more than adequate to defend the kingdom. Even so, Kellermann dispatched a Berg regiment to Kassel where it arrived at the end of June. While the regiment saw no action, its presence allowed Jerome to employ his Royal Guard for operations. At that point the bulk of 10 Corps was distributed with the Royal Guard, a combined battalion of French depot troops and the Berg infantry regiment at Kassel, the line units and the companies of the French 22nd Line in Magdeburg, and a Dutch division under GD Pierre Guillaume Gratien between Hamburg and Bremen. Although command and control of 10 Corps was totally ineffective, the situation not improved by rivalry between the various commanders, by 20 May it had become clear that Schill had but a tiny force and now Gratien set off in pursuit. After some delay Gratien, reinforced by some 2,100 Danish troops to around 6,000 men, stormed the fortress on 31 May. Schill was killed during the fighting. His remaining officers and men surrendered. Randomly selected, fourteen troopers were shot between 18 and 22 July; the remainder were sent to the galleys at Cherbourg and Brest. The eleven officers captured faced court-martial at Wesel and were shot on 16 September. Only a handful of Schill's men escaped into Prussia, where the officers were cashiered and the men imprisoned.

THE BLACK BAND AND
AUSTRIAN INCURSIONS INTO SAXONY

Among the various revolts raised in Germany in 1809, the efforts of the Black Brunswickers, a force raised and commanded by the 38-year-old deposed Duke of Brunswick-Oels, Friedrich Wilhelm, were perhaps the most effective and certainly the luckiest. His duchy had been absorbed into Westphalia and he had retired to Baden. When it became clear that Austria was intent on war with France, he hurried to Vienna to sign a convention that he would raise a small corps, about 2,000 strong, and join the war against France as an independent ally not as part of the Austrian Army. Obsessed by thoughts of revenge against Napoleon and France, he clothed his men in totally black uniforms, hence their name, the 'Black Band'. On 21 May he issued a proclamation calling on all Germans to revolt and began to engage a small war against French communications, depots and such like in Saxony from where most line troops had departed as the 9 Corps under Bernadotte. But the duke's forces displayed an unfortunate proclivity to loot and plunder and became little more than brigands. Meanwhile, his appeals for volunteers fell on deaf ears: fewer than 200 men were enlisted. Even the support of an Austrian division under FML Carl am Ende, arriving from Bohemia in late May, did not improve the Brunswickers' effectiveness or their recruitment effort and neither did other Austrian detachments sent from Bohemia on raids into Saxony.

They were none the less an embarrassment to the French and their German allies when they occupied Dresden on 16 July, this despite improving Saxon attempts to raise or organize new troops even to the extent of recalling units from Poland. This annoyed Napoleon. The region's defence was the responsibility of Jerome's 10 Corps, but the prince had done very little. Now stung into action by several harsh reprimands from the emperor, he finally sent Westphalian and Dutch units to drive the Black Band out of Saxony. Main elements of 10 Corps arrived in the combat area on 1 July, but on 13 July the Znaim armistice ended the fighting between France and Austria, and on orders from Archduke Charles, the Austrian contingents, ultimately commanded by FML Kienmayer, were withdrawn on 21 July. As an independent ally of Austria, the Duke of Brunswick refused to acknowledge the armistice between the Napoleonic and Habsburg empires and with a small mixed force, some 2,200 men, set out towards north Germany passing through Brunswick. He had expected popular support in his ancestral lands, but little emerged and though he managed to defeat a scandalously poorly led Westphalian column, mainly the 5th Line, on

1 August at Halberstadt, he had no option but to continue to the North Sea. Evading an extremely badly handled Westphalian and Saxon pursuit, the duke and his remaining 1,600 men – three light battalions, one sharpshooter company, a hussar regiment, a lancer squadron and a horse artillery battery – managed to embark on Royal Navy ships near Bremen on 3 and 4 August. Thus they escaped the fate of Schill's men and, reorganized on the Isle of Wight and designated as the Brunswick-Oels *Jäger*, in October 1810 they were sent to join Wellington's army in Spain.

SIDESHOWS IN DALMATIA AND POLAND

The Austrian war plan had included offensive operations into Dalmatia and the Grand Duchy of Warsaw. Although Marmont's Army of Dalmatia was part of the forces under Eugène, there was little co-operation until the Austrians had retreated from the Adige. Marmont's immediate task was to contain the greatest number of Austrians and Stojevic and his Croatian *Grenzer* reserve battalions and *Landwehr* levies made small advances, but within weeks stalled in the fire of the veteran French divisions. In early May, Marmont counter-attacked into the Lika region of western Croatia. And when the Muslim Bosnians, instigated by Marmont, raided into the almost undefended Military Border region, torching a number of villages, Stojevic's corps virtu-ally dissolved as men deserted to protect their homes. With Austrian resistance crumbling, he made a fast march along the coastal road to join Macdonald's forces in Carniola and Styria.[17] He arrived near Graz on 26 May where he combined with the weak French rearguard to take Graz that day and pursued the retreating Gyulai towards Feldbach, where orders reached him to move at once in forced marches to Vienna.

Finally, there was the campaign in the Grand Duchy of Warsaw and in Galicia, a sideshow at best, but the only Polish military success of the eighteenth and nineteenth centuries. Commanded by Archduke Ferdinand d'Este, its overly ambitious mission was to knock the Grand

Duchy of Warsaw, now ruled by the king of Saxony, out of the war and then, with misplaced expectations of Prussian support, turn west to strike into the French rear. Ferdinand's VII Corps, 32,000 strong including a major cavalry component of forty-four squadrons with 5,000 troopers, crossed the border on 15 April to begin his advance on Warsaw. Prince Poniatowski commanded the Polish Army, only some 15,000 strong though another 22,000 were serving Napoleon elsewhere. It was reinforced by a small Saxon contingent under GM von Dyherrn. Aware of his numerical inferiority – 14,000 Poles against 26,000 Austrians – Poniatowski had taken up a defensive position at Raszyn, six miles south-east of Warsaw. Defeated after tenacious resistance on 19 April, the Polish commander evacuated the capital, retiring east over the Vistula to the fortified Praga suburb which he successfully held against an Austrian attack on 26 April. At this point the recalled Saxons went north to make their way back home, while Ferdinand sent a detachment north to link up with the Prussians, a futile move. Prussia would not intervene

During the last weeks of April and into May, the Austrian main effort was directed to cross the Vistula and come to grips with the main Polish force, but they made little progress. On 2 May they were repulsed at Gora Kalawara and forced to retreat south, where on 18 May they sustained another defeat when 3,000 Poles forced a 4,000-strong Austrian garrison at Sandomierz to capitulate. Meanwhile, in accordance with their undertaking at Erfurt in 1808, a Russian auxiliary corps moved slowly towards Lublin while in the Austrian rear western Poland and Galicia flared into open rebellion. By 21 June the Austrians had recovered Lemberg, only to be driven out within days by a Russian column. With small-scale engagements continuing, on 9 June Ferdinand was informed about the outcome of the Battle of Wagram and received orders to withdraw west to protect the fortress and depots at Olmütz in Bohemia. Meanwhile, in eastern Galicia the local commander, FML Prince Hohenlohe, with only between 4,000 and 5,000 men, managed to repulse some small Polish detachments and even advance east, reaching Tarnow on 15 July. Here he was informed of the Armistice at Znaim and hostilities ended.[18]

For the Austrians the Polish campaign had been a dead end, perhaps even a defeat. Poniatowski had tied down substantial Austrian forces and yet there was nothing in Poland that could not have been recovered in the event of victory over Napoleon's main army. It illustrated the problem created by Austrian strategic decision-makers trying to fight on several fronts with inadequate resources. As for Russia, its intervention had been late and largely concerned with grabbing pieces of Poland, in the process revealing that the alliance with Napoleon was coming under severe strain. Overall, except perhaps for the Italian campaign, the various sideshows in 1809 had but little influence on the central campaign in the valley of the Danube.

CHAPTER FIVE

Aspern-Essling: Napoleon repulsed

THE STRATEGIC SITUATION

Although much had changed since Napoleon had arrived on 17 April at Donauwörth to take charge of the situation in Bavaria to defeat Archduke Charles and force the invading Austrian forces to retreat, he had not broken the enemy army or any of its corps. His capture of Vienna on 12–13 April had also not produced the expected Austrian peace offer. He had driven a thin wedge along the Danube into the Austrian heartland, but his line of communications was vulnerable and required a substantial troop commitment to protect it. Davout's corps and Vandamme's Württembergers were deployed along the Danube to protect Napoleon's southern flank, and Bernadotte's Saxon 9 Corps, stiffened by Dupas's small French division, was moving towards the area. In Italy, to be sure, Eugène's Army of Italy had pushed the Army of Inner Austria east into Hungary, while from Dalmatia, Marmont's two divisions were moving slowly – far too slowly, the emperor thought – into Styria. But with the main army having escaped through the Bohemian mountains and now reorganizing north-east of Vienna and

John reinforcing what Napoleon believed to be his still combat-capable army in Hungary, the emperor's immediate objective was to prevent the union of these two Austrian armies. Moreover, the Tyrolean revolt was threatening his rear, Germany was restive, there remained the possibility of Prussian intervention and the Tsar was not making any substantial moves to implement the promises he had made at Erfurt. Napoleon's strategic situation was potentially precarious. His most urgent operational objective was to locate and defeat Charles's army, but he found himself in almost total ignorance of his enemy's where-abouts. His light cavalry had failed to locate the enemy and for once his staff had failed to provide adequate geographic intelligence. On 13 May he wrote indignantly to General Henri Clarke, his war minister, that, 'I must express my extreme displeasure that you have left me without any maps or topographical reports … [of] the neighbourhood of Vienna'. He continued that Clarke was to send the maps, plans, reconnaissance reports and notes concerning Moravia, Bohemia and Hungary – originals, not copies – within twenty-four hours.[1]

Napoleon clearly realized that his most urgent operational task was to transport his army across the broad Danube, the river in effect serving to mask the location of his enemy. At the same time, it was also evident that the presence of Charles's main army, now deployed north of Vienna, provided potential offensive opportunities for the Austrians. The most attractive option for Charles was to cross the river upstream and into the French rear and threaten Napoleon's line of communications, a move that would have forced Napoleon to evacuate Vienna and fight a battle on ground of the Austrian's choosing. But such an enterprise was far too daring for Charles while his army, having returned to the old column system, was no longer able to fight a mobile battle. Even so, the archduke came under considerable and repeated pressure to take immediate offensive action. Emperor Francis urged him 'to get the armies scrapping', while his beautiful but bellicose wife, the Empress Maria Ludovica, complained that 'Charles has become indifferent to a soldier's honour and only longs for peace'.[2]

In fact, Charles had no intention of taking the offensive, especially when an attack by Kolowrat's II Corps against Bernadotte's bridge-head at Linz was easily repulsed on 17–18 May. While the archduke let it be known that a cross-river operation was still his 'favourite project', he welcomed and most probably inspired his chief-of-staff's memorandum of 17 May advocating a Fabian strategy. By remaining on the left bank of the Danube, so General Wimpffen argued, the army retained its freedom to manoeuvre. Replacements, stores and *matériel* were close at hand, and just by remaining in position the army tied down a large part of Napoleon's total forces. Ultimately Napoleon would have to attack across the Danube and if repulsed his army might well be annihilated during the retreat. On the other hand, if the Austrians crossed the river and were defeated, this might well spell the end of the Habsburg state. Therefore, Wimpffen asked, why risk total disaster? 'Fabius had saved Rome as Daun had saved Austria not through rashness but through delay … these are the examples we should follow.'[3]

Charles now decided that any French crossing should not be resisted at the water's edge. The enemy should be allowed to transfer a substantial number of troops into the plain beyond and, with part of his army still crossing, should be concentrically attacked while deploying. Meanwhile, the archduke encamped his army, about 120,000 strong if reserves are included and 98,000 strong if not, on the forward slopes of the Bisamberg.[4]

At this point, Charles enjoyed numerical superiority in men and guns. With much of his army still dispersed, Napoleon could only immediately muster Masséna's 4 Corps with its corps cavalry under Marulaz and with Lasalle's light cavalry division attached. Then there was Lannes's 2 Corps and Bessières's cavalry reserve, eighteen regiments of heavy cavalry. Also at hand were elements of the Imperial Guard: six battalions of the newly formed Young Guard commanded by General Philbert Curial, and General Jean Dorsenne's four battalions of the Old Guard. Finally, Davout's 3 Corps, perhaps the best line formation in the army, with a strong component of veteran troops, was ordered to march on Vienna.

In all Napoleon's army for the coming battle comprised 85,000 men. Inferior numbers, however, did not worry the emperor. Archduke Charles's curiously submissive letter had convinced him that the enemy's fighting spirit was broken, and he worried above all that the Austrian army might slip away into Bohemia or Moravia.

CROSSING THE DANUBE

Of course, Napoleon was also well aware of the need to transfer his army to the left bank and the day after his troops had occupied Vienna he ordered a crossing at Nussdorf, a few miles upstream from the city. Here the river narrowed, though this made for a very rapid current, and the heights of the Bisamberg dominated the crossing site. Still, an attempt was made to seize the Schwarze Lacken Au, an island close to the left bank. Marshal Lannes ordered General Saint-Hilaire to embark 500 *tirailleurs*, 250 each from the 72nd and the 105th Line, to seize the island which, unknown to the French, was connected to the left bank by a short bridge. Then, too, the two majors commanding the two detachments did not coordinate their action and left themselves no combat reserve. Within a very short time Austrian reinforcements, the IR 49 Kerpen from Hiller's VI Corps, arrived and though Napoleon and Lannes, who observed the action, ordered in reinforcements, after six hours of bloody fighting the French were forced to withdraw having lost 96 dead and 386, many wounded, taken prisoner. It was a debacle, though given the location and the lack of deployment space on the opposite bank it would appear that this operation had merely been a reconnaissance in force and perhaps also designed to draw Austrian attention to this sector.[5] In this it succeeded. Throughout the coming great battles, Archduke Charles maintained V Corps in this area. Actually, on 11 May, Napoleon had already ordered General Nicolas-Marie Songis, the army artillery commander, to reconnoitre the river line between Vienna and Pressburg to find a suitable crossing location.[6]

But meanwhile General Henri Bertrand, chief of army engineers, had located a possible crossing site at Kaiser-Ebersdorf some 4 miles downstream from Vienna. Some miles below Klosterneuburg, the Danube divided into four separate channels, a tangle of islands large and small and a number of sand bars providing the opportunity to bridge the wide river in several stages. The largest of these islands below the Schwarze Lacken Au were the Tabor, the Prater, the heavily wooded Lobau and the adjoining Lobgrund islands. The last were roughly 3 miles square, large enough to serve as an assembly area for several corps, with the woods and undergrowth also providing concealment for bridgework. The Lobau crossing was particularly suited for bridging because here the bridgework could be subdivided. From the south bank the distance to a large sand bar, the Schneiderhaufen, was 450 yards; from there to the Lobgrund, an island separated from the Lobau proper only by a narrow channel, was 225 yards. The final stretch, from the Lobau to the left bank across the sluggish Stadler Arm, was but 130 yards wide.

Once across the Danube from the Lobau there was the Marchfeld, a vast flat and fertile alluvial plain, gently sloping up north from the Danube to the foothills of the Bisamberg in the west and north. In the east the river March and an escarpment, the Wagram plateau, delimited the Marchfeld. Coming from the Lobau, the compact villages of Aspern and Essling flank a salient, the Mühlau, the entrance to the Marchfeld proper. Save for some artificial elevations, a couple of yards at best, at Aspern, Essling and Gross Enzersdorf, the immediate terrain on the north bank consisted of meadows interspersed with some woods and thick brush. Most importantly, however, numerous drainage ditches, which interfered with operations by troops in close formations but favoured fighting in open order, cut the area. The Marchfeld was well known to the Austrian staff and frequently had served as a manoeuvre area and here, on the plain and in the foothills, the decisive battles of the 1809 campaign were fought: at Aspern–Essling on 21–22 May and Wagram on 5–6 July.

Worried about the archduke escaping into the interior of the monarchy or linking up with John's army from Hungary, Napoleon decided on an immediate crossing at the location recommended by Bertrand even though his Engineer Park, specially formed for the 1809 campaign, had not yet arrived. It consisted of nine *sapeur* companies, three *pontonniers* units and three companies of miners, and was reinforced by three battalions of marine artificers and 1,200 sailors, commanded by Capitaine Pierre Baste of the French Navy. The reinforced park would not arrive until after Aspern–Essling. Meanwhile the engineers, sappers, miners and gunners of the corps would have to handle the bridging operations.

Napoleon ordered the construction of a single consecutive set of pile and pontoon bridges from Kaiser-Ebersdorf across the various islands and the great sandbar to the Mühlau salient. Relying on a single set of pontoon bridges was a risky undertaking. Experts warned that it was the season when the river, already high though still below the high-water mark, was prone to sudden surges in floodwater because of spring rains and runoff from melting snows in the Alps. They also warned that the current was already swift enough that, from positions upstream, the Austrians could launch ram devices – stone-laden barges, heavy tree trunks and such – to smash the long and flimsy pontoon bridges and trestle across the main channel. Napoleon, however, was not deterred. Entrusting Masséna with constructing the bridges and providing the spearhead of the crossing, Napoleon had materials, ropes, timber and pontoons brought to Kaiser-Ebersdorf. Just above this small town there was a creek suitable for collecting pontoons and building rafts and trestles. By 18 May enough material was at hand for a single and narrow bridge, though anchors and chains were in short supply and makeshift expedients – boxes filled with iron scrap and cannon balls – were substituted.

On 18–19 May elements from Molitor's division carried by six large boats occupied the Lobgrund and, reinforced the next day, ejected the small Austrian garrison from the Lobau. Also on 19 May engineers linked the Lobau islands to the south bank by a single, rather ramshackle bridge of sixty-eight pontoons, nine rafts and some trestles.

That evening 200 *voltigeurs* rowed across the Stadler Arm to establish a bridgehead in the Mühlau salient, driving back outposts from Klenau's Advance Guard. By about 6 p.m. the next day, driving in Austrian forward elements with artillery and musketry fire and despite harassing Austrian counter-fire, the *pontonniers* and *sapeurs* of Legrand's division managed to complete the final bridge – three trestle sections and fifteen boats – across the Stadler Arm into the Mühlau. At dusk on 20 May, Molitor's infantry division and Lasalle's light cavalry crossed into the salient. While the light horse advanced to reconnoitre, the infantry occupied the villages of Aspern and Essling. Hiller had observed the French crossing and had at once ridden to inform Charles in person that an immediate counter-attack was required. But Charles would not hear of it. Napoleon's crossing of the Danube relieved him of having to take the offensive and agreed with his own plans. He waited until the late afternoon but then issued orders to begin moving his corps into positions for the planned concentric attack the next day.

Meanwhile the build-up of French troops on the Lobau continued. Though it had been temporarily interrupted during the afternoon of 20 May when an Austrian ram-barge brought down the bridge span between the Schneidergrund and the Lobau, engineers repaired the breach by evening and Lasalle's light cavalry division filed across to support Molitor. As dusk fell, Lasalle's horsemen attempted to explore north of the Mühlau, but Klenau had sent in reinforcements to block their progress and the French cavalry could not penetrate their screen, leaving Napoleon with no intelligence about Austrian positions or movements. This failure of the French reconnaissance effort induced the emperor to believe that the Austrians were retreating and had only left some squadrons behind to screen their movement. Still seeking to confirm the whereabouts of the Austrian army, at midnight he ordered Masséna to climb the church tower at Aspern to assess whether there were any Austrian movements. Detecting but a few campfires on the slopes of the Bisamberg, too few for a large army, he reported that the

Austrians were retreating. In reality, of course, they were marching to their new assembly areas.

With the bridge holding during the night and traffic fully restored at dawn on 21 May, Whit Sunday, the emperor, who had moved his command post to the north bank, ordered additional forces into the Mühlau. These were two additional infantry divisions of Masséna's 4 Corps, Boudet's and Legrand's, and two heavy cuirassier divisions, d'Espagne's and Saint-Sulpice's, from Bessières's Cavalry Reserve. These were to be followed by Lannes's corps, then Masséna's 4 Corps, the remainder of the Cavalry Reserve and the Imperial Guard, and finally by Davout. But it would not be possible to execute this schedule in full. The Danube had risen almost 3 feet and at 10 a.m. another ram-barge again destroyed the second part of the bridge. By mid morning Napoleon had three infantry divisions, 20,000 men, 8,500 cavalry troopers and 44 guns in the Mühlau bridgehead. The heavy proportion of cavalry reflected the emperor's intention to pursue a retreating enemy, but meanwhile the French reordered their deployment. Molitor's reunited division, supported by elements of Legrand's, took up positions in and around Aspern, while Boudet's division, temporarily commanded by Lannes, was to hold Essling. The cavalry remained to protect the centre.[7]

Curiously, the French command had taken no measures to fortify the bridgehead. Neither Aspern nor Essling, both only a few hundred yards from the riverbank and a mile-and-a-half apart, were prepared for defence. The houses were not loop-holed and the approaches not barricaded. Even so, the villages were naturally strong positions. Aspern, the larger of the two villages, had 106 stone houses with a church, a solidly built vicarage with an adjoining cemetery surrounded by a chest-high stone wall (though this could not withstand cannon fire) on slightly elevated ground at the western end of the village. Two main streets ran parallel though Aspern, with narrow side streets providing cover to shift troops. To the west, north and east of Aspern ran the remains of a now abandoned flood dike. South of the village was a heavily overgrown area, the Gemeinde Au, stretching to the Danube. However, the terrain to the west of Aspern was covered by thick brushland, forest and broken by rivulets, though between Aspern and Esling the terrain was more suitable for deploying major closed formations. An earth-banked ditch along a narrow road connected the village to Essling. This was a smaller place, with only fifty-six houses, and divided in two by a public square. The eastern half provided no strong points, but in the western part an important defensive stronghold was provided by a massive three-storey stone granary, its walls several yards thick, with an iron gate, windows with iron shutters and a heavy tiled roof. Garrisoned by 300 men provided with a triple ammunition issue, rations and water, it would withstand repeated assaults during the coming battle. In all, the French frontage was little more than 3 miles wide and, to protect against an enemy breakthrough, Napoleon himself traced a final fortified bridgehead covering the bridge to the Lobau.[8]

DAY ONE: 21 MAY

The Austrian dispositions had been made the previous day and, marching through the night, their forces had reached their jumping-off areas along the north-west edge of the Marchfeld by the morning of 21 May. Ahead of the army and forming a screen came Klenau's Advance Guard. The main force was deployed in five columns. From left to right, that is roughly west to east, came Hiller's VI Corps and Bellegarde's I Corps, both directed against Aspern. Hohenzollern's II Corps, forming the third column, was also directed against the village. Liechtenstein's Cavalry Reserve was stationed a short distance back between the third and the fourth column. Further to the east, Rosenberg's IV Corps, launched against Essling, was divided into two columns. The fourth column, Dedovich's division, was to take the village while the fifth column, Hohenlohe with Rohan's and Hohenlohe's divisions, was to bypass Essling, secure Gross Enzersdorf and close up to the Danube. These concentric operations, always a favourite Austrian manoeuvre, depended on concerted timing and actions by the different columns, something that with poor staff work and approach marches of different length was difficult to achieve and contributed to the favourable, but certainly not decisive, outcome of the battle which given the Austrians numerical superiority – 83,000 foot, 14,000 horse and 293 guns – should have delivered a crushing victory.

The initial Austrian deployment was poorly planned and very slow. Committing the bulk of their forces against the two villages left the Austrian centre weak, and the Cavalry Corps held in reserve was reduced in strength when each of the column commanders, worried about being caught by cavalry on flat ground, demanded and received cavalry support. During the coming battle the mounted arm did not act as a major striking force, but was primarily employed to protect infantry formations.[9] Finally, the line of contact from west of Aspern to east of Essling was less than 4 miles. Assuming a battalion frontage of 200 yards each, thirty battalions should have sufficed in the fighting line, but around Aspern the Austrians initially committed three corps, with the result that troops, horses and guns got in each other's way. Immediately, however, heavy fog rising from the Danube valley obscured the opposing armies. At 9 a.m. the archduke issued orders to cook breakfast but when the fog started to lift at around 10 a.m. the Austrians began to advance. That morning the bridge had been ruptured again, and Napoleon had considered a withdrawal but was reassured by Molitor that he could hold Aspern and Essling. Marshals Masséna, Lannes and Bessières supported this assessment though Berthier remained silent. Meanwhile Napoleon, by now able to observe the area from the Aspern church steeple, became aware that the Austrians were approaching in force and pushed all possible reinforcements across the hastily repaired and still shaky bridge. By 6.30 in the evening Saint-Cyr's division of 4 Corps – about 9,000 men and 18 guns – Saint-Germain's cuirassier brigade of Nansouty's heavy division, as well as Saint-Sulpice's heavy division, had managed to get across to the damaged and partially underwater bridge to the Mühlau.

FIGHTING FOR ASPERN AND
THE CAVALRY CLASH IN THE CENTRE

Still, the Austrian fighting system was exceedingly cumbersome, and it took Hiller and the rest of the army several hours to shake themselves from march order into fighting formations. At about 1 p.m. the Advance Guard of the first column, VI Corps, commanded by GM Armand von Nordmann, came into contact with French outposts and pushed Marulaz's cavalry, Baden and Hessian light horse, covering a French battery back on to Molitor's left flank. This created confusion among the French defenders and, supported by the fire of three batteries, three battalions of IR 60 Gyulai managed to penetrate the western part of the village, to be halted by point-blank fire at the church-cemetery position by French reserves, the 37th and 67th Line from Viviez's brigade. Hiller made no attempt to exploit his initial success, but positioned the remainder of his thirty battalions and squadrons in a defensive position and only renewed his assaults using eight battalions – line, *Jäger* and *Grenzer* – at 3.30 p.m. Poorly coordinated, the attack was repulsed with heavy casualties. Meanwhile, the second and third columns, I and II Corps, were finally coming to their start lines and, to support Hiller, opened a preparatory bombardment of the village, by now in flames. Realizing that the Austrians intended to converge against the two villages, Napoleon ordered his few guns into the centre, primarily to support the defence of Essling, which he believed the weaker of the two positions. Also, at around 3.30 p.m. scouts from Liechtenstein's Cavalry Corps in the centre recognized that the French line between Aspern and Essling was only held by cavalry, d'Espagne's cuirassier division and Piré's light horse brigade from Lasalle's light division. Seeing an opportunity, Liechtenstein ordered a charge, but mindful of his orders to protect the fourth and fifth columns still marching on Essling, he divided his force and shifted his left wing into the area northeast of Essling. Meanwhile, Bessières, with 7,000 sabres, charged the remaining Austrian cuirassier regiments of the right wing, but these managed to hold until hastily summoned detached cuirrassiers, uhlans and reserve hussars gave the Austrians a slight numerical edge. After a brief mêlée, the now outnumbered French fell back behind the ditch connecting the two villages. Even so, for the moment Liechtenstein's horse was no longer capable of offensive action and the Austrian centre was thinly covered.

About one hour later the fourth column, half of IV Corps, had arrived north of Essling, while the fifth column was deploying east of the village near Gross Enzersdorf. At about 4.30 p.m. Hiller, Bellegarde and Hohenzollern were preparing for a joint attack on Aspern where intense fighting raged from house to house, from roofs to cellars and behind gravestones and walls. Ultimately, the outnumbered defenders lost their hold on the church and cemetery position. With Molitor's division now exhausted, Napoleon ordered Legrand's division into Aspern. First to arrive was the 26th Light, which halted the Austrian advance and, when reinforced by the 18th, drove the Austrians out of the village. With casualties near 50 per cent, Molitor's troops were pulled back into reserve and relieved by Legrand's troops, his two French regiments now joined by the Baden IR 3 Graf Hochberg and Saint-Cyr's division. To ease pressure on Aspern, Marulaz's light horse had begun to advance against the Austrian cavalry to the north, but then ran into Austrian infantry deployed in solid masses and holding firm, firing only when the enemy closed to within fifteen paces, driving the light horse back. Even when Bessières ordered d'Espagne's cuirassiers and two just-arrived heavy regiments to support and attack the Austrian masses, the heavies achieved nothing of moment, clashing with some reconstituted Austrian horse in another mêlée. On the Austrian side Hohenzollern's corps, whose presence north of Aspern had merely congested the tactical situation, was now shifted to the centre.

Meanwhile, fighting continued to rage in and around Aspern, seen by both commanders – Napoleon as well as Archduke Charles – as the most important, even decisive, position. Charles ordered Bellegarde to take and hold the location, now a smoking ruin, at all costs. Six battalions of GM Wacquant's brigade from Dedovich's division led the attack, supported by the rest of the corps. Again the fighting was especially fierce around the church-cemetery position. The Austrians captured it but were ejected, but with Archduke Charles appearing to encourage his troops and artillery moving to fire canister at close range, at around 6.30 p.m. Legrand's troops were driven out. Napoleon at once ordered the newly arrived Hesse-Darmstadt Leibgarde Brigade of Saint-Cyr division to recapture the village, but the Austrians were too strong. By now both sides were exhausted. Legrand's battered battalions and the Hessians held on to the south-east of Aspern and to the Gemeinde Au leading to the Danube. Fighting died down with only sporadic firing during the night.[10]

Even though the French had not been completely ejected from Aspern, Charles was satisfied and attempted to storm Essling before darkness fell. Because he intended to break the French centre the next morning, he needed to occupy the village flanking his planned advance. But Lannes, his defences anchored on the granary, had few problems holding his positions. Charles, who had moved his command post to Breitenlee, now issued orders for a concentric attack. But poorly coordinated, his columns attacking in sequence instead of together, the attack failed, and Lannes ordered Bessières to pursue the retreating Austrian infantry. When the French cavalry, led by Saint-Germain's cuirassiers, just arrived from the Lobau, failed to make much of an impression, Lannes sent a second message to Bessières repeating his order in terms the marshal considered offensive. As the fighting died down, Bessières confronted Lannes, claiming he had been insulted. For many years there had been bad blood between the two marshals and a heated discussion ensued during which both officers made as if to draw their swords. A duel between the two marshals was only avoided when Masséna, senior to both of them, intervened. 'I am your senior,' Masséna shouted, 'you are in my camp and I shall not permit to give my troops the scandalous spectacle of seeing two marshals draw on each other, and that in the presence of the enemy.'[11]

At about 7 p.m. an Austrian ram-boat again disrupted the bridge, but French engineers had it back in operation three hours later. During the night, despite repeated breaks in the bridge that were always repaired, Napoleon received substantial reinforcements. They included the Saint-Sulpice cuirassier division, the bulk of Lannes's strong 2 Corps, commanded temporarily by Oudinot, eight battalions of the Young and four of the Old Guard, a total of 7,800 men, as well as eighty-six artillery pieces. Napoleon had also sent urgent orders for Davout to bring up his corps, but by the time it arrived at mid morning on 22 May the bridge had collapsed. Even so, by dawn on 22 May, Napoleon had some 56,000 infantry, 12,000 cavalry and 144 guns against Austrian effectives remaining at about 80,000 foot, 14,000 horse and 150 guns. The numerical odds had improved considerably, but still were weighted heavily in favour of the Austrians.

THE SECOND DAY: 22 MAY

Both commanders were reasonably satisfied with the course of events and both intended to attack at dawn the next day. For once optimistic, Archduke Charles, unaware that he had only fought a portion of Napoleon's troops and that the enemy had been reinforced, assumed that the French were preparing to evacuate the Mühlau. At about 10.30 p.m. on 21 May he issued orders for the coming day, ordering all commanders to be ready to advance by dawn to resume their methodical attacks against the wings of the French position and eliminate their rearguard. For his part, Napoleon had decided to use 2 Corps to break through the Austrian centre. When this had been achieved, the corps was to turn left and, in conjunction with Masséna, drive the Austrian right wing upstream along the Danube. At the same time Lannes was to drive the Austrian left wing back. Aspern was the key point of this plan and Masséna was told that his primary task was to retake and hold the entire village.

Before dawn Masséna had formed two attack columns from the 18th and 4th Line, reinforced by detachments from the 26th Light and the 46th Line. Their charge managed to penetrate the Austrian positions but ultimately they were forced to withdraw. Despite this success, GM Waquant, the local commander, asked Hiller for reinforcements and retired his troops from the village. Aware that the troops still had ample ammunition, a livid Hiller ordered them to take up new positions to the rear and use their artillery pieces to prevent the French emerging from the village.

At about the same time Lannes had successfully repelled Rosenberg's IV Corps, once again attacking Essling piecemeal. After some bitter fighting the Austrians were evicted and by 7 a.m. were driven back east to Gross Enzersdorf. The prerequisites for Napoleon's attempt to assault the Austrian centre had been achieved. Since 6 a.m Lannes's three assault divisions – from left to right, Tharreau, Claparède and Saint-Hilaire – had been assembled along the Aspern–Essling Road. Although dense fog once again hampered visibility, the Austrian artillery, using area fire, was inflicting substantial losses. Unwilling to keep his troops taking unnecessary casualties, at 7 a.m. Napoleon ordered the advance. Moving in echelon, with the Saint-Hilaire division spearheaded by the 'terrible' 57th Line leading the assault, backed by the light horse from Marulaz and Lasalle, and the heavies from Nansouty and Arrighi who had replaced the mortally wounded d'Espagne, the attack went in, though suffering substantial losses from the Austrian artillery. Smashing into the Austrian front in heavy battalion columns, the 57th captured a battalion of IR 54 Froon and a 6-pounder battery. Some front-line Austrian battalions were wavering, but rallied in the rear and were repositioned to lengthen the left of the centre. Meanwhile, Austrian artillery slowed Saint-Hilaire's advance while the conscripts of Tharreau's and Claparède's divisions were unable to change formations under fire and lost heavily. 'The fire of grape-shot and musketry', General Savary wrote, 'threw our columns into confusion and compelled us to stop and open a fire of cannon and muskets, with the disadvantage of numbers against us.'[12]

As the French infantry stalled, the white-coated Austrian infantry retired into the shelter of Liechtenstein's cavalry. Bessières now threw in his supporting cavalry, formed up in two massive blocks of 4,000 and 5,000 troopers. Penetrating the first lines of Liechtenstein's cavalry, the French breakthrough panicked and broke two regiments of *insurrectio* hussars while the nearby IR 15 Zach began to waver. This was the crisis of the battle for the Austrians. Never lacking in personal courage, at this moment Archduke Charles galloped forward to steady the regiment. According to legend, memorialized in many pictures and the famous equestrian statue outside the imperial palace in Vienna, the archduke seized the regimental colours as he led the unit forward. However, he later told an inquirer: 'You know how heavy the colours are. Do you really believe that a little chap like me could have gone off with them?' Whatever the exact circumstances, his personal intervention stabilized the line and gave time for the Grenadier Corps from the Reserve to intervene.[13]

THE FRENCH RETIRE

By about 9 a.m. the French were running low on ammunition and, with casualties mounting, including Saint-Hilaire killed, could not advance any further. Lannes had asked for reinforcements, but there was none. Napoleon had just been informed that a major part of the bridge had been carried away, eliminating any prospect of Davout's entering the battle. Hoping for a favourable report from his engineers, the emperor kept Lannes in his advanced positions for another hour. At about 10 a.m. another floating object, a large water mill, slammed into the bridge resulting in an irreparable breach and Charles emplaced a grand battery, about 200 guns, against the French centre. Napoleon now ordered a gradual retirement to the Aspern–Essling road and, in fact, realized that a general retreat had become inevitable, though it could only be carried out under the cover of darkness. Until then the perimeter around the bridgehead had to be held. By now many French guns had been put out of action and ammunition was running short. At 12.30 the emperor, who had taken up position ahead of the Imperial Guard, stationed parallel in unshakeable lines behind Lannes, sent an urgent dispatch to Davout. 'The enemy is employing two hundred cannon against us, to which, low on ammunition since ten, we cannot reply ... send ammunition and rations.'[14]

Napoleon realized that both Aspern and Essling were vital bastions for holding the defensive perimeter and both were under heavy attack. For his part, the archduke had seen that Napoleon's advance in the centre had left him exposed to a thrust from the flank and already at 7 a.m. he had issued orders to Hiller to take Aspern whatever the cost. A bombardment by the combined artillery of the first and second column razed still standing buildings, especially the church, and an assault by IR 51 Splényi briefly regained control of the village. Masséna now ordered in his last reserve, a battalion of the Hessian Leibgarde, which retook much of the location, but the heavy smoke forced an evacuation of the village by both sides. At round 11 a.m. the Hessians re-entered the smoking ruins already reoccupied by the Austrians, retook it briefly only to lose it again to an assault by volunteers from IR 31 Benjowsky and IR 14 Klebek. Napoleon now committed three battalions of the Young Guard and, inspired by the example of Masséna's fighting sword in hand among his troops, regained control. An Austrian counter-attack changed the situation and after continued fighting, by late afternoon Hiller's seventh attack had taken the village and environs, except for the ditch and dike leading to Aspern and some grazing land between the houses and the river. When FML Vogelsang hesitated to push the attack further, Charles, who had meanwhile arrived at the spot, ordered that this last position be taken at once. 'Shoot down all who do not obey, cashier officers on the spot, but take that ditch.'[15]

At the other end of the line, at Essling, Rosenberg had failed to achieve much in the morning. His repeated and uncoordinated attacks failed, the granary proving a stronger defensive position than the church-cemetery position at Aspern. Liechtenstein arrived after noon to organize the first organized assault and Charles in person arrived with d'Aspre and Merville's four-battalion Grenadier Brigade to reinforce the action. At about 3 p.m. Boudet was forced out of the small village, but the general and a few hundred grenadiers were able to maintain themselves in the granary. Aware that the loss of Essling would endanger any orderly retreat, Napoleon ordered Colonel Seruzier to support efforts to retake Essling. 'I count on you,' Napoleon told him, 'to save the army.'[16] He also dispatched Generals Georges Mouton and Jean Rapp, both senior aides, to restore the situation with five battalions of the Young Guard. Interpreting their orders liberally, the two stalwarts not only evicted the Habsburg troops from the village but also pressed Rosenberg back toward Gross-Essling. The effective action of these two young generals had an important, perhaps decisive, effect. Essling remained in French hands, protecting the retreat. The only French reserves now were the Old Guard battalions stationed near the bridge to the Lobau. Perceiving that the battle was dying down and his presence in front of the Old Guard was no longer required, and with the Guardsmen threatening to down arms if he did not remove himself to safety, Napoleon retired to the rear and Lannes was entrusted with the overall command of all troops on the left bank.

In the centre, though hard pressed, Lannes, assisted by a number of mounted charges, had, retiring step by step, managed to maintain his line. This, combined with the counter-attack at Essling, convinced Charles that Napoleon had received major reinforcements and at about 3.30 p.m. he halted action in the centre and assumed a defensive posture, though maintaining the bombardment of the French infantry with some fifty guns. Between 3 and 4 p.m. this fire mortally wounded Lannes. A small cannon ball, presumably a 3-pounder ricochet, shattered both his knees. Taken to the rear and eventually to a hospital on the right bank of the Danube, the marshal would linger on until 31 May. It was a great pity because the battle was practically over. Charles's reasons for his decision to halt are not clear. To be sure, his troops were exhausted and he no longer had any reserves, though the story that he was also low on ammunition does not appear to be correct, while the outnumbered French were in any case even worse off. The sudden shift to the defensive was perhaps best demonstrated at Aspern where at around 4 p.m. Hiller, after seven assaults, was preparing to roll up the French line along the river. He was stopped when Wimpffen, accompanied by several senior staff officers, appeared to order a furious Hiller to 'halt and not start a new battle'. And when Hiller insisted that this was the opportunity for a final and decisive assault there was a violent scene.[17] In the end, of course, Wimpffen, acting with the archduke's authority, prevailed.

There would be no determined pursuit of the French rearguard as, harassed only by intermittent skirmish and artillery fire, they fell back in good order. They first moved to the bridgehead defences and then during the night retired in phased order over the bridge to the Lobau, artillery first, then the Guard, heavy cavalry and finally the infantry. The marshal remained almost to the last in the bridgehead until, at dawn, the last defenders left their fortifications and the bridge was taken up. Even then pockets of French troops still held on along the river-bank and in the Essling granary. The last of this rearguard, the *voltigeurs* of the 18th Line of Legrand's division, were only taken off by two large boats on the morning of the next day, 23 May.

Napoleon had left the Mühlau salient for the Lobau in the after-noon and towards evening he summoned his marshals to a conference. Berthier and Davout, the latter having come over from the right bank, were already present, while Masséna arrived after some delay. Lannes, however, failed to appear. At 7 p.m. the conference proceeded. Initially all the marshals favoured a retreat to the right bank but Napoleon changed their mind. He pointed out that the artillery and the wounded brought to the Lobau would have to be abandoned, encouraging the enemy to believe he had gained a great victory. This, the emperor maintained, was not the case, but the perception of such a French defeat might turn allies and neutrals against him and force a retreat to the Rhine. No, he maintained, the battle had been a victory and only the Danube had defeated him. But with the Lobau held in preparation for a second crossing, the Austrian main army would be fixed, while rein-forcements, the rest of the Imperial Guard and the Armies of Italy and

Dalmatia, would arrive within a short time. His reasoning was persuasive. Masséna was entrusted to accelerate the retreat and given command of all troops on the left bank, the islands in the river and the Lobau.

As the meeting broke up Napoleon was shaken by the news that Lannes, the marshal closest to him, and Saint-Hilaire had both been seriously wounded. Napoleon dictated some additional instructions for Masséna, who had already returned to the north bank. Accompanied by Berthier, Napoleon then left the Lobau by boat to Kaiser-Ebersdorf. The battle was over. The attempt to cross the Danube by a sudden assault had failed.

THE BATTLE EVALUATED
AND ITS IMMEDIATE AFTERMATH

It had been a bloody soldier's battle. Neither commander-in-chief performed brilliantly. Despite being celebrated as the victor, Archduke Charles had not been able to exploit his vast superiority in men and guns for a decisive victory. His plan of operations repeated the preferred Austrian tactics of a concentric attack, failing to take into account the need for coordination of movement on an extensive battlefield. As for Napoleon, he had gambled, though he would claim then and later that victory had been snatched from him by the collapse of the main bridge on the second day. Indeed, had the bridge held for a couple more hours, enabling Davout's 3 Corps to pass, Napoleon probably would have achieved a major victory.

Losses were heavy on both sides. The Austrians lost 5,200 dead and 21,500 wounded; French losses, contrary to Napoleon's claims, were about the same. As usual, casualties of French senior officers were heavier than the Austrians'. Besides Lannes, the first marshal to be killed in battle, three generals were killed and eighteen wounded. Austrian losses included one general killed and thirteen high-ranking officers wounded. Both commanders had reason to be satisfied with the conduct of their troops. Despite a minor panic towards noon of the second day, soon ended by the Guard, the French had maintained good order

127

during a difficult retreat. The Austrians captured only three dismounted guns, seven ammunition wagons and one set of colours, though also picked up some 14,000 muskets. But facing a numerically superior enemy and superior firepower, their backs to the river and with no assurance of reinforcement, all fighting units of Napoleon's forces, veterans and recruits alike, Frenchmen as well as Confederation of the Rhine troops, had fought tenaciously. The Austrian combat performance, especially that of their line infantry fighting in defensive masses, had been excellent, though their cavalry had been disappointing. Their artillery also had done very well. If Aspern–Essling remained only a tactical victory, the troops could not be blamed.

As was his habit, the archduke had fought a cautious defensive battle aiming to repulse but not destroy the enemy. By the end of the second day, his earlier optimism had faded and he did not order an all-out pursuit. Only on the evening of 23 May did he issue orders to Hiller and Rosenberg to 'disturb the French'. Hiller and his advance guard were to bombard the Lobau while Rosenberg was to throw a pontoon bridge across the Stadler Arm and attack into the Lobau with one brigade of infantry and one squadron of cavalry.

The proposed scale of the operation indicates that nothing more than a raid was planned and the orders also warned the commanders to take no risks that might require commitment of strong reinforcements. In the end, nothing came of this half-hearted scheme. Hiller limited himself to some light cannon fire. Rosenberg, finding that the rise of the Danube had swollen the Stadler Arm and made it uncommonly rapid, was unable to throw a bridge across the stream. The French were astonished and relieved by the Austrian inaction. While crossing into the Lobau would have been a losing gamble, a heavy bombardment would have inflicted serious casualties on the dense masses huddling on the island.

But having repulsed Napoleon, Charles believed that a tactical victory was enough to fan the embers of revolt in Germany and to induce Prussia and Russia to join Austria, prospects that might persuade

Napoleon to come to terms. But although newspapers in Bohemia, Prussia and elsewhere trumpeted that Napoleon had been totally defeated, the emperor himself killed and his army in complete disarray, in the end the truth emerged. Repulsed, yes, but not crushed and a partial success would convince neither Prussia nor Russia to risk intervention; meanwhile, there was still no sign of the promised British support. Napoleon was not dead or even wounded, but he was exhausted and for a day and a half remained in a state of near indecision. Crucially, the fighting morale of his army remained high, he still disposed of substantial reserves and a second and better-prepared attempt was likely to succeed.

CHAPTER SIX

Across the Danube

THE AFTERMATH OF ASPERN–ESSLING

The reaction to the battle varied between the French and Austrians, revealing marked differences of character and style of command between the two commanders as well as between their respective objectives. Napoleon refused to evacuate the Lobau and rejected suggestions that he fall back to Vienna. Aware that the rebuff might have wider consequences in Europe, he was determined to attempt another crossing of the Danube from the Lobau: his objective remained the destruction of the main Austrian army. But he realized that this would take the most careful preparations: secure bridges would have to be constructed, more troops assembled and additional artillery procured. Recovering his enormous energy, he was everywhere, supervising and spurring on preparations. By contrast, Archduke Charles, curiously depressed, seldom left his headquarters in Deutsch-Wagram. Although defeated in Bavaria, his troops had fought well at Aspern–Essling but the heavy losses incurred in the battle had sapped his confidence. His main objective was to exploit his success and use his improved strategic position to enter peace negotiations on favourable terms. But he failed to convince his imperial brother and had to continue his struggle against the intrigues of the war faction. Anton Baron Baldacci, an ever-scheming confidant of the Emperor Francis, observed that 'Napoleon was an utterly common general and certainly would have been destroyed if Archduke Charles had not been an even more incompetent leader'.[1] Such intrigues could not remain hidden, and contributed to the lack of cooperation from his corps commanders, above all Archduke John. Meanwhile, though his forces were still well over 90,000 strong and being further reinforced, the archduke lapsed into lethargy and remained passive for the next crucial weeks. By contrast, with Napoleon's sole authority unchallenged, he alone on the French side took the important strategic and administrative decisions and he was determined to reverse his defeat.

LOBAU ISLAND CONVERTED
INTO AN OFFENSIVE BASE

After recovering from his physical exhaustion, Napoleon worked furiously. His first priority was to restore firm communications with the south bank to the Lobau, now packed with 60,000 men – including 20,000 wounded – guns and limbers, wagons and other impedimenta. There was no shelter and hardly any rations, and the energetic Surgeon-General Larrey commandeered and slaughtered the horses even of senior officers and used inverted cuirasses to make a nourishing broth for his charges. The emperor pushed hard to replenish Masséna's ammunition, provide rations and evacuate the wounded. With the Danube subsiding, by 25 May a provisional bridge had been built, largely by the effort of the just-arrived naval battalions. The wounded were taken off the island first, then the empty ammunition wagons, then the Imperial Guard, 2 Corps, which reincorporated Saint-Hilaire's division, now commanded by Pacthod, and Demont's reserve division.

In contrast with his precipitate actions at Aspern–Essling, the next battle was minutely prepared by Napoleon, with the river crossing designed almost like an attack against a fortress. The Lobau, now designated as the Ile Napoleon, was to be the jumping-off place and the emperor remained concerned about its security. On 27 May the bridge collapsed again, and that day he detailed Colonel Charles Sainte-Croix, serving on Masséna's staff, to visit all outposts and report on the situation on the island every morning. On 31 May he instructed Generals Rogniat, a gunner, and Foucher, an engineer, to determine the work necessary to construct solid bridges to support another crossing and to establish batteries to secure the Lobau. They reported back to Masséna on 3 June and the marshal endorsed and forwarded their recommendations two days later. The generals recommended that multiple strong trestle-bridges be built from Kaiser-Ebersdorf to the Lobau, but advised against a repeat crossing at the location used on 20 May, though they suggested that this might well serve as a deception. They proposed crossing on a broad front making use of the small islets in the Stadlau branch on the east side of the Lobau as stepping stones. Going from west to south-east, these were designated as the Ile Masséna, upstream from the original crossing, then a small island named Ile Saint-Hilaire, both providing excellent fields of fire towards Aspern–Essling. Directly across from Essling was the Ile Bessières, and further downstream the Ile de Moulin and the Ile Montebello. Facing east were Iles Pouzet, Lannes and Alexandre. Because the riverbank below the Ile Alexandre was swampy and covered with thick brush, they suggested a possible amphibious landing further down river below the Ile Alexandre, close to where the Stadlau branch rejoined the main stream of the Danube, an area called the Hanselgrund. With the Austrians apparently fortifying the river line from Aspern to Enzersdorf, a landing near this point would enable the emperor to turn their positions. In this report, endorsed on 6 June by Masséna, the basic elements of Napoleon's evolving battle plan for Wagram can be discerned.

BUILDING THE BRIDGES ACROSS THE DANUBE

Never a man to lose time, Napoleon had already instructed Bertrand to organize the construction of several great bridges protected by a palisade upstream and capable of withstanding the current and the ramming craft that had destroyed the original bridge connecting the south shore with the Lobgrund–Lobau Island. After consulting with his fellow engineer officers, Bertrand reported to Napoleon. Given time, manpower and equipment, he assured the emperor that such bridges could be built. Napoleon ordered their immediate construction, providing Bertrand with command of all the engineer and pioneer companies, the naval artificers and all the necessary civilian workers and bridge-building and maintenance engines from the Austrian stores in Vienna. 'I will', Bertrand boasted to a fellow engineer, 'build solid bridges.'[2] Actual work started on 1 June. By then the three naval battalions (not to be confused with the marines of the Imperial Guard who arrived only after the battle), one battalion of naval artificers and two battalions of sailors, each about 500 men strong, commanded by Captain Baste of the imperial navy, joined the hard-pressed corps engineers and *pontonniers*. In addition, the Army Engineer Reserve was pressed into service. The naval battalions proved especially versatile. Carrying their own tools, the sailors performed an amazing amount of work. They built bridges, gunboats, landing barges capable of holding 200 men, and a floating battery. They repaired damaged pontoons, organized water transport and, manning ten gunboats (including three gunboats captured from the Austrians) and several lesser craft, gave Napoleon control of the Danube.

Material for the bridging projects, captured or manufactured in the huge depots of the river administration in Vienna, was assembled at Kaiser-Ebersdorf. Over 4,000 wagons carried wooden beams, cordage, iron fastenings and anchors to the bridge depot there, while pontoons and rafts manufactured in Vienna were floated downstream. While the main bridges were built, a forward depot on the Lobau received materials for the smaller bridges to be thrown from the various islands to the left bank. Iron-shod and ordinary beams were no problem, but there was a shortage of cordage and anchors. Austrian civilian artisans manufactured cordage and, when this did not suffice, Napoleon had the church bell ropes dismantled. Though only French troops were allowed near the bridges, civilian labourers were employed in manufacturing bridging components, while Davout and Eugène were instructed to bring everything in the way of bridging material they could find. But this proved difficult, especially the problem of finding enough anchors to replace the provisional stone-filled barrels used in May. In the end Davout could find only seven anchors, but Eugène managed to procure sixty heavy iron anchors which he sent to Kaiser-Ebersdorf.[3]

The bridgeworks envisaged by Napoleon and his engineering staff were indeed impressive. Utilizing seven large and a number of smaller floating pile drivers from the magazines in Vienna, an 800-yard double stockade of strong iron-shod piles was driven into the bed of the fast-flowing river from the shore to the Schneidergrund and from there to the Lobgrund. This provided protection against any future Austrian attempts to rupture the bridgeworks. The main bridge was to be a reinforced trestle-bridge. To make its piers withstand the strong current, they were placed in groups of five about 2 feet apart, tied together with diagonal and horizontal trusses. In all there were sixty piers, forty-one over the first arm of the river to the Schneidergrund and nineteen from there to the Lobgrund, providing a firm base for the heavy planks of the three-carriage-wide roadway.

Actual construction was directed by one of Bertrand's senior battalion commanders and a specialist in bridge building, Colonel Feraudy, known among his peers as the 'Grand Pontife'. Napoleon, who had now taken up residence in the splendid Schönbrunn Palace south of the city, frequently rode down to visit the site to encourage his officers and men to make even speedier progress. They responded. The main bridge, complete with night illumination and strong railings, was completed by 21 June, as were three additional short pile bridges, each about 25 yards long, connecting the Lobgrund with the Lobau. These were designed for the movement of artillery, ammunition and supplies. Some 50 yards upstream from the main bridge the engineers constructed a second trestle-bridge for the evacuation of the wounded. In addition, during the construction a smaller service bridge, composed of sixty-eight heavy boats and nine substantial rafts, had been placed some 30 yards downstream, and was designated to carry infantry reinforcements only. The ten gunboats, including three captured Austrian craft, armed with small bow howitzers and manned by thirty to fifty sailors each, were assigned to patrol the Danube upstream from the main bridges and were supplemented by another twenty armed river craft. A huge iron chain that the Austrians had employed two centuries earlier to bar the river against the Turks was also sent to Kaiser-Ebersdorf, but proved too heavy and unwieldy and was not used. By working night and day, the French completed the construction of the main trestle-bridge and its subsidiaries – major engineering achievements surpassing the bridges constructed by Caesar and Trajan – in less than a month. Napoleon was justified when he boasted in his 24th Bulletin of 2 July: 'the Danube no longer exists for the French Army.'

THE LOBAU ISLAND BASE

Even while construction of the bridges proceeded there was much additional activity. On 29 May, Napoleon had already decided on a simultaneous multi-corps assault that would require at least four crossings. In the event there would be ten assault crossings by raft and pontoon bridges, as well as a number of amphibious assault landings, with all necessary *matériel* prepared on the Lobau. The various small streams and creeks cutting the island were bridged, in some cases widened to that they could conceal the pre-positioned assault barges and bridging equipment until the actual moment of the assaults. Among the assault craft, pontoons, rafts and such, there was one ingenious piece, a special pre-assembled one-piece flexible bridge, made of fourteen captured pontoons in four sections tied together by rope hinges, which was to be used for crossing from the Lobau to the Ile Alexandre. Moored near the south-east end of the Ile Alexandre, it was to be released into the Stadlau branch. The current would unfold the sections and float them downstream. Then, pulled by a boat, they would swing towards the opposite bank where they were anchored. Iron rods would then be slid into iron brackets from one pontoon to the other, creating a solid bridge, more than 100 yards long with a roadbed wide enough for a three-rank column or one line of led horses.

The intended locations for the assault bridges indicated the continued refinement of Napoleon's battle plan. Frequently scouting in person along the north and north-east shore of the Lobau, dressed in a sergeant's greatcoat, he had noted that the Austrians were fortifying the line from Aspern to Gross Enzersdorf, but had pulled their main army out of artillery range. But he had no intention of repeating his crossing into the Mühlau, though he planned to deceive the enemy by demonstrations and feints in this area. He planned that the actual crossings would be mounted during the night from the east side of the Lobau through and around the Ile Alexandre in the direction of Gross Enzersdorf. The most southerly attack would protect the flank while in the north the Lobau batteries would provide support. As he pointed out to Berthier, this plan provided an element of surprise, deceiving the Austrians and avoiding a frontal attack against the Austrian fortified line.[4] Once across and on the Marchfeld, the army would wheel west and roll up the Austrian left flank along the river.

The Lobau became the advanced fortified base, supply depot and assembly area. There were two main roads on the island. The first led from the Lobgrund to the site of the crossing used on 20 May, the second ended up opposite the Ile Alexandre. A complete network of secondary roads, graded and signposted, gave easy access to all points of the island where magazines, depots, workshops and field hospitals, as well as a large bakery were established. The stores included 300,000 bread rations, 200,000 bottles of wine and 15,000 pints of brandy. By the end of June, 4 Corps was encamped on the Lobau while 2 Corps was assembled around Kaiser-Ebersdorf. To secure the island against an Austrian coup, Napoleon had ordered the construction of small defensive works. A small battery protected the inlet between the Lobgrund and the Lobau in the south-west. On the north-west side, going from west to east, since the end of May the Tabor islands, north of the

Leopoldstadt suburb, had been garrisoned by troops from General Friant's division of Davout's 3 Corps. Designed to defend Vienna, but perhaps more as a deception, the two islands were each armed with a four-gun 6-pounder battery, while on the Leopoldstadt river bank a battery of four captured 18-pounders was emplaced.

Napoleon intended to use Lobau Island and the various islets in the Danube as concentration areas and forward artillery bases to cover the assault crossings, destroy the Austrian works and guns along the river line and provide fire support during the initial stages of his deployment on the Marchfeld. In their report of 3 June, Generals Foucher and Rogniat had estimated that a minimum of seventy heavy and medium pieces would be needed to support the planned operations. In the event, 124 captured pieces were installed or kept ready in reserve. Emplaced during June and the first three days of July, there were 31 pieces on the north side and 75 on the east side, with a reserve of 18 mobile 12-pounders with some of the batteries positioned on the islands, especially the Ile Alexandre. Napoleon ordered all guns supplied with 300 rounds of ammunition. By type there were 28 heavy 18-pounders, 24 lighter 12-pounders, 17 heavy 28cm-mortars, 10 howitzers and a variety of smaller pieces, mainly 6- and 4-pounders. A carefully worked out fire plan envisaged the elimination of the Austrian fortifications and the demolition of Essling and Gross Enzersdorf. Other designated targets included individual works from Aspern east and south, down to the small Austrian position known as the Maison Blanche, about a mile-and-a-half below the Ile Alexandre. General Aubry, later replaced by Jean-Louis Ebénézer Reynier, was appointed in overall command of the Lobau artillery.[5]

CONCENTRATING THE ARMY

Napoleon always attached supreme importance to artillery, and had been shaken by the fire of the numerically superior and concentrated Austrian artillery at Aspern–Essling. Therefore he and his director of artillery, General Gaston Lariboisière, who had replaced Songis de Courbons, mortally wounded at Aspern–Essling, took steps to strengthen the artillery assigned to the corps. Immediately after the battle, on 25 May, he ordered Lariboisière to redistribute corps artillery and to issue captured guns to 2, 3 and 4 Corps as well as the Cavalry Reserve. Oudinot's 2 Corps received an additional forty-eight pieces, while Davout's 3 Corps and Masséna's 4 Corps were each allotted sixty-six guns, making these two elite corps the most artillery-heavy in the army.[6] The Cavalry Reserve had twenty-six guns. But this was still not enough for the emperor, and more guns were collected from everywhere in his empire. Eugène was instructed to bring as many guns as possible, eventually arriving with 100, some of them pieces captured at various Austrian fortresses and depots. Towards the end of June the emperor was delighted by the arrival of Colonel Antoine Drouot with the bulk of the field artillery of the Guard, including three cherished 12-pounder batteries, bringing the total Guard artillery to sixty pieces. By 4 July, inclusive of the Lobau and island batteries, Napoleon disposed of 617 pieces of artillery and could deploy 488 guns in the field for the next battle.

The emperor was determined to fight this battle with superior numbers and he brought up all possible reinforcements. A substantial number of wounded returned to duty and units were brought up to strength with replacements. All the depots of the Rhine and Italy were emptied and refilled with 40,000 recruits of the class of 1809. Two strong corps, Masséna's 4 Corps (21,300 infantry, 6,100 cavalry, 2,800 artillery, 186 guns) and Oudinot's 2 Corps (26,000 infantry, 1,600 cavalry, 1,900 artillery, 64 guns), were already deployed on the island or near the main bridge. But in order to maintain the element of surprise, the emperor did not concentrate additional large formations until the end of June, and orders to concentrate near Vienna were issued only on 24 June.

At this time Davout's powerful 3 Corps, which once across the Danube would constitute the right wing of the deployed army and therefore had three cavalry divisions attached, Grouchy, Pully, and Montbrun, shifted from its position downstream at Pressburg towards

Vienna. Concentration speeded up during the last week of June as the emperor called in his outlying corps to assemble at Kaiser-Ebersdorf. These included Eugène's army, which had pushed John's forces into Hungary, defeated them on 14 June in the battle of Raab and then driven them across the Danube where their positions around Pressburg, including a small bridgehead across the Danube, were to be screened by Severoli's Italian division. The Army of Italy – two French corps under Generals Macdonald and Grenier, as well as the two mounted brigades of the Royal Italian Guard, a total of 19,000 infantry, 2,000 cavalry, 1,700 artillery and 33 guns – moved towards Vienna. Also ordered to Vienna was Bernadotte's 9 Saxon Corps, which consisted of two Saxon divisions with the weak French Dupas division attached. In all, Bernadotte had 15,500 infantry, 3,100 cavalry, 900 artillery and 38 guns. Hustling up from Styria, harried by peremptory orders to move his corps, described by the emperor as 'the most beautiful in my army', to a faster pace was Marmont's Army of Dalmatia, the 11 Corps. Though small – only two divisions with 9,700 infantry, 300 cavalry, 700 artillery and 28 guns – almost all its units comprised hardened veterans.[7] Assembling east of Vienna was the three-division cavalry reserve under Bessières (8,200 cavalry, 500 artillery, 28 guns). Once reinforced, the Bavarian division under General Wrede, a combined force with 5,400 infantry, 1,100 cavalry, 700 gunners and 24 guns, after marching 125 miles in six days, would arrive late on 4 July. Meanwhile Vandamme's 8 (Württemberg) Corps (8,600 infantry, 2,200 cavalry, 900 artillery and 40 guns), secured Vienna and guarded the riverbank upstream. Napoleon boasted that he would attack with 180,000 men, but this number included the Lobau garrison, engineers and sappers and his medical staff and other non-combatants. Actually, the emperor disposed of between 150,000 to 175,000 effectives in the coming battle: 260 battalions, 207 squadrons and 617 guns.[8]

FORMULATING THE ATTACK PLAN

Napoleon's concentration of his forces was a considerable achievement. It assembled the great bulk of the Army of Germany. Only Vandamme's Württembergers, positioned along the Danube upstream from Vienna, two divisions of Lefebvre's Bavarians, detailed to contain the Tyrolean insurrection, and one division of the Army of Italy, detailed to screen Pressburg out of the battle, were left out of the attack. The date for the assault was fixed on 24 June when, instructing Eugène and Davout to arrive at Kaiser-Ebersdorf by 2 July, Napoleon told them that 'I intend to attack the enemy on the 5th'. Five weeks after having been repulsed and driven back across the Danube, Napoleon had converted the Lobau into an impressive fortified fire base, built three substantial bridges across the Danube and prepared eight assault bridges. In addition, he had procured a Danube flotilla of ten gunboats and other armed craft, as well as five large ferries, each capable of carrying 300 men, and a number of flatboats and barges. He had also had elaborated an overall battle plan. The enemy would be confused by several feints north from the Lobau, while the main thrust would be delivered from its east side. During the night the Stadlau branch would be crossed from the north and south ends of the Ile Alexandre to the Marchfeld plain, with amphibious assaults on the Hanselgrund from the south end of the Lobau to precede this movement. Once across the Stadlau branch, the army would deploy in three battle lines and, rolling up the Austrian positions along the river and pivoting on Gross Enzersdorf, envelop the enemy and destroy him.

THE FINAL PREPARATIONS FOR THE CROSSING

Napoleon was always an improviser and did not believe that it was possible to plan a battle in detail, but he realized that a multi-corps night crossing had to be planned meticulously. As usual, Berthier and his staff worked out the details. To deceive the enemy, on 30 June Napoleon ordered one of Masséna's divisions, Legrand's, to cross the Stadlau branch into the Mühlau at the same spot he had crossed in May and establish a bridgehead there. Covered by the fire of thirty-six guns, some 800 infantry made the 100-yard crossing by boat. French engineers then emplaced a short pontoon bridge and by 5 p.m. Legrand had crossed it, pushing back three Austrian battalions and immediately throwing up substantial earthworks and emplacing six artillery pieces.

There was no major Austrian reaction until the next day when Charles moved his main force close to the river. But after being fired on from the Lobau and realizing the threat from the massive French batteries, the next day he pulled his men back to their original positions on the line of the Russbach to the Bisamberg. During the following night Napoleon moved his headquarters to the south-west part of the Lobau, where he was joined by the Imperial Guard. As a further deception, four additional bridges were built from the north shore of the Lobau to the opposite bank, and on 2 July a small feint was undertaken towards Stadlau, upriver from Aspern. On this occasion French guns bombarded the Austrian positions, 500 men landed on the Schierling Grund, while further east Masséna was directed to seize the Ile Bessières just below the Mühlau and place an eight-gun battery there to dominate the river bank up to Gross Enzersdorf. The same day, heavy batteries on the Lobau again opened fire on Austrian works and troops near Gross Enzersdorf, inflicting heavy damage and 300 casualties. Archduke Charles, who had advanced II and III Corps close to the river line, now pulled his main forces back and issued orders that they were not to support the units of the Advance Guard and VI Corps holding the river line without his direct orders.

Napoleon prepared and issued final movement orders between 2 and 4 July. His plan was based on deception, the demonstrated slow reaction of the Austrians and sheer weight of numbers and firepower. Late on 2 July, Berthier issued Napoleon's instructions regarding the placement of the formations on the Lobau and the order and timing of their crossing to the left bank. As far as possible they were to bivouac close to their designated crossings and in the order of battle they were to assume once across the river. During the day the bridges, policed by gendarmes of the Imperial Guard, were reserved for transport of stores; troop movement was to be under the cover of darkness. The first line of battle was to consist of 4, 2, and 3 Corps with attached cavalry. Masséna's 4 Corps, still minus Legrand's division, deployed on the north-east side of the Lobau, and Oudinot's 2 Corps crossed soon after darkness on the night of the 3rd to take up positions in the south-east. The Imperial Guard, 7,400 infantry, 3,400 cavalry, 1,600 artillery and 60 guns, followed at 8.30 p.m. Finally at 11 p.m. 9 Corps, which was to assemble on the north-west of the island to convey the impression of an attack north, crossed into the Lobau. The movement of stores occupied most of the daylight hours of 4 July, but after dark Davout was to cross, taking his station slightly to the rear between Masséna and Oudinot.

The second line was to be formed of the Army of Italy, two French divisions and the Royal Italian Guard, crossing at 1 a.m. on the 5th to deploy on the left, followed before dawn by Bernadotte's corps taking up positions on the right. The Imperial Guard, already encamped on the Lobau, would occupy the centre, while the light cavalry was to cross at 3.00 a.m. followed by the Reserve Cavalry, three heavy divisions under Bessières. Marmont's corps and the Bavarians were not expected until late on 5 July and were to act as reserves on the second day.

Also on 2 July, specific fire plans were issued for the Lobau and the batteries on the adjoining islands. Here General Reynier was to take command at noon on 4 July. In addition to the gunners and such, he was to have a number of detached infantry units: one Baden regiment from Masséna, two battalions from Oudinot, two battalions of Saxons from Bernadotte as well as Berthier's Neuchâtel battalion. The various units were to defend the batteries on and around the Lobau while the Neuchâtel battalion, Berthier's own, was to replace Legrand's division in the Mühlau bridgehead during the night of 4–5 July. The timing of the first amphibious assaults, the placing of the assault bridges and the order of march for correct deployment on the other side were crucial. That close-on 150,000 men with their horses, guns and ammunition trains were able to cross the river in a single night was a triumph of staff work. There was only a minor mix-up, between elements of Davout's and Oudinot's corps when, because of an oversight by Berthier's staff, Davout crossed by the centre instead of the right bridge, causing each corps to cross the other's line of march during the night.

A complication had threatened on 2 July when Masséna was incapacitated after being thrown from his horse, but much to Napoleon's delight the marshal refused to stand down and told the emperor that he would utilize his light carriage. 'With you on my left flank,' the emperor remarked, 'I feel assured'. Though in considerable pain, Masséna conducted his corps during the days of battle by riding in a phaeton drawn by four white horses and handled by two elaborately uniformed civilian coachmen. If his visibility encouraged his own troops, it also made him a clear target for the Austrian gunners. Indeed one horse was killed during the second day, but Masséna remained unscathed. In vivid contrast to Masséna, on the Austrian side, General Hiller, commanding VI Corps, was so unhappy with his dispositions – 'I repeatedly have warned that the fortifications are too weak', he complained – that on 4 July he asked for and received permission to leave the army on the grounds of ill health.

THE OTHER SIDE OF THE RIVER

While Napoleon has spent six weeks preparing for his next attempt to cross the Danube, the Austrians wasted much of the same period. They did nothing to prevent Napoleon's converting the Lobau into a fortified base or to summon all possible reinforcements. Charles continued his attempts to exploit his success at Aspern–Essling as the basis for peace negotiations, but, lacking support from his imperial brother and undercut by the war faction, was losing control over his subordinates, his generals as well as his extraordinarily self-willed and uncooperative brothers. Personal rivalry and dissension reappeared in the Austrian high command and government. While Quartermaster-General Wimpffen was preening himself as the victor of Aspern–Essling and became ever more arrogant, Hiller was sulky and told all who would listen that the French could have been annihilated if his corps had not been held back from pushing his final attack. On 24 May Archduke Charles took the Emperor Francis, Foreign Minister Stadion and other dignitaries on a tour of the battlefield. Here in the broiling sun were those corpses and horse cadavers that had not yet been buried, and Charles apparently wanted to impress his brother and his entourage with the horrors of war and make them amenable to peace negotiations. Hiller, however, spoiled his efforts. This, the general argued, was not the time for peace but the very moment 'to ring the tocsin, mobilize every available man and attack the enemy with your courageous army'. In a week, so the general asserted, 'the enemy will be destroyed and Your Majesty can dictate peace terms'. The emperor and Stadion seemed impressed by the argument; the archduke remained silent. On 26 May, during a war council at headquarters now in Breitenlee, Hiller again pressed for an offensive. If an attack into the Lobau appeared too risky, then the army should march to Pressburg and cross the river into the rear of the enemy, while 30,000 men were to deliver a diversion from their present positions. The last proposal met opposition from Wimpffen who argued that if the army were defeated at Pressburg it would be pushed into Hungary, leaving Bohemia, the province with the most resources and remaining magazines, uncovered. In the end nothing was resolved.

But the army could not remain for long in the battle zone along the river where during the unseasonably hot weather the presence of dead bodies in the sweltering heat – men and horses alike – created an increasing health hazard. On 24 May Archduke Charles had issued orders to bury them, a slow process not finished until 13 June. Meanwhile, leaving behind only Hiller's VI Corps and the Advance Guard along the river, he had retired the bulk of his army to the edge of the Marchfeld, establishing his headquarters first at Markgrafneusiedl, then, after an accidental fire destroyed the village, at Deutsch-Wagram. I, II and IV Corps camped on the escarpment plain beyond the Russbach,

The Archduke Charles was the first European general to defeat Napoleon in battle. At Aspern–Essling he repulsed the French Emperor's initial attempt to cross the Danube. Charles faced Napoleon twelve years earlier when he commanded the remnants of the Austrian army in Italy in 1797. (Bridgeman/Chateau de Versailles, France)

ABOVE Napoleon underestimated Austrian determination at Aspern–Essling. In this picture French cuirassiers are repulsed by Hungarian grenadiers on the first day of the battle. (AKG Images)

Marshal Jean Lannes (AKG Images)

Marshal André Massèna (AKG Images)

ABOVE The Emperor and his marshals review plans for the crossing of the Danube. Note the bridge and engineering barges in the background on the left. (Bridgeman/Apsley House, The Wellington Museum, London)

BELOW Repulsed at Aspern–Essling, Napoleon made careful preparations. Building strong bridges, he turned Lobau Island into a powerful fire base and a vast assembly area. Here between 2 and 4 July 1809, artillery and cavalry are crossing over the southern branch of the Danube to their concentration areas. (Bridgeman/Chateau de Versailles, France)

Within the limitations of available technology, Napoleon tried to control his battles closely. Here he is shown at a critical point of the battle, shortly after noon on the second day of Wagram, 6 July 1809, observing Davout's envelopment of the extreme left of the Austrian position at Markgrafneusiedl. (Bridgeman/Giraudon/Chateau de Versailles, France)

ABOVE After bitter fighting, on the second day of the battle of Wagram, shortly after midday on 6 July 1809, Napoleon and his staff ride forward to observe Eugène's Army of Italy attack the Austrian centre. The Russbach hills can be seen in the rear of the picture. (AKG Images)

BELOW Napoleon's counter-attack, led by Macdonald's divisions (not depicted) and supported by the Young Guard (left) and a grand battery (right), stalled the Austrian attempt to envelop the left flank of the French army. (Bridgeman/The Stapleton Collection)

Marshal Etienne Macdonald
(AKG Images)

Prince Eugène de Beauharnais (AKG Images)

Marshal Auguste Marmont (AKG Images)

Marshal Jean-Baptiste Bernadotte (AKG Images)

Marshal Louis-Nicholas Davout (AKG Images)

ABOVE Archduke John (AKG Images)

LEFT The Archduke Charles was the ablest of allied commanders. Here he seizes the banner of Infantry Regiment Zach and directs a counter-attack against Prince Eugène's divisions on the evening of the first day of Wagram. (AKG Images)

Prince von Liechtenstein (AKG Images)

General Heinrich Bellegarde (AKG Images)

Napoleon contemplates plans on the night of the battle of Wagram. (AKG Images)

while III Corps, soon to be joined by V Corps called in from guarding the Danube near Linz, took station on the slopes of the Bisamberg. The Reserve Corps, the cavalry and the grenadier battalions were quartered in the villages of the plain below.

Despite his defensive victory, Charles found himself in a difficult situation. He realized that none of the grand strategic assumptions made when war had been decided on had come true. Aspern–Essling had not been enough to convince potential allies to join Austria. Prussia had not joined the war. There was no general uprising in Germany. Russia, a French ally, albeit an uncertain one, was becoming more aggressive in Galicia, supporting the Poles invading from the Grand Duchy of Warsaw. The promised British diversionary attack into the Low Countries had not materialized. On 23 June the archduke wrote to the Emperor Francis that 'the first battle lost is a death sentence for the Monarchy'. Some days later he wrote to Field-Marshal Duke Albert, his uncle and close friend, with whom he maintained close relations throughout his career, that, if unavoidable, he would 'strike one more blow against the French, though you may rest assured that I shall risk nothing or as little as possible'.[9] Austria, he continued, cannot continue to fight on several fronts and 'only a major success against Napoleon can save the war'. But he considered the outcome of another major battle as most doubtful.

Tactically the Austrian staff was well informed of French preparations on the Lobau and Charles was also aware of his own army's short-comings. There was considerable traffic between Napoleon's camp and the other side of the Danube, while pickets along the river and above all the observatory on the Bisamberg could see the French preparations. 'The steady work of the carpenters and shipwrights,' one contemporary, Varnhagen von Ense, noted, 'the arrival of artillery and ammunition wagons – none of this escaped our notice.'[10] While Austrian observers on the Bisamberg could observe traffic across the main arm of the Danube and then in the plain of the Marchfeld, from the roof of the Maison Blanche (*Uferhaus* to the Austrians) it was possible to see only a short distance into the densely wooded east shore of the Lobau. In any case, with most of the troop movements conducted at night during the critical last days before the second crossing, much of the final concentration escaped observation.

THE AUSTRIAN BATTLE PLANS

The Austrian army had suffered substantial losses at Aspern-Essling and replacements and reinforcements were trickling in only slowly. Given this situation, Archduke Charles was in no mood to chance another major battle, and certainly not in a position to take the offensive. The question was how best to fight a defensive battle. Charles expected a renewed French attack, but he and his staff believed it would come across from the Lobau north, essentially in the same direction as on 20 May. He pulled back his main body to the line of the Russbach-Bisamberg, leaving only VI Corps and the Klenau's Advance Guard to watch the river line and begin construction of a chain of sixteen defensive redoubts. The former quartermaster-general, von Heldenfeld, who had been one of the young archduke's military mentors, observed rather scathingly that only Turks would throw up such poorly designed earthworks.[11] Not always well sited and providing no all-round protection, the majority of these rather weak works, emplacing some seventy-two field pieces, were concentrated between Aspern and Gross Enzersdorf. The last work, located at the extreme left of the Austrian line, was established below the Ile Alexandre in the Hanselgrund, an area of meadow and brush near the junction of the Stadlau branch into the Danube. But this left a 3-mile stretch along the water unprotected. Curiously, although it would have been feasible within three weeks, Charles made no effort to draw on the heavy artillery available in the arsenals in Bohemia and Moravia to strengthen his works along the river line.

The archduke was concerned with strengthening his army but he was unwilling and unable to concentrate all available major combat formations. From Linz, he brought the bulk of Kolowrat's III Corps, but left about a third behind. Then there was FML Ignaz Gyulai's corps near Graz, about 20,000 strong, also left in place. Also not available were two mixed detachments under Generals Ende and von Radivojevic, some 12,000 men, who in June had been sent from northern Bohemia to raid into Saxony and the Main region in the hopes of raising the population. Although initially well received, their appeals for volunteers yielded but a total of eighty-six men, illustrating that hopes of a popular rising in Germany were illusory. Clearly he could not recall Archduke Ferdinand's corps from Galicia. Though on 2 July the Emperor Francis, never shy of interfering in military affairs and of bypassing Charles, would write to Wimpffen, that 'unless you intend to conduct a major action in the next few days, 12–15,000 men should be sent to Galicia'.[12] Meanwhile, Hungary provided the noble mounted *insurrectio*, the old feudal levy called out by Archduke Palatine Joseph, but who was reluctant to make demands for more men and was not inclined to cooperate with either John or Charles. In any case, the mounted *insurrectio* and the Portal militia, untrained infantry, lacked combat capabilities and the palatine feared that further call-ups might only provoke uprisings. This left Archduke John's Army of Inner Austria, repeatedly defeated but still 11,000 foot, 2,200 horse, and 34 guns and now encamped near Pressburg with a small bridgehead across the Danube. Although relations between the two brothers were strained, the archduke counted on John to reinforce his left wing during the coming battle but would be disappointed.

Charles, however, was able to find reinforcements from the *Landwehr* units of Lower Austria, Bohemia and Moravia. Individuals were used as filler replacements and thirty-one *Landwehr* battalions, not all well trained, were brigaded with regular formations. Initially there were some jurisdictional problems because the Bohemians and Moravians quite properly objected to serving outside the boundaries of their kingdom, but after being assured of equal treatment with the line infantry they came willingly enough and in the end all, especially the Vienna *Landwehr* Volunteer battalions, fought well. By the first week of July Charles had 119,000 infantry, 15,000 cavalry and 414 guns, not counting V Corps, which would not participate in the fighting and was left on the Bisamberg to protect a line of retreat into Moravia and Bohemia if necessary, or John's army, which arrived too late. Although Charles was clearly weaker than his enemy, the court strategists in Vienna continued to interfere. Bypassing the commander-in-chief, Minister Stadion kept insisting that the situation was better than pictured by Charles, and maintained a private correspondence with Wimpffen claiming that if the main army was not prepared to challenge the enemy, at least it could send reinforcements to Saxony and Galicia. None the less, though hampered by intrigues at court and dissension among his commanders, it is also clear that Charles did not put in every ounce of effort to prepare for battle. He was never a commander willing to risk all in order to gain a decisive victory, and as late as the first days of July he remained preoccupied with the hope that Napoleon would negotiate.

As was, and remains, common in many armies, Charles did use the time before battle to smarten up his troops. There was much drilling and many inspections, and to deal with what appeared a deterioration of discipline Charles reintroduced corporal punishment, abolished in his army code only two years earlier. Not too much should be made of this. Napoleon also tightened up discipline and threatened – and carried out – draconian punishments for looting and desertion at this time. More important was that despite shortcomings exhibited in the Austrian army in Bavaria and at Aspern–Essling, no effort was made to improve skirmishing, the control of large formations or staff procedures. Fighting instructions issued on 5 June merely restated points made before the war, though there was one, mainly administrative, change. Charles had abolished the corps designation and reintroduced columns operating under a centralized battle command, but nothing else had changed and the designation corps will continue to be used here. The reorganization made the conduct of operations even more sluggish, especially when corps commanders were reminded to keep their formations aligned with adjoining formations, though at the same time also told not to follow this rule too rigidly. If a neighbouring formation was forced back, commanders were not to conform but to act against the flanks of the enemy force pursuing the retiring column. This of course made sense, but what remains less easy to understand was Charles's neglect to fortify the defensive positions of his army in depth. Although he had plenty of civilian labour available, he did not employ it. Beyond the thin chain of earthworks between Aspern–Essling–Gross Enzersdorf along the Stadlau branch, nothing was done to fortify the Russbach position until 4 July, when it was too late. There was also no effort made to fortify any of the small villages and hamlets such as Mühlleiten on the left or Aderklaa in the centre, on the generally featureless March-feld plain, located on a small elevation and surrounded by a dam.

A partial explanation may be that the Austrian high command had failed to come up with a single battle plan. Basically there were three options. Charles was above all concerned not to risk his army and he wanted to be able to break off the battle at any point. This precluded fighting close to the river, an area exposed to the heavy French batteries and with wooded terrain, cut up by rivulets, brush and small streams and with few roads, ground in which the French, better at fighting in open order, had the clear advantage. Also, in the event of a retreat becoming necessary, the army would suffer heavy losses extricating itself from this position. Giving battle further up in the open and basically flat terrain of the Marchfeld was more suited to the Austrian fighting methods but, given the pronounced superiority of the French cavalry and artillery it was also extremely risky. The third option was to let the French penetrate to the edge of the Marchfeld and oblige them to attack the excellent defensive position on the far edge of the Russbach plateau from Wagram to Markgrafneusiedl on the left of the Austrian line. Strong forces, the Reserve Cavalry and the Grenadier Corps, would bar this position against an envelopment from the plain while at the same time a strong right wing stationed on the lower slopes of the Bisamberg would hit the French flank. The position remained vulnerable and exposed on the left where the Russbach plateau gently sloped down to the plain, enabling the position to be outflanked, but

Charles was confident that Archduke John's army marching up from Pressburg would extend the line to the river.

There are strong indications that Charles, expecting the French to attack north into the Mühlau, repeating their May operation, initially favoured bringing up the entire arm down the Marchfeld close to the river. It would appear that the archduke had decided to repeat the Aspern model, intending to smash the enemy with his back to the river. This was a sound manoeuvre in the event Napoleon did indeed cross north into the Mühlau, but even then needed better odds, especially in cavalry and artillery, than he had available. When on 1 and 2 July Napoleon's feints indicated such a move, on 2 July Archduke Charles did advance his main forces on a broad front, with the main concentration between Essling and Gross Enzersdorf, his troops arriving in their new positions by sundown. The French bombardment commencing about noon that day convinced him that this was dangerous and, with the Bisamberg observatory reporting that while there was heavy vehicular traffic across the bridges into the Lobau no concentration of troops was visible, he became uncertain. The next morning, 3 July, he retired the bulk of his troops to their previous positions and returned his headquarters, which had advanced to Breitenlee, back to Deutsch-Wagram.

Only the Advance Guard, now commanded by FML Armand von Nordmann, a French *emigré* and an able officer, who took command when Klenau became commander of VI Corps after Hiller departed, remained on the east end of the river line. The Advance Guard, reinforced by brigades from III, IV, and V Corps, numbered just short of 12,000 foot, 2,500 horse and 48 guns, and covered the line from Essling down towards the outflow of the Stadlau ranch into the Danube. Klenau's VI Corps, 12,500 foot, 1,300 cavalry, 1,400 artillery and 64 guns, was deployed from Essling west to Am Spitz. The bulk of the army, II, III and IV Corps, comprising 72 battalions, 22 squadrons and 196 guns (a total of 63,115 foot, 2,110 horse and 164 guns), was placed in the Russbach line, with I Corps at Wagram, II at Baumersdorf, and IV above Markgrafneusiedl. With its steep bank on the far side, the Russbach, complemented by boggy terrain and heavy brush along its course, was a substantial obstacle, but the plateau position could have been improved by fortifications. Then too on its right around Gerasdorf, the terrain provided no substantial defensive assets. Here Charles placed his Reserve Cavalry with his Grenadier Corps in reserve. Finally, III Corps, some 16,000 infantry, 668 cavalry and 58 guns, was stationed at Hagenbrunn and the east slopes of the Bisamberg. He stationed V Corps, only 7,500 infantry and 12 guns strong, though with an additional brigade from III Corps attached, with detachments guarding the Danube upstream at Krems on the Bisamberg. It was not included in the battle plan but was assigned to protect an eventual line of retreat.

The final decision, reached only on the evening of 4 July, called for the Advance Guard and VI Corps, supported by the Reserve Cavalry, to offer the most protracted resistance against a French advance, cause delay, disorder and inflict casualties and then fall back. Nordmann was to retire towards Markgrafneusiedl and Klenau to fall back to Stammersdorf, aligning with III Corps to his left. These dispositions created an extended line over 13 miles wide, with the left and the right wings at sharp angles to each other, though the apex was weak. It was planned that if Napoleon attacked the Russbach line the Austrian right wing would fall on his flank, but if he turned towards the Bisamberg then the heavy Austrian left would attack his flank. The basic plan was sound, but it took no account of the slow Austrian staff work and the difficulty of coordinating two widely separated wings. Above all it needlessly exposed the Advance Guard and VI Corps. If the objective was merely to delay the French advance, then fewer troops would have sufficed. But if resistance was protracted, then the 25,000 men of these formations were too weak in number and would suffer heavy casualties to no great effect.

To keep the Austrians in doubt about his intentions for as long as possible, on 2 July Napoleon ordered Berthier to open negotiations regarding an exchange of prisoners on 4 July, a move that seemed to confirm the archduke's hope that a peaceful solution was still possible. But it was just another ruse and he was duped. In the morning of 4 July, the Bisamberg observatory signalled the approach of large numbers of troops from the road east along the Danube: Davout's 3 Corps and the Army of Italy. Also a few hours earlier the heavy French batteries on the Lobau and adjoining islands bombarded Aspern and Essling and demolished work no. 11, west of Gross Enzersdorf. At about 2 p.m., a sudden thunderstorm left the Bisamberg observatory unable to see the French movements. It made little difference. The archduke realized that the feared battle had already begun and that by now it was too late to change his dispositions.

Although his engineering staff had previously suggested that the Russbach line should be fortified, Wimpffen had rejected the idea, asserting that this would dishearten the troops. This failure to strengthen a naturally strong position would cost the Austrians dearly. Belatedly, on 4 July, Charles had issued orders for redoubts to be built in front of I, II and IV Corps, but with neither engineers nor tools available, little was accomplished. Finally, becoming aware that an all-out French attack was imminent and that the stakes were high indeed, at 7 that evening he sent an urgent message to John: 'The battle here on the Marchfeld will determine the fate of our Dynasty ... I request you march at once, leaving behind all baggage and impediment and join my left wing.'[13] The archduke expected John to cover the 24 miles rapidly and to arrive the next day. In the event, the message arrived only at 6 the next morning and then, moving with no particular haste and requiring a second order sent on the morning of the 5th, it took John nineteen hours to get his troops moving. Finally, aware that something big was afoot, at 11 p.m. on the 4th and again at 2.30 a.m. on the 5th, Charles ordered all guns of VI Corps to fire a one-hour barrage against the Lobau, the French-occupied islands and the bridges in the Stadlau branch.[14] Needless to say this blind area-fire had no practical effect and did not disturb the crossing. French amphibious assault troops were already ashore at 9 p.m. on the extreme left of the Austrian line.

From the outset, if the French crossed to the north bank in substantial numbers and in good order, given the abilities of the two commanders and their chief subordinates the outcome of the battle was not really in doubt. Napoleon disposed of superior numbers, especially in cavalry and guns, and never wavered from his objective. Archduke Charles, by contrast, vacillated between offensive and defensive battle plans and only on the night of the French crossing decided on a defensive–offensive strategy. However, his intentions were certainly not made clear to his forward elements. Telling them to 'offer determined resistance' in the end led to the near destruction of the Advance Guard, while VI Corps and the Cavalry Reserve spent much of the day needlessly manoeuvring, suffering losses but hardly delaying the French deployment.

CHAPTER SEVEN

Wagram: The first day

THE OPPOSING ARMIES

Shortly after noon on 4 July, Napoleon issued an order of the day for his army. 'Soldiers,' it went, 'one month after Austria has declared war against us, we have entered its capital, have destroyed its best troops, have taken more than 200 guns and 60 flags and have captured 100,000 prisoners.' Only the Danube's high water and rapid flow had delayed final victory, but with bridges built and other preparations in place, 'we now shall move on the enemy and destroy the power which for 15 years has menaced our fatherland and our children'.[1]

During the afternoon, as French troops moved to their embarkation points and bridge-crossing locations, the searing heat of the last three weeks was broken by a series of heavy thunderstorms. With bucketing rain and occasional thunder lasting well into the night, further observations from the Bisamberg became impossible, hiding the final French preparations and blinding the Austrian command. In accordance with Napoleon's meticulously prepared plans, the first wave across the third arm of the Danube consisted of three corps. Oudinot's 2 Corps and Masséna's 4 Corps were the first to cross to the north bank, followed within hours by Davout's 3 Corps. Their mission was to gain room to deploy the Army of Germany on the Marchfeld. This required driving the Austrian Advance Guard from its forward positions, including Gross Enzersdorf, and pushing Klenau's VI Corps east beyond Essling and Aspern. Earlier Oudinot would execute the initial crossings on the right, clearing the minor Austrian outposts, and then drive north-east towards Wittau and Rutzendorf. In the centre Davout, on the right of the battle line, was to swing north, while Oudinot was to deploy in the direction of Gross Enzersdorf. On the left, Masséna was to follow the river, support Oudinot, take Essling and Aspern and drive Klenau's VI Corps towards the Bisamberg. After the capture of Gross Enzersdorf, projected for about 9 a.m. on the 5th, the three corps with their attached cavalry were to align and then pivot east from Gross Enzersdorf to gain room to deploy the army in line of battle on the Marchfeld.

Behind the first line, with additional bridges built, a second line deployed, with the Saxon Corps on the left, the Army of Italy in the centre and the Imperial Guard on the right. A third line was constituted by the heavy cavalry reserve. Napoleon's objective was achieved. All the crossings and the initial engagements were successful. By the afternoon of 5 July, Napoleon had the great bulk of his forces, 134,000 infantry, 27,600 cavalry and 433 guns, not including the Lobau batteries, deployed on the Marchfeld.

Excluding V Corps, which would not participate in the fighting, and Archduke John's small army, which arrived too late to affect the outcome, Charles disposed of a total about 140,000 effectives. This included 121,500 infantry in 160 2/3rd battalions, 14,700 mounted men in 150 squadrons and 414 guns. Although, as is common, the figures given by the various authorities and even archival records differ, it is clear that in contrast to Aspern–Essling Napoleon enjoyed a substantial numerical advantage, especially in cavalry.[2]

Nordmann had only assumed command of the Advance Guard and the weak and poorly sited defensive earthworks nos. 6–16 at 5 p.m. on 4 July. Even when reinforced by two infantry brigades and two hussar regiments, his force was far too weak to offer the 'protracted and determined' resistance ordered by Charles at 6 p.m. on 4 July. Including the guns in works nos. 7–16, Nordmann had only forty-eight guns and some 14,240 men, a total of four brigades including five good *Landwehr* battalions, two *Jäger* battalions and one regiment of Wallach-Illyrian *Grenzer*. Covering the stretch between VI Corps at Essling and work no. 8, he had the eight squadrons of the Hessen–Homburg Hussars. His main force was posted at Gross Enzersdorf, a small town but defensible with a crenellated wall, ditch and flood dyke and a walled cemetery on an elevation. Brigade Mayer, including two excellent infantry regiments, IR 4 Hoch und Deutschmeister and IR 47 Kerpen, was stationed between work no. 8 and Gross Enzersdorf, while the battalions of Brigade Riese were formed behind the town. Along the shallow parapets connecting works nos. 8 and 9, the latter almost levelled by the French bombardment on 2 July, there was IR 58 Beaulieu, while Gross Enzersdorf was held by IR 44 Bellegarde. Two *Grenzer* battalions supported by two squadrons each of the Stipsicz and Primatial Hussars held works nos. 14 and 15 south of Enzersdorf, while the road to Wittau was held by IR 64 Chasteler. Finally there were the small outposts. Two companies of the 1st *Jäger* battalion were at the Uferhaus, another two companies were in the Hanselgrund, and one and a half companies occupied work no. 16. At Mühlleiten there was a half company of 7th *Jäger* Battalion, small detachments held various hamlets, and one company occupied the manor house at Sachsengang. The balance of Nordmann's cavalry patrolled the banks of the Danube eastwards. Clearly, except for the concentration of troops and works around Gross Enzersdorf, this disposition offered no hope for 'determined and protracted resistance', though a few positions held through the night and into the early morning. Advance Corps had been deployed for outpost duty only. The decision to have the main army stand on the defence had been taken only late the evening of 4 July and the Advance Corps now had to fight where it stood.

THE NIGHT CROSSINGS, 4 JULY

With a cold rain mixed with hail pelting down, at 8 p.m. Colonel Conroux of Tharreau's division, Oudinot's 2 Corps, embarked 1,500 *voltigeurs* in five large flatboats that had been specially furnished with bulletproof bulwarks. Their task was to cross from the south-east shore of the Lobau near the outflow of the Stadlau branch to the Hanselgrund. There they were to seize the small 3-pounder-armed Austrian work no. 16 and drive off its garrison, just one and half companies of the 1st *Jäger* battalion. Eight gunboats of Captain Baste's flotilla, armed with 6-pounders and some boat howitzers, supported their passage while the two remaining boats of his flotilla were to bombard the shoreline near the Mühlau salient. A six-gun battery posted on the Lobau was to provide additional suppressive fire. Although detected on their final approach at about 9.30 p.m., the supporting fire silenced the small Austrian 3-pounder battery. After landing, the French light infantry, distinguished in the darkness by white armbands and ordered to advance with the bayonet only, drove the vastly outnumbered defenders north through the dense woods. Encountering little further resistance, the assault cleared the Hanselgrund up to the 'canal', the Steigbügel creek that divided the island from the mainland. Meanwhile, in less than two hours Oudinot's engineers had completed a pontoon bridge allowing the bulk of his corps to cross to the left bank. Leaving behind his 1,450-strong Portuguese Legion to fortify the bridgehead, Oudinot split his corps, ordering one division north along the river towards the Maison Blanche, a second north-east towards the small town of Mühlleiten. In fact, the speedy progress of Masséna's corps compelled the Austrians to hastily evacuate the Maison Blanche position, allowing Oudinot to direct his entire corps to push towards Mühlleiten. After throwing three small bridges across the canal, Tharreau's division had already cleared the Hanselgrund. Meanwhile, Captain Baste proceeded as ordered north to occupy the Rohrhaufen, a swampy islet in the Stadlau branch opposite the Steigbügel, where he landed some 100 musket-armed sailors and established a small battery covering the left flank of Oudinot's advance and then serving to protect Masséna's crossings.

By 10 p.m., with the success of Oudinot's crossing assured, the French batteries on the north-east of the Lobau, on the Ile de Moulin and on the Ile Alexandre, opened a heavy and steady bombardment against Austrian positions and troops in the Essling–Gross Enzersdorf area. Soon thereafter, Masséna's 4 Corps began to cross from the Ile Alexandre to the left bank just below the Maison Blanche, encountering only minor resistance. First across, embarking from the lower end of the Ile Alexandre and ordered to establish a small bridgehead, was Colonel Sainte-Croix with 2,500 *voltigeurs* and ten guns from Boudet's division, 100 rounds per piece, carried in five specially constructed barges also with bulletproof shielding. Simultaneously, the ingenious one-piece bridge anchored on the Ile Alexandre was put to use. With Napoleon present – the French emperor was extraordinarily active all night – Captain Heckman of the engineers swung the bridge out into the stream where the current unfolded it across to the opposite bank, where it was secured by heavy ropes. The entire manoeuvre took but five minutes and even before the bridge was fully anchored the first of Masséna's infantry columns pounded across. Additional troops, infantry and artillery, were transferred by boats and rafts, and using pre-positioned materials within an hour engineers completed seven further boat and raft bridges, each immediately secured by a fortified bridgehead. Across poured the rest of Masséna's corps, the rear elements of Boudet's division, followed by Molitor and Saint-Cyr divisions, Marulaz's light horse brigade and Lasalle's attached light cavalry division.

Conspicuous in his open carriage, Masséna, surrounded by his staff officers and with his physician in attendance to change compresses, followed the first divisions. With Napoleon determined to avoid shortages of ammunition on the far side, each division was followed by ammunition wagons. Throughout the crossings, rain and thunder continued, while massed bands struck up martial airs and the troops sung 'Partant pour

La Syrie,' a popular marching song. Including Legrand's division, by 4 a.m. on 5 July Masséna's entire corps was across and forming up in the Schusterau. He placed his divisions at right angles to the waterway. Boudet on the left, then Molitor and Saint-Cyr, with Legrand on the right, relieved from his duties in the Mühlau where he had been replaced by a number of Rhine Confederation units which arrived only during the afternoon of the 5th. His corps cavalry brigade under Marulaz, joined by Lasalle's light cavalry divisions, was posted on the extreme left along the Danube. Pushing north, Masséna moved to take Gross Enzersdorf.

Almost simultaneously, Davout had begun to transfer his 3 Corps, perhaps the best line formation in the army, and his attached cavalry to the left bank. His four infantry divisions, Morand, Friant, Gudin and Puthod, crossed in the order they arrived, followed by his three attached cavalry divisions, two of dragoons commanded by General Grouchy and a light division, *chasseurs à cheval* and hussars, under Louis-Pierre Montbrun. Davout's powerful corps was to anchor the right wing of Napoleon's line of battle with his attached cavalry ranging to the east to intercept the possible arrival of Archduke John's army. Having been assigned a crossing just south of Masséna's and marching on Wittau and Probstdorf, his troops moving east crossed Oudinot's column moving north, causing a two-hour delay. But this was only a minor planning mistake. Sorted out by experienced officers, the crossing had largely been accomplished to plan, and with additional bridges completed from the north-east shore of the Lobau, the entire second line arrived in the early afternoon.

GAINING DEPLOYMENT ROOM

During the night and early morning the vastly outmatched and surprised Austrian command had offered little effective opposition, though individual units and soldiers, especially the *Jäger* battalions, operating in small clumps in the woods, had fought well. The first major French objective was Gross Enzersdorf where Nordmann had positioned the bulk of his troops around the town and in the surrounding works, especially nos. 14 and 15 to the south. Behind the town the Brigades Riese and Mayer formed up in reserve. With the dawn, there came an end to the rain and the promise of an extremely hot day. Nordmann ordered IR 58 Beaulieu of Riese's brigade to charge the advancing French columns with the bayonet. Despite initial success, the attack was driven back with heavy casualties, and by 6 a.m. the regiment had to retreat to Stadl-Enzersdorf. At the same time Masséna took the partially demolished and staunchly defended works in the vicinity, clearing the way for an attack on Gross Enzersdorf. Heavily pounded by twelve heavy mortars and six 24-pounders emplaced on the Lobau, the town was soon in flaming ruins, though the attack, spearheaded by the 46th Line led by Saint-Croix and supported by Saint-Cyr's division, met with stiff and determined resistance. By 8 a.m., however, the crenellated town walls were stormed. Most of the defenders got away, but many were taken prisoner. Nearby Pouzet Island was also taken and a new bridge, completed by evening, thrown across to the north bank. Nordmann now withdrew to Essling with orders from Klenau, who throughout the morning maintained an unwarranted and over-optimistic assessment of the situation, to continue tenacious resistance.

Oudinot meanwhile had encountered determined opposition at Sachsengang, a strongly built two-storey stone manor with a tower and a modest moat on the road to Wittau. This position was held by the 7th *Jäger* Battalion with two 3-pounder guns and reinforced by elements of the 1st *Jäger* Battalion that had retired from Mühlleiten. Surrounded and attacked by Tharreau's division, though Oudinot's main body moved on, the position surrendered only at 2.30 a.m. on 5 July when its ammunition was exhausted. But this small delay had hardly interfered with the French deployment on the edge of the Marchfeld plain. On Nordmann's far left wing the Primatial and Stipsicz Hussars of Frelich's brigade, considering themselves in danger of being cut off, had retired north until they found support from advanced units of Rosenberg's IV Corps at Rutzendorf. On the right wing, in accordance with Klenau's orders, the Austrian Advance Guard was making a slow fighting retreat east towards Aspern, defending works nos. 8 to 6, all fairly good positions but, facing the river, now attacked in the flank.

At 10 a.m. there was a short halt in the French forward movement to sort out troops and to redistribute munitions from the ammunition carts that had followed each division and rations from the supply wagons. Crucially, though, Napoleon now had his corps deployed, as planned, facing north. With Gross Enzersdorf as the pivot, the French battle line formed to move across the Marchfeld. The line up was as follows: Masséna's 4 Corps on the left; Oudinot with 2 Corps in the centre, where he had taken up his position by 8 a.m.; and Davout's 3 Corps, its cavalry division probing east looking for John's expected arrival, advancing well beyond Wittau on the right. Additional corps had transferred during the morning and afternoon and began to form the second battle line. Eugène's Army of Italy arrived at noon. It was followed some hours later by Pacthod's small division, only two brigades strong, of Grenier's corps. Bernadotte's 9 Corps reached its position at 2 p.m., the Imperial Guard and the Cavalry Reserve at 4 p.m. Marmont and Wrede had crossed to the Lobau ready to enter combat the next day. Shortly after noon, Napoleon, soon joined by the Imperial Guard, as always in full dress, had taken up his position on a hillock some 700 yards west of Aderklaa behind Oudinot's corps, from where he gave orders to continue the advance swinging north across the Marchfeld towards the Russbach plateau.

THE AUSTRIANS DRIVEN FROM THE RIVER LINE

On the Austrian side there had been confusion. Informed of the French crossings at 5 a.m., Charles had ordered an all-out alert and tried to speed up his belated and futile efforts to dig redoubts, each large enough for 400 men and five guns, in front of the Russbach position. He also sent another messenger to John, still over 20 miles away, to urge speed. On the other hand, as late as 6 a.m. on 5 July Nordmann and Klenau had reported to army headquarters that they did not expect a major attack that morning, an opinion supported by Wimpffen who had ridden forward to Gross Enzersdorf. At 6.30 a.m. Charles therefore ordered the Advance Guard and VI Corps to hold their positions tenaciously, an order that may have encouraged both Klenau and Nordmann to expect support by the main army. But this did not happen. After the loss of Gross Enzersdorf, Nordmann took advantage of the pause in French movement to redeploy his remaining troops between work no. 8 at Essling to Rutzendorf, with cavalry positioned at both flanks. Klenau's VI Corps was positioned to the west of Essling with Splenyi's brigade under orders to fall on the French left as it advanced. But it was a battered force and at this point Charles or Klenau – the senior field commander on the spot, but not a man to take the initiative – should have ordered Nordmann to extricate himself. Instead Charles merely sent elements of Liechtenstein's Cavalry Reserve forward to prevent Nordmann from being cut off. FML Schwarzenberg and FML Nostitz with seven regiments of light horse took up station at Pysdorf. GM Roussel d'Hurbal's brigade of two cuirassier regiments went to Neu Wirtshaus, and the four cuirassier regiments of Brigades Lederer and Kroyher were kept in reserve at Raasdorf to shield the Advance Guard's flank during an eventual retreat. As it turned out, Nordmann's troops, moving in masses to hold off cavalry and supported by some forty-eight guns, took the brunt of Napoleon's main attack, in the process suffering major losses. Further west, Masséna, pivoting on Boudet division, spread his divisions to the right, advancing with Molitor's division pushing on Hirschstetten, Saint-Cyr on Breitenlee and Legrand towards Süssenbrunn. Only Boudet continued to push west. This relieved pressure on Klenau, whose rearguard held work nos. 2 and 3 at Aspern until 5 p.m. and allowed VI Corps to make an orderly retreat, forming masses to hold off Lasalle's and Marulaz repeated cavalry charges. As at Aspern, steady masses deterred cavalry and Klenau reached Stammersdorf about 8 p.m.

THE ADVANCE TO THE RUSSBACH LINE

Napoleon had now deployed the bulk of his army on the Marchfeld. Masséna was to advance north-west between Aspern and Breitenlee, behind the light cavalry of Lasalle and Marulaz, on the extreme left; Oudinot was to advance to the Russbach opposite Baumersdorf (Parbasdorf); and Davout was to seize Glinzendorf in the plain below Markgrafneusiedl. Unsure about the location of the enemy's main army, Napoleon sent three brigades of light horse forward to Rutzendorf, where they swung north-west to Pysdorf, coming across Austrian cavalry. Neither side, however, wished to engage and the encounter consisted mainly of an exchange of long-range horse artillery fire in which the more numerous and better-handled French cavalry batteries gained the upper hand. Behind them advanced Davout's infantry, who occupied Rutzendorf before continuing north. As the three corps fanned out across the Marchfeld, marching on a broad front through the ripe corn in extreme heat, artillery well to the front, a large gap opened between Masséna and Oudinot, which Napoleon filled with Eugène's Army of Italy and Bernadotte's Saxon 9 Corps.

At about 1 p.m. Nordmann, concerned about French cavalry turning his flank, had decided to fall back to Grosshofen and Markgrafneusiedl. At 1.30 p.m., Charles ordered Liechtenstein's cavalry forward to protect the retreating Advance Guard, but, moving east with his five regiments towards Glinzendorf, Liechtenstein showed no inclination to attack. Nordmann withdrew in good order, keeping his infantry in masses to fight off the French cavalry though suffering heavy losses from French artillery fire. An attempt to delay the French advance at Glinzendorf was brushed aside at about 3 p.m. as Davout reached the line between Glinzendorf and Raasdorf, closing up on Oudinot. At about the same time and to Oudinot's left at Raasdorf, the advance element of Bernadotte's corps, Dupas's division, ran into resistance from Riese's brigade, which had now been joined by the remnants of the Wallach-Illyrian *Grenzer* and the Chasteler Regiment. But the defenders were speedily ejected by two battalions of the 5th Light and driven in on

Hohenzollern's II Corps. The bulk of Bernadotte's corps now swung to take Aderklaa where at about 3.30 p.m. its leading cavalry encountered d'Hurbal's cuirassier brigade. There followed a clash between the Saxon light cavalry and the Austrian cuirassiers. As some units on both sides shared the same regimental patron, Duke Albert of Sachsen-Teschen, the encounter came to enjoy a degree of celebrity. In reality, however, it was a minor clash only. To allow the French horse to deploy, the Saxon Prinz Klemens Chevaulegers charged repeatedly but were repelled by Austrian carbine volley, delivered in defiance of regulations and contrary to the best practice of the day from a standing position, an indication of the poor command and training now common in the Austrian mounted branch. Undeterred, the Saxons, now reinforced, charged again and Rousell's troopers were driven off, their escape covered by Lederer's brigade. At around 4 p.m., Liechtenstein withdrew most of his cavalry to their original locations between Wagram and Gerasdorf, leaving behind five regiments with IV Corps at Markgrafneusiedl. Overall, the Austrian cavalry achieved little on this opening day of the battle, despite suffering 1,000 casualties, a painful loss considering that the Cavalry Reserve Corps numbered only 12,000 effectives. Also, throughout the day, the grenadiers of the Reserve Corps had remained stationary at Seyring.

To the east, Nordmann finally reached safety in a new position between Markgrafneusiedl and Ober-Siebenbrunn. His losses in the fighting during the night and day of 4 and 5 July were estimated at 6,000 men, about 50 per cent of his strength. The Advance Guard had been sacrificed to let Klenau escape, but these losses could have been reduced if Charles had permitted the Guard to retire earlier that morning. Incorporated into Rosenberg's IV Corps, the remnant of the Advance Guard would be in combat again the next day. Few units in history have suffered such heavy casualties and remained capable of fighting the following day.

By 6 p.m., Napoleon's army, the infantry marching in battalion columns behind a light cavalry screen, had reached the Russbach. Masséna was at Breitenlee, his divisions spread out widely from Boudet near the Danube to Legrand at Süssenbrunn. Bernadotte was at Aderklaa with Dupas's division opposite Baumersdorf and the Army of Italy behind him. Oudinot's corps, to the right of Baumersdorf, stretched back to Grosshofen, with Davout deployed between Grosshofen and Glinzendorf, his attached cavalry divisions further out on the right. The French left wing was only 27,000 strong while the bulk, some 110,000 men, faced the Russbach line. The Imperial Guard, 11,000 strong, was in reserve in the centre near Napoleon's command post and Bessières's heavy cavalry was moving up. Marmont's corps and Wrede's 2nd Bavarian division were still crossing the bridges.

On the Austrian side the left wing was deployed behind the Russbach from Wagram to Markgrafneusiedl with I Corps on the right, II Corps in the centre and IV Corps on the left. West of this position the terrain provided no major defensive assets. Here, at Gerasdorf, Charles stationed the Cavalry Corps, backed up at some distance by the Grenadier Corps. Klenau's VI Corps had pulled back to the foothills of the Bisamberg and aligned with III Corps to its left. The Austrian line therefore formed a sharp angle. Potentially, it could take the French in a double envelopment, but the apex was weakly held and the line stretched for over 12 miles, making coordination and control of the two separate wings problematic. Napoleon, meanwhile, held the advantage of the central position and a shorter line.

THE ATTACK ON THE RUSSBACH LINE FAILS

That evening Charles was not expecting any more major action. Napoleon, however, still uncertain about the location and intentions of the Austrian main force, decided to use the remaining daylight hours for an immediate attack against the Russbach line. Perhaps the emperor was dissatisfied with his failure to come to grips with the main army or wanted to discover the strength of the enemy; perhaps, relying on false reports that the Austrians were retreating, he wanted to prevent Charles from slipping away during the night. In any case, it was the wrong decision. His men were dead tired and not all of his formations were properly concentrated and positioned forward. None the less, he ordered an immediate assault against the Russbach line with the aim of breaking the Austrian line around Deutsch-Wagram. Orders were issued shortly after 6 p.m., but with units requiring different approach times, Napoleon specified neither a clear time for the assault to begin nor clear objectives. He also failed to assign specific targets for the supporting artillery. These shortcomings were compounded by assigning the key objective of Deutsch-Wagram to some of the weakest formations in his army. Oudinot's corps, for example, was largely composed of new recruits. Similarly, to have expected much from Bernadotte's 9 Corps Saxons, even when augmented by Dupas's division, Sahuc's light division and eventually by Macdonald's exhausted and depleted French divisions of the Army of Italy, can only be considered a mistake. But the flow of battle had brought these formations into attack positions at this point and this could not be changed.

At about 7 p.m. the French batteries opened their preparatory bombardment and, with the sinking sun at their back, the attack columns, supported by cavalry, went forward. Oudinot had orders to attack II Corps, Dupas, followed by the Army of Italy, was to drive between I and II Corps, while on the flanks Bernadotte, supported by twenty-four horse-drawn guns of the Imperial Guard, was to take Deutsch-Wagram, and Davout was to storm Markgrafneusiedl. With orders hastily issued and the timing of the assaults poorly coordinated, no ground was taken and all the attacks were repulsed.

Oudinot was first to attack, at about 7.30 p.m., against Hohenzollern's II Corps at Baumersdorf. These were well-positioned troops protected in part by hastily built or dug fortifications and supported by sixty-eight guns. Behind its heavy skirmish line, II Corps was drawn up in two lines. Elements of Frère's division managed to cross the Russbach and reach the escarpment where the small hamlet of Baumersdorf, some thirty houses with a small wooden bridge straddling the brook, was on fire. But although vastly outnumbered, the troops of MG Ignaz Hardegg's brigade, the 8th *Jäger* Battalion and the 2nd

Battalion of the Erzherzog Karl Legion, stubbornly defended the position. They had prepared hasty field defences, including rifle pits (*Jägergruben*) and trenches. Oudinot now launched a flanking attack, committing the 10th Light and the 57th Line Regiments of Grandjean's division. The 'terrible 57th', perhaps the most renowned line regiment in the French Army, broke into the village but was not able to make much progress against the defenders. Meanwhile, the 10th Light made its way across the boggy terrain along the brook and up the steep incline to the plateau. But here it ran into heavy cannon fire and point-blank musketry from battalions of MG Buresch's brigade of II Corps before being charged by the Vincent Chevaulegers, a depleted regiment only some 500 troopers strong but personally led by Prince Hohenzollern. The isolated French light infantry broke and, fleeing down the escarpment, took the 57th with it. Both units eventually regrouped north of Raasdorf where they were confronted by the steady battalions of the Imperial Guard. With darkness closing in, the Austrians did not pursue but merely reoccupied their former positions. By 8 p.m., Oudinot's attack had been repulsed with substantial losses.

To the west, also at about 8 p.m., Dupas's small mixed division, temporarily attached to the Army of Italy, made use of the smoke from the burning buildings of Baumersdorf to advance across the Russbach. By lucky accident Dupas had hit the seam between I and II Corps and, though sustaining substantial losses, he inclined his units along the brook west towards Deutsch-Wagram before climbing up the escarpment. But his force was small, a mere five French battalions augmented by two Saxon battalions, the Metzsch light infantry and the Radeloff grenadiers, and his divisional guns were to be supported by some horse batteries of the Guard. After Dupas's infantry reached the plateau it came up against the eastern edge of Deutsch-Wagram, defended by a brigade of Austrian regulars from Dedovich's division, and ground to a halt in house-to-house fighting. Shortly thereafter troops of Macdonald's corps from the Army of Italy, Lamarque's division, followed while in turn the divisions of Serras and Durette also managed to gain footholds on the plateau. They were supported by Sahuc's light cavalry, which had found a way across the brook and ridden up the edge of the plateau where they began to attack the Austrian positions.

Attacked by infantry and cavalry, the Austrian gunners panicked and abandoned their pieces to shelter behind the infantry of Bellegarde's I Corps. The Austrian first line broke. It had been disposed in masses and this, of course, made it much less effective in a fire fight. IR 47 Vogelsang fell back in disorder, in turn disrupting IR 35 Argenteau. The position of I Corps looked dangerous, but the corps commander, Bellegarde, managed to rally his regiments and, by refusing his flank, restored his battle line. Luck was on his side. At this point, with visibility sharply reduced by smoke from the burning buildings, clouds of black powder and falling darkness, Lamarque's assault columns faltered amid heavy point-blank fire. The situation became confused. Follow-up French reinforcements from Macdonald's corps, with Macdonald in person, sword in hand, trying to restore order, mistook the two white-uniformed Saxon units of Dupas's division, the Metzsch Schützen and the Radeloff Grenadier battalions, for Austrians and fired on them. The attack failed in the confusion and the reformed Argenteau regiment immediately counter-attacked, driving the stunned Saxons and French back. Meanwhile, Seras's division had gained the plateau, posing a new danger. But Archduke Charles himself rode up, and using the flat of his sword, restored discipline among the wavering Vogelsang infantry. Amid the confused close fighting, the archduke was slightly wounded and almost taken prisoner, but saved through the intervention of Lt von Weidenfeld. Now IR 42 Erbach counter-attacked the French. In addition, the position at Baumersdorf secured, Hohenzollern returned with the Vincent Chevaulegers and the Hessen-Homburg Hussars and completed the rout of the outnumbered French. Here, too, the Austrians did not pursue beyond the Russbach, in Macdonald's opinion saving the demoralized French divisions from destruction. Despite the initial orderly conduct of the retreat, Austrian pressure turned retreat into a near rout at the return crossing over the Russbach. But the Austrians halted at the Russbach. Night pursuit was risky and the main concern of all generals was to keep troops under control in a confused situation. As it was, Eugène spent the rest of the night restoring order among his shattered battalions.[3]

A second, belated attack against Wagram from the west by the Polenz's 2nd Division of Bernadotte's corps also failed. Later Bernadotte would claim that he had pleaded for hours for the intervention of this division, but with only ten battalions available and with the Austrian Reserve Cavalry Corps deployed in the plain on his left flank, he had hesitated to commit it. Even though he had received his orders shortly after 7 p.m. he did not move until 9.30 p.m. He was also short of artillery after various detachments had left him with only eighteen guns. On reaching the plateau, three Saxon battalions of Lecoq's brigade of the 2nd Division ran into heavy fire from two battalions of IR 17 Reuss-Plauen and one battalion of 2nd *Jäger* and stalled. Additional Saxon reinforcements, arriving rather late, were soon absorbed in the confusion of a night combat where everyone, except the *Jäger*, wore white uniforms. The final blow came at about 10.30 p.m when MG Hartizsch arrived with the last of the Saxon infantry, elite grenadier battalions, which, however, had not been informed that Saxon troops were already fighting in the village. Once again, confronted by white-uniformed soldiers they opened fire. Although the mistake was cleared up in a few minutes, the friendly fire and the critical wounding of Hartizsch was the last blow to the Saxon morale. Believing themselves surrounded, at about 11 p.m., having sustained over a third of their number in casualties, they fled in disorder from the escarpment and into the plain beyond Aderklaa.

Given its limitations in training, the Saxon infantry had fought well enough, but it was not trained to fight in flexible open order. With street fighting always confusing, especially at night, the Saxons soon became muddled in the smoke-filled side alleys of Deutsch-Wagram. The debacle was not only an indication of Bernadotte's diminished leadership – he later complained to the emperor that a 'hidden hand' at headquarters had prevented him from receiving proper support – but also a sign that the French Army of 1809 was no longer the cohesive force of 1805.[4] During the night, while continuing to complain about his mistreatment at headquarters, Bernadotte attempted to rally and reform the Saxons around Aderklaa, but he was hardly inspiring and had only limited success.

Finally, Davout, on the French right, had received his orders to attack Markgrafneusiedl too late. At about 9 p.m., following a hasty artillery bombardment which caused little damage, he advanced Gudin's division followed by Puthod's forward frontally from Grosshofen, while Friant's and Morand's divisions were instructed to cross the Russbach further down river, their flanks supported by cavalry. But Markgrafneusiedl, a naturally strong position made stronger by light earthworks, could not be taken easily. When at around 10 p.m. Davout realized that the attacks on Baumersdorf and Deutsch-Wagram had failed and that his tired troops faced Rosenberg's fresher IV Corps with strong cavalry support on its left flank, he called off his attack and withdrew his corps to Glinzendorf for the night. In years to come, quite unfairly, Napoleon was critical of Davout's decision and claimed that it had cost him the first day battle.

Napoleon was wrong. All along the line of contact the attacks had been uncoordinated and badly prepared. Overall, the losses sustained by the French, especially the divisions of the Army of Italy, had been substantial. Three divisional commanders had been wounded, Serras, Sahuc and Grenier, the last with a shattered hand that prevented him from fighting the next day. If it had been Napoleon's objective to fix the enemy in position and to defeat him the next day, he had succeeded. But if he had hoped to destroy substantial elements of the Habsburg army during the night, he failed. It has been argued that the archduke's defensive success that night lured him into adopting an offensive plan of operations for the next morning. Even though concerned that Archduke John's army, designed to close the ring into which he thought he had drawn Napoleon, was not yet in place, he had no doubt that his brother would arrive.

By 11 p.m. all was quiet along the battle line. For Napoleon, though occupying only the same positions he had reached that evening, the first day of battle had been a qualified success. He had crossed the Danube and successfully deployed his army and stores. If he had not destroyed the main Austrian army, it is unlikely that there had ever been a realistic chance of a victory on the opening day. On the Austrian side, the troops, especially the infantry, had performed exceedingly well, and fighting on good defensive ground had repelled the evening attacks. At the same time, there had been shortcomings in the high command, wavering in decision-making and slow communications, all combining to cause unnecessary casualties. It would appear that as late as the morning of 5 July, Archduke Charles was still uncertain whether to let the enemy cross the river for a decisive battle or merely replay the battle of Aspern–Essling. In fact, observing the rapid advance of the French across the Marchfeld from their observatory on the Bisamberg, the Emperor Francis had asked Charles whether this development formed part of the Austrian plan. Charles replied that all was going to plan, the French would be allowed to cross, attack the Austrian position and then be thrown back into the river. Somewhat less than convinced Francis responded, 'That is alright then, just do not let too many across.'[5] Both sides then were determined to renew battle the next day.

CHAPTER EIGHT

Wagram: The second day

BATTLE PLANS ON BOTH SIDES

At about 10.30 p.m., combat petered out. Only an occasional shot by a nervous picket, touching off a brief exchange of fire, disturbed the night. Troops on both sides were exhausted and slept fitfully on their arms. This was especially true of the French, who had been on the move since the afternoon of the previous day, drenched during the evening and night and then exhausted by the extreme heat of 5 July. By contrast, the night of 5 July was unseasonably cold. Campfires were lit, meals cooked and horses fed, but rations for man and beast were meagre at best, though the marshals and generals certainly did better for themselves. Meanwhile, exhaustion notwithstanding, with the battle so evenly poised, the senior commanders and their staff on both sides made their plans to resume fighting the next day.

At his command post near Raasdorf, Napoleon issued his orders for the coming day to his assembled marshals and senior officers. (Still trying to reorder his Saxons, Bernadotte alone was absent.) Retreat was clearly not an option: the emperor's principal objective remained the destruction of the main Austrian army behind the Russbach. Holding the central position, Napoleon planned that 9 Saxon Corps, which he still considered combat capable, and Oudinot's 2 Corps would pin down the archduke around Wagram. Davout's 3 Corps, with its strong attached cavalry shielding its right, was to deliver the main thrust, turning the Austrian left at Markgrafneusiedl and then rolling up the Austrian line. When Davout had taken the plateau, the decisive moment would arrive for the Army of Italy, Macdonald's corps leading, to breach the Austrian line around Wagram. With this in mind, and also to be able to react to any contingency, such as the possible arrival of Archduke John, at about 2 a.m. Napoleon reinforced his centre, ordering Masséna's 4 Corps closer to Aderklaa, leaving only Boudet's division near Aspern to guard the Lobau and its vital bridges. During the night and early morning, the French were further reinforced by the arrival of Broussier's and Pacthod's infantry divisions from the Army of Italy, Marmont's XI Corps and Wrede's Bavarian division. These formations, however, would not come into action until after midday. The Imperial Guard, Marmont's corps, Wrede's Bavarians and the Reserve Cavalry were kept at his disposal in reserve. Orders issued, Napoleon, protected only by a wind-break formed by twelve stacked drums and guarded by the sentries of his Old Guard, snatched a few hours of sleep.

Across the Russbach, Archduke Charles returned to his head-quarters in Wagram about 11 p.m. He was satisfied with the outcome of the first day. Although he had not prevented the French from deploying on the Marchfeld – in fact, bringing them there had been part of his plan, though the speed of their advance had come as a surprise – they had been decisively repulsed in their unexpected evening assault on the Russbach line. Except for the damage done to Nordmann's Advance Guard, its remnant now attached to Rosenberg's IV Corps, all his major formations were intact, and his soldiers had fought well. But it had been a defensive battle and the terrain, especially along the Russbach, had been a vital factor. Charles was convinced that Napoleon would have to attack the next day and, given his superiority in infantry, cavalry and guns, that he might well succeed in breaking the apex of the Austrian position in the plain west of the Russbach, where the terrain offered no defensive advantage. Therefore he had decided not to cede the initiative to the French. The only possible salvation was to launch a preemptive attack at dawn the next day.

The conception of the operational plan adopted for the coming day, known as the 'Disposition' in Austro-German military usage, has been much disputed. It followed the plan already discussed before the battle. Though certain historians have continued to claim that Grünne and Wimpffen foisted the scheme on a sick Charles, who allegedly suffered a severe epileptic attack around midnight, such claims must be considered a legend. Certainly the archduke was tired; moreover he had been lightly wounded in the combat at Baumersdorf earlier in the evening. Equally certainly, however, he was capable of authorizing the Disposition.[1] The basic idea was daring: a near-simultaneous general attack along the whole front at 4 a.m. 'The generalissimus had decided to attack both wings of the enemy at dawn.'[2] It envisaged a double envelopment of the French army between the right and the left wings of the Austrian army, with the apex held by the Reserve Cavalry and grenadiers. Theoretically, it was sound. Given Napoleon's numerical superiority, it was perhaps the only option. There was, however, a fatal flaw. The Austrian battle frontage extended for over 11 miles, while the more compact French front was less than 6 miles wide. These distances were especially serious for the two corps on the Austrian right wing, the most distant from the enemy, though a well-mounted staff officer could ride the distance in less than twenty minutes. The inevitable delay between the issue of the operational orders and their receipt, coupled with the time then required for them to be acted on – troops assembled, marched to their start lines and finally deployed in battle – made coordinated attacks on both wings impossible.

None the less, shortly after midnight, orders went out for a general attack at 4 a.m., just before sunrise. The French left was to be driven in by VI and III Corps advancing aligned, supported to the north by a simultaneous attack by part of the Cavalry Corps joined by the

Grenadier Reserve. On the Austrian left, IV Corps, supported by I Corps artillery and then, as deployment room was gained, joined by I Corps, was to attack Davout. To avoid congestion, II Corps in the centre was to remain in place and only provide artillery support until there was enough space to bring its formations beyond the Russbach. Actually IV Corps was not all that strong, but then Charles still expected the arrival of Archduke John on his left wing. Tactically, infantry was to advance in masses, cavalry in chequerboard formation. Charles and his battle staff were to locate themselves behind I Corps.[3] Significantly, and much criticized by later commentators, Charles did not retain a battle reserve, except for one brigade and one battery of III Corps at Stammersdorf, another provision to secure the potential line of retreat. Also V Corps was kept out of action. Its role, indicative of Charles's inclination never to risk all, was to remain in position to protect a possible retreat by the right wing of his army across the Bisamberg to Moravia and Bohemia.

The success of the Austrian operational plan depended on synchronized movement, always a difficult task for the command and control apparatus, the battle management, of the Austrian staff. In fact, on this occasion, as already pointed out, cooperation was impossible because the instructions were issued far too late. III and VI Corps on the right wing, farthest both from the Austrian command and the enemy, should have received their orders by 1 a.m. but did not receive them before 3 a.m; they therefore could not possibly arrive at their start line between Kagran and Breitenlee one hour later and be in action before 8 a.m. For that matter, the Grenadier Corps, still in reserve at Seiring, who were supposed to join these two corps, also came into action several hours late.

THE ADVANCE OF AUSTRIAN IV CORPS

On 6 July the archduke and the emperor took the offensive almost simultaneously. Unaware of the delay on the right flank and centre, IV Corps moved out on time at about 4 a.m. advancing in three columns.

The Hessen-Homburg Brigade, six battalions strong, pushed on Grosshofen; the second column, with twelve line and four *Landwehr* battalions, advanced on Glinzendorf. FML Radetzky commanded a ten-battalion advance guard, supported by ten squadrons of the Erzherzog Ferdinand Hussars. The third column to the left of the infantry with Leopoldsdorf as their objective rode a thirty-squadron-strong cavalry column. Commanded by FML Nostitz, it consisted of ten squadrons of Blankenstein Hussars and eight of O'Reilly's Chevaulegers, both from MG Wartensleben's brigade, as well as six squadrons of Riesch and Erzherzog Johann Dragoons from MG Rothkirch's brigade. Finally at Ober-Siebenbrunn there were remaining units of Nordmann's former Advance Guard, the Hessen-Homburg, Primatial and Stipsicz Hussars.

Although Archduke Charles had ordered absolute silence so commands could be heard, the Austrians proceeded with much noise and disorder. Nevertheless, they might have achieved a tactical surprise. At about 2 a.m. Berthier had dispatched one of his trusted aides, Colonel Lejeune, to cross the Russbach to try to discover any signs of Austrian movement. At Markgrafneusiedl, he found Rosenberg's IV corps forming up for an attack, but he was unable to penetrate the Austrian outposts and had to make a wide detour to the south-east before he could return to imperial headquarters.[4]

But even so, any tactical surprise that the Austrians might exploit here was at best limited. Almost simultaneously Davout's troops were preparing to move against Markgrafneusiedl. On his left, along the embankments of the road from Grosshofen to Glinzendorf, Friant's division, still 8,000 strong, had posted a heavy skirmish screen with the bulk of the division deployed in two lines behind it. Grosshofen itself was held by one regiment from Puthod's division while behind Friant, who was down to 4,000, Morand's division was in reserve. Gudin held Glinzendorf. On the right flank Montbrun with nineteen and Grouchy with twenty-one squadrons opposed the Austrian cavalry column, with Montbrun sending some squadrons forward towards Ober-Siebenbrunn. At about 5 a.m., after driving in the French outposts,

Radetzky's Advance Guard, displaying uncommon bravery in the face of heavy musketry and the fire of one battery, managed to penetrate into Grosshofen. Davout's main body now arrived and, with units from Puthod's division attacking frontally and units from Gudin attacking the flank, the Austrians were evicted.

The sound of the guns had disturbed Napoleon and his staff at breakfast. In fact, the emperor feared that they signalled the arrival of Archduke John. He therefore mounted and rode post-haste to Davout, ordering the Imperial Guard and the cuirassier divisions of de Casanova' (who had replaced d'Espagne, killed at Aspern) and Nansouty's to follow him. When he arrived at about 6 a.m. he found that the Austrians were already retreating on Markgrafneusiedl on the orders of Archduke Charles who had become aware that neither his right wing nor Archduke John had come into action and was afraid of leaving IV Corps in an exposed position. Radetzky covered the retreat. He deployed MG Provenchères's brigade in a heavy skirmish line, backed by a second line in masses supported by his cavalry battery. Against an enemy who followed somewhat cautiously, he successfully returned to his line of departure. By 6 a.m. the corps was back in its original position, though having suffered about 1,100 casualties and with lowered morale. Even so, Rosenberg's sally had consequences. After his personal inspection of the terrain, Napoleon, who had originally envisaged a frontal attack against the heights, now changed his orders to Davout. He instructed the marshal to use two of his divisions frontally, but sent his other two divisions and his attached cavalry to cross the Russbach downstream to deliver a flank attack up the gentle slope to the east of the Austrian position. The change forced Davout to reorder his troops, build a bridge for his artillery some miles downstream and delayed his attack on Markgrafneusiedl by about two hours.

Informed by his far-ranging cavalry scouts that as yet there was no sign of John, Napoleon rode back to his command post, directing the Guard and Nansouty's division back to their original positions in reserve. He left Arrighi's cuirassiers as well as a 12-pounder battery with Davout, who was instructed to continue his operations against Rosenberg and take Markgrafneusiedl, while Oudinot and Eugène were directed to pin the Austrian forces on the Russbach. On his way back to his interrupted breakfast, he halted briefly to confer with Oudinot when an Austrian shell exploded nearby, grazing the general, who exclaimed: 'Sire, they are firing on the general staff!' to which an unfazed Napoleon replied, 'Oh well, in war every accident is possible'.[5] Then, passing the cheering ranks of Tharreau's division, he returned to his command post.

THE STRUGGLE FOR ADERKLAA

No sooner had the emperor returned when he was faced by a major crisis that nearly shattered his centre. Bellegarde's I Corps had also moved on time. Leaving behind General Dedovich with seven battalions on the plateau, advance elements from Fresnel's division, one battalion each from the Legion Archduke Charles, the 2nd *Jäger* and the Kolowrat Infantry Regiment, accompanied by six squadrons of the Klenau Chevaulegers, had been surprised to find Aderklaa, a stoutly built village, undefended. Protected by an embankment, the village was important strategically. For the French it was a jump-off position to take Wagram from the west, while for the Austrians it protected the right flank of the Russbach position. But during the night Bernadotte, under the pretext that his troops were too exposed, had irresponsibly, and without notifying the emperor, withdrawn his shaken Saxon infantry – by now no more than 6,000 effectives – some 1,000 yards south-east of the village while placing his cavalry on the left. Almost not believing his good fortune, Bellegarde at once occupied Aderklaa. He used his main force to extend his position in two lines to Wagram while the grenadiers, finally arriving at 6 a.m., deployed to the left of Aderklaa to Breitenlee and the Cavalry Corps, less one cuirassier regiment sent to II Corps, formed up behind the infantry. To counter the Austrian move, Bernadotte established a twenty-six-piece gun line in front of his corps and soon artillery of both sides came into action and inflicted heavy casualties. Enfiladed by the Austrian batteries from Wagram, the Saxon gunners suffered terribly and during the next three hours fifteen guns were dismounted.

The time was about 7.30 a.m. Napoleon, furious that Bernadotte had abandoned his position, realized the threat of an Austrian break-through and after a short conference in Masséna's carriage ordered the marshal, whose corps had come up, to recapture Aderklaa at once. The marshal detailed Saint-Cyr to take the village and, when the general hesitated, looking for an opening into the defended village, Masséna commanded him to attack at once while Bernadotte was to assist on the right. The counter-attack by Saint-Cyr's division, led by the 24th Light and the 4th Line Regiment supported by two regiments of the excellent Hessian Leib Brigade formed in battalion columns, was preceded by skirmishers. On his right, Bernadotte's Saxons and Dupas's division, now reduced to little more than two French battalions and three weak Saxon battalions, attacked between Aderklaa and Wagram. Saint-Cyr's 24th Light and 4th Line swept through the village and then proceeded to pursue the panicked defenders beyond. But here they ran into Bellegarde's steady masses of the second line and were driven back in disorder to Aderklaa, which they and some Hessian units tried to hold. Meanwhile on the right the Saxons had also been halted and begun to retreat.

This would have been the moment for Bellegarde to mount an all-out attack, but he had no instructions, his second line was disordered and his right wing as yet lacked contact with III Corps. However, the Grenadier Corps was at hand and for a short time the Austrians enjoyed numerical superiority, not counting the troops left under Dedovich, 44,000 men against some 35,000 French and Saxons. From Wagram, Archduke Charles ordered the recapture of Aderklaa. By 8 a.m., GM von Stutterheim commanding, three grenadier battalions, Scovaud, Jambline and Brzeczinski, and two battalions from the IR 42 Erbach took the village in bloody hand-to-hand fighting. Meanwhile, under pressure from the Klenau Chevaulegers and the threat of

Liechtenstein's Reserve Cavalry, the Saxon gun line was overrun and their retreat south-east of Aderklaa degenerated into a rout, joined by some French troops.

Masséna at once launched Lasalle's and Marulaz's light horse to attack the Austrian guns deploying before the village. The charge put the Austrian gunners to flight, but was then pushed back by Liechtenstein's Reserve Cavalry. To avoid being stalled by the panicking mob, the marshal ordered his troops to fire into the Saxons to clear the way for another infantry assault by Leguay's brigade joined by the 67th Line from Viviez brigade, both from Molitor's division. Taking horrendous casualties, one in three according to some reports, and with Molitor down to 3,000 men, the French regained control of Aderklaa at about 9.45 a.m. and held it until about 11 a.m. when fresh Austrian grenadier battalions evicted them in disorder. Masséna ordered Legrand's division to cover their retreat. The combat's outcome clearly favoured Charles. By 10 a.m. I Corps had formed between Wagram and Aderklaa and his Grenadier Reserve, albeit in skirmish formations and not in masses, extended his line towards Süssenbrunn.

Continuing to flee towards Raasdorf, the Saxons, accompanied by a good many Frenchmen and with Bernadotte galloping ahead, ran into Napoleon. It was standing military practice that to turn fleeing troops around, their commander should meet them head-on, but relations between Napoleon and Bernadotte were already strained and that morning the emperor was angry. As Marbot tells it, the emperor had been informed that the night before Bernadotte had boasted that Napoleon had mishandled the evening attacks and that had he, Bernadotte, been in command he would have used 'scientific manoeuvre' to overcome the Austrians almost without combat. Already infuriated by Bernadotte's boasting of the previous night, Napoleon was not now in a mood to listen to excuses and demanded to know if this was the 'scientific manoeuvre' that would win the battle. As Bernadotte tried to justify himself, the emperor angrily dismissed him from command. 'I remove you, sir, from the command of the army corps you handle so badly ... A bungler like you is no good to me.'[6] For the rest of the day, except for its ten remaining cannons and its cavalry squadrons, 9 Corps was out of action, reforming between Neu Wirtshaus and Raasdorf. The Saxon foot were good enough soldiers, but they had taken heavy casualties the night before, their tight formations were unsuitable under heavy fire and, having attacked, been repulsed and then charged by Austrian cavalry, they were at the end of their fighting strength that morning. Other troops, including French, notably Saint-Cyr's division, had also been routed but the Saxons became a convenient scapegoat.

NAPOLEON'S LEFT FLANK THREATENED

But Napoleon's overall situation on his left continued to deteriorate. From 7.30 a.m. onwards Austrian III and VI Corps were finally intervening in the battle, with Kolowrat linking up with Prochaska's Grenadier Brigade at Süssenbrun at about 9.30 a.m. At this point, however, having received no instructions to change his standing order to align with the corps on either side, he halted with his main force. Klenau, who had the longest approach march and had to reorder his troops, advanced his VI Corps in battalion columns down the Kagran–Aspern road with cavalry support on his flanks. Opposed only by Boudet's division of Masséna's corps, at about 8 a.m. he closed on Aspern and Essling. In a reckless effort, Boudet had sent one of his batteries forward to enfilade Klenau's advance, but Wallmoden's light cavalry brigade, the Liechtenstein and Kienmayer Hussars, had captured the guns. Although a gallant counter-attack by the 56th Line retook the guns there were no horses to pull them back and, under heavy fire from Klenau's 64 guns, Boudet fell back to the old bridgehead area. Meanwhile MG Vecsey's Saint Georg and Brod *Grenzer* entered Aspern and advanced to reoccupy the works east of Essling. Under heavy pressure and vastly outnumbered, Boudet, who after attempting to hold Aspern with the 93rd Line behind the cemetery wall and the 3rd Light in Essling, made a hasty retreat towards the Mühlau salient.

By 10 a.m. Klenau, now only some 3 miles from Breitenlee, was in position either to strike into the rear of the French army or to attack the bridges. But he did neither. He positioned two batteries to fire on the bridges south of Gross Enzersdorf, causing near panic among the supply drivers and miscellaneous non-combatants, but, except for a feeble attack on the bridgehead, repelled by the garrison, one Baden and one Neuchâtel regiment, made no further advance.[7] His orders made no provision for such a move and, aligning his troops with III Corps, as his operations journal tells it, he 'waited for developments in the centre'.[8] Moreover, Boudet's retreat had uncovered the Lobau batteries and Klenau's battalions and guns were coming under intense bombardment from the heavy guns and mortars on the Lobau. It should be remembered that Klenau had only 14,000 men, was not in direct contact with Kolowrat and that his orders specifically directed him to keep his corps aligned with the adjoining formation. Probably a combination of lack of orders and personal initiative along with the weight of fire from the Lobau batteries contributed to Klenau's hesitation.

Klenau was not alone in hesitating. By this time, except for the two corps behind the Russbach and V Corps on the Bisam, the entire Austrian army was facing east in line between the Danube and Wagram, outflanking Masséna and leaving a large gap in the French line, the Austrians did not attack. The favourable turn of events in the centre had not been expected. While the Austrian corps commanders did not dare to act on their own, the slow and cumbersome Austrian command-and-control system could not take advantage of the opportunity. Meanwhile Napoleon, always at his best in a crisis, acted rapidly.[9]

NAPOLEON STABILIZES HIS LEFT FLANK

From his command post on a small knoll near Raasdorf, conspicuous on his white charger, Euphrates, and surrounded by his staff, Napoleon had observed the attack on his left. He and his staff were under constant fairly heavy artillery fire (some twenty-six headquarters officers were killed that day). But unmoved, Napoleon now displayed an outstanding example of battle management. Holding the central position within a curving battlefront, he issued his orders. Prince Eugène, who at Wagram had revealed himself a competent commander, had on his own initiative already refused his flank. With Grenier's corps, consisting of Durutte's and Pacthod's divisions, facing the Russbach, he pivoted Macdonald's corps – Lamarque's, Seras's and Broussier's divisions – to face west, keeping his small Italian Guard in reserve.[10]

The emperor also pressed Davout to intensify his effort against Markgrafneusiedl, the all-decisive operation, which once it had reached beyond the tower above Markgrafneusiedl would be the signal for the general attack. Meanwhile, Masséna was ordered to disengage and march south across the Austrian front to deal with Klenau. To disengage Masséna's corps out of line and gain time preventing Liechtenstein's cavalry from forming up to attack Masséna's vulnerable march columns, Bessières's cavalry was launched against the weakest link in the Austrian front, the seam between the Grenadier Corps and Kolowrat near Süssenbrun. To cover the gap that would appear in his front and unwilling to engage his remaining infantry reserves, the Guard, Marmont and the Bavarians, Napoleon concentrated a Grand Battery, the famed 'battery of 100 guns' (some sources make it 112 pieces). It included all sixty of the Guard's guns as well as guns from the Army of Italy and the Bavarian 12-pounder battery. The time was now about 11 a.m.[11]

The cavalry attack was hastily organized and poorly handled, but none the less it achieved its main purpose, protecting Masséna's disengagement. No orders seem to have reached the Guard Cavalry. Saint-Germain's cuirassier brigade was kept back in reserve while the rest of Nansouty's heavy cavalry division, some 4,000 cuirassiers and carabiniers, was committed to the charge led by Bessières in person. As they passed Napoleon each regiment raised a loud cheer. Advancing towards the enemy line they received heavy converging defensive fire. Bessières was wounded and only Brigadier's DeFrance's carabiniers came into close contact with the enemy, who remained drawn up in masses backed by the Hessen-Homburg Cuirassiers. DeFrance's troopers had little choice but to retreat, pursued by Austrian fire. Coming into action too late, the Guard Cavalry, four squadrons of Polish Chevaulegers and four squadrons of *chasseurs à cheval*, no more than 2,000 sabres combined, attacked but also achieved no breakthrough. In all, the French cavalry lost some 1,200 horses but they stopped Liechtenstein from interfering with Masséna's move and halted the advance of the grenadier's right and Kolowrat's left wing.

Thus covered, Masséna proceeded to disengage and begin his spectacular and daring flank march south, while around 11 a.m. Napoleon deployed his Grand Battery which he ordered to drive the enemy from the area between Aderklaa and Süssenbrunn. Under the overall command of General Lauriston, a gunner and one of the emperor's senior aides, the Grand Battery came into action. First came the Guard Horse Artillery, six batteries with 6- and 8-pounders and 24-pounder howitzers, led by Colonel d'Aboville, galloping to their appointed positions. They were followed by Lieutenant Colonel Drouot's four foot batteries, three equipped with six 12-pounder cannons each. Joined by the pieces from the Army of Italy and the Bavarian 12-pounders, the Grand Battery, with the Italian guns on the left, Drouot in the centre and d'Aboville on the flanks, formed a 2,000-yard-wide gun line. Deploying within heavy canister range, as each battery reached its designated position it unlimbered and immediately opened fire while attempting to advance the gun line. At a range of between only 400 to 600 yards from the Austrian infantry, it poured a heavy volume of fire on Kolowrat and Liechtenstein, over 200 rounds of solid shot as well as canister for each gun in the Guard Artillery. Here, the weight of the shot fired by the heavier 8- and 12-pounder guns was most effective. Not only did they have a longer range both with solid round shot and heavy canister, the heavier shot, due to the kinetic energy that varies directly with the weight but according to the square of the velocity, had much more hitting power. The heavier pieces fired larger and more far-reaching canister; they also produced a much more terrifying noise.

Gradually pushing forward, the Grand Battery inflicted substantial casualties on the Austrian infantry, forcing Kolowrat to retire on Breitenlee. The Austrian counter-battery fire, mainly light- and medium-brigade batteries, some now out of ammunition, but augmented by position batteries, including two 12-pounder batteries at Wagram only 1,000 yards away and firing solid round shot, inflicted heavy losses in men and horses on the French batteries. In addition, there was the musketry of the Austrian infantry. There was no safety even in the rear. Overshooting cannonballs hit Napoleon's staff and tore into the imperturbable ranks of the Old Guard. With several senior officers wounded, including Drouot and d'Aboville, whose right arm was torn off (in all, twenty-eight officers were put out of action), and with gun crews seriously weakened, Napoleon called for volunteers from the infantry of the Guard. He asked for twenty men from each company; an average of fifty stepped forward, double-timed, to the guns, and according to Drouot, behaved 'with the greatest gallantry'.[12] Meanwhile the high corn around the guns on both sides had been set alight by sparks and discarded match. Those wounded, on both sides, unable to crawl to safety, were burned alive.

Behind the left of the Grand Battery Napoleon, who kept a close watch on Davout's progress, instructed Macdonald to form up his three divisions in an attack column to exploit any opportunity arising. It now was near noon and Masséna's 4 Corps column was approaching Klenau. Its 5-mile march across the front of two Austrian corps had been an impressive performance. Along with Saint-Sulpice's cuirassier division, with its light cavalry shielding its right and with Masséna conspicuous in his carriage, the corps marched in column across Kolowrat's front. This was a dangerous manoeuvre but Kolowrat did not move except for one easily repulsed attack by a hussar regiment. The column, partially concealed by man-high cornfields, remained out of musket range and was only impeded by artillery fire. Shortly after noon, advance elements of Legrand's division arrived at the Neu Wirtshaus, in sight of Essling, while Marulaz's troopers, galloping ahead, drove off some Austrian light horse harrying Boudet's rearguard and then surprised and captured the Austrian batteries firing on the bridges. By this time, however, Davout had gained a decisive success. He had stormed Markgrafneusiedl, with Oudinot joining the attack during the last phase, and was now pushing beyond. Napoleon declared the battle won and issued orders for a general advance.

DAVOUT TAKES MARKGRAFNEUSIEDL

Napoleon considered the capture of Markgrafneusiedl, the bastion of the Austrian left line, as essential for victory. Located below the escarpment, which here turned north-east, sloping gently down into a plain and providing an opportunity for an outflanking attack, the village was a strong position. The Russbach also turned south-east here, widening its valley. The houses of the village were well built and there were number of larger defensible stone buildings including a mill and a monastery. On the plateau above were a disused church crowned by a square stone tower and surrounded by a dry moat and some remains of old earthworks, survivals from earlier times when it had served as an outpost against Hungarian mounted raiders.

Davout's attack had been delayed by two hours. Originally his orders had been to make a frontal assault north, but early in the morning Napoleon had instructed him to envelop Markgrafneusiedl and destroy Rosenberg. It took him a further two hours to transfer the bulk of his corps across the Russbach some miles downstream in preparation for an outflanking attack utilizing the sloping approach to the plateau in the east for his main effort. Following an intense bombardment by his reinforced corps artillery, including some twenty-three 12-pounders, and supported by some guns from Oudinot's corps, which silenced most of the Austrian guns in the plain and damaged some of the artillery on the escarpment, Davout began his attack at 9.30 a.m. Two of his four divisions, Puthod on the left and Gudin on the right, were to advance frontally against the village, now on fire, while a short distance downstream at Leopoldshof his engineers threw a bridge across the Russbach. This allowed his substantial cavalry force, Pajol's light cavalry and the attached divisions of Grouchy, Pully and Montbrun, to cross and drive the Austrian cavalry near Ober-Siebenbrunn, Fröhlich's brigade, to the rear. Once accomplished, this gained deployment room for Morant and Friant, accompanied by their artillery, to cross the Russbach and form up facing the left wing of Rosenberg's IV Corps. The presence of the cavalry divisions not only secured the infantry against a counter-attack by the Austrian cavalry on the plateau but protected its flank against John's army, still expected to come into action. Against this contingency and to keep a battle reserve, Arrighi's cuirassier division and its horse battery remained in reserve at Grosshofen. The deployment went more slowly than expected and it was 10.15 a.m. before Davout's infantry reached their assault positions, Morand on the right and Friant to his left extending to the Russbach, aided by the movement of Arrighi's 8-pounder battery to a small elevation in the ground from where it was able to enfilade the Austrian line on the plateau.

Rosenberg, commanding IV Corps, was desperately hoping for the arrival of Archduke John. Earlier that morning he had voiced his doubts to Archduke Charles that IV Corps, even bolstered by the remnants of Nordmann's Advance Guard, was strong enough to withstand assault. But except for leaving Nostitz's cavalry division behind, the archduke disposed of no reserves, a major shortcoming of his operational plan, and could only offer the optimistic assurance that the Army of Inner Austria would arrive on his left flank. Though Rosenberg enjoyed the advantage of an uphill and partly fortified position, and his attached cavalry divisions far outnumbered those of his opponent, overall his strength was inferior to Davout's. Including Nordmann's battered units, he disposed of some 18,500 infantry and sixty guns, albeit two 12-pounder batteries, while Davout, counting the horse batteries of his attached cavalry divisions, deployed 114 pieces.

The weakest sector in Rosenberg's battle line, a hook-shaped line along the rim of the plateau with Markgrafneusiedl and the square tower serving as the hinge, was on his left flank, to the south-east, where the plateau sloped gently down towards the Ober-Siebenbrunn plain. At its southern end there was a ditch defended by five battalions; where it ended to the north, Rosenberg placed GM Mayer's brigade, the IR 4 Hoch und Deutschmeister and the IR 49 Kerpen as well as two *Landwehr* battalions. Some 200 paces behind and forming a second line were the remaining troops of IR 44 Bellegarde, 46 Chasteler and 58 Beaulieu together with the combined *Landwehr* battalions, 1st and 2nd Wiener Wald and 3rd Manhartsberg. On the extreme left wing, around the Siedichfür farmstead, Nostitz, detached from the Cavalry Reserve, assembled the bulk of his division. The dragoons of Brigade Rothkirch extended the line on the heights while the light horse of Wartensleben's brigade was posted in the plain together with the remainder of Frölich's cavalry from the Advance Guard. Facing south in the original position across the Russbach there remained three weak brigades and on the escarpment near the tower Rosenberg emplaced a 12-pounder battery covered by one battalion of IR 3 Erzherzog Karl and the Unter dem Manhartsberg *Landwehr* battalion. An additional 6-pounder battery on the rim of the plateau was defended by two battalions. Given the absence of prepared field fortifications and his numerical inferiority, Rosenberg made the best dispositions he could, hoping that a tenacious defence of his east-facing line, coupled with strong and effective shock action by Nostitz's cavalry squadrons against the French flank, might hold the French attack until the hoped-for arrival of Archduke John.

The fighting for Markgrafneusiedl, in which MG Peter Vécsey was killed, was fierce, and the outcome not finally determined until some time after noon. As the Austrian guns in the plain were silenced, a mounted Davout personally led Gudin's and Puthod's divisions forward. Despite receiving heavy defensive musket fire, the two divisions managed to enter the village, now in flames. Gudin was wounded and Davout had his horse shot from under him. Even so, the defenders, having now evacuated the building below the escarpment, had regrouped, still willing to fight, around the tower position. Gudin's skirmishers scaled up to reach the rim of the plateau. On the right flank, Morand's division, attacking in two lines with the 13th Light and the 17th Line leading, reached the crest of the slope, but was immediately countercharged by the Hoch und Deutschmeister and Kerpen infantry supported by eight squadrons from the Erzherzog Ferdinand Hussars. The French attack was temporarily halted with the 17th Line in some disarray. But Morand received support from Friant who sent in Gilly's brigade with the 15th Light and the 33rd Line against the Austrian flank. Despite Nordmann's effort to rally the troops, an action during which this gallant officer was killed by a musket ball, the Austrians, having suffered heavy casualties, were soon pushed back to their original position. Then, instead of executing a mass charge, successive separate charges by the Blankenstein and the Hessen-Homburg Hussars also failed and by 11.30 Montbrun and Friant were firmly established on the plateau.

Around the tower position, Gudin and Puthod were gaining the upper hand, with counter-attacks by the remaining troops of the Riese Brigade, the much-reduced regiments Chasteler, Bellegarde and Beaulieu, all failing. Their morale was not improved by the absence of their brigade commander, GM Riese, who as one Austrian historian scathingly commented 'was not to be seen'.[13] Friant's men consolidated their hold on the tower position and moved forward to roll up the Austrian line. But for a while the determined resistance continued as Rosenberg tried to regroup in a new line on the plateau north-east of the tower and the Austrians repeatedly counter-attacked, stalling further French advances. Davout now ordered Arrighi's division to charge the enemy infantry, but executed reluctantly and conducted up an incline across difficult terrain, it failed and Davout then sent it back to the plain.

THE CAVALRY CLASH AT OBER-SIEBENBRUNN

The time was just past noon. At this juncture, recognizing the critical situation developing on his right and leaving Archduke Ludwig in temporary charge on his right wing, Archduke Charles arrived with reinforcements from Hohenlohe's II Corps that in its positions at Baumersdorf had not been engaged thus far. He ordered Hohenlohe to send five battalions from IR 57 Joseph Colloredo and IR 15 Zach, and the 6-pounder brigade artillery battery from Buresch's brigade, as well as four squadrons of Hessen-Homburg Hussars. In addition, he sent the Hohenzollern Cuirassiers from the Reserve Cavalry. The infantry joined the attempt to hold back Davout's advance; the cuirassiers, reinforcing Nostitz's cavalry, were ordered to drive off Montbrun's and Grouchy's cavalry before falling on the flank of the French infantry.

Now, in the vicinity of Ober-Siebenbrunn, the battle's major cavalry encounter took place. With over forty squadrons Nostitz at first drove back the outnumbered nine squadrons of Montbrun's division with Wartensleben's brigade, the Blankenstein Hussars and the O'Reilly Chevauxlegers, repelling the 7th Hussars. Following this, the Hohenzollern Cuirassiers attacked Montbrun's second line, which curiously tried to repulse the Austrian charge at the halt with a futile carbine volley, a blunder that allowed the Austrians to break the line and capture ten cavalry guns. But then, as Montbrun sent in new squadrons, the 11th and 12th Chasseurs, the 11th hitting the flank of the O'Reilly Chevaulegers, while at the same time Grouchy's dragoon division formed up in line to countercharge, the balance tilted in favour of the French. In the mêlée that followed, Nostitz and MG Rothkirch were wounded, the Austrians retired to reform and the French recovered their guns. Contributing to this outcome was that the Austrian cavalry was poorly handled. Not trained for a massed charge, instead of attacking in divisions or brigades, they attacked in single regiments that could not withstand the massed charge by Grouchy's division. For instance, the after-battle report of the Riesch Dragoons claimed that it had faced a six-fold superiority of hostile horse. By 1 p.m., the disordered Austrian cavalry fell back on its shaken infantry to join Rosenberg's IV Corps in a gradual and orderly retreat north in the direction of the Wendling-Hof.

At about noon both Napoleon and Charles realized that the end of the battle was in sight. A messenger from John informed Charles that his army would arrive only at 5 p.m., too late, the archduke recognized, to affect the outcome of the battle. In fact, John's troops, following Austrian Army custom, were resting and cooking their rations at Marchegg, still some 10 miles away from the battle. Charles now began to think about extricating his army in good order. At about 2.30 p.m., he issued instructions to begin a phased withdrawal.

Since mid morning Napoleon had anxiously trained his spyglass to watch the progress of his right wing. When the powder smoke showing Davout's firing line had moved west well beyond the square tower, Napoleon told his staff that the battle was won and issued orders for a general assault. Oudinot was to press forward to the escarpment against Hohenlohe, Eugène was to storm Wagram, and Macdonald's attack column, supported by cavalry on his flanks, was to break the Austrian centre between III Corps and the Grenadier Corps. Finally, he informed Masséna that with the battle won he was to mount an immediate all-out attack against Klenau.

MACDONALD'S ATTACK COLUMN

Macdonald had begun his advance shortly before 1 p.m. Contrary to the views of many writers, its purpose was not to achieve a breakthrough but to prevent Charles from detaching troops to his left wing. Macdonald, who would win his marshal's baton for this action, later wrote that 'I was far from thinking that this demonstration was to be the main attack on the enemy's centre'. He had formed his three divisions – twenty-three battalions now shrunk to approximately 8,000 men – in a large hollow rectangle, not the massive column so often described. The front of the column consisted of eight battalions, four each from Broussier's and Lamarque's divisions, formed in two lines three deep and 365 metres wide. The front was sustained on the right by eight battalions in column and on the right by four battalions also in column. Three battalion columns from Seras's division, deployed side by side, formed the rear, resulting in a hollow rectangle with a front of some 900 yards and a depth of about 600. This unusual formation was not adopted because the troops were inexperienced but because of the probability that it would be attacked from three sides. Both divisional artillery and a forward move by the Grand Battery on its right were to support the column. Cavalry – Sahuc's light division of the Army of Italy and the Guard Cavalry on its right and Nansouty's division on its left – was to cover the column. Conspicuous on his white charger, Napoleon had ridden through Austrian fire to be present when the column moved out in the direction of Süssenbrunn, flags flying, drums beating the charge and the men cheering.

To confront this array, which on the flat ground appeared to the Austrians as an enormous solid breakthrough mass supported by cavalry and artillery, Charles had decided to refuse the flanks of III Corps and the Grenadier Reserve. This exposed the column to some close musketry and canister fire from three sides. As the column and the artillery moved into point-blank range, the Austrians opened up with everything they had, disabling fifteen artillery pieces before they had advanced far, and then pulled back out of canister range. Macdonald's column continued forward, sustaining heavy losses from converging fire that within an hour had reduced it to little more than half-strength; most historians speak of just about 1,500 men. The column dented the Austrian line, but could not achieve a breakthrough. To buy time for the Austrians to reform their battle line, Liechtenstein threw all available cavalry frontally against Macdonald's column but was repelled by hastily formed squares.

To Napoleon's disgust the French cavalry had put in a disappointing performance. The accompanying heavy cavalry achieved little. Nansouty had kept his division, already battered during the last two days, too far to the rear, and when called forward by Macdonald the squadrons arrived too late. The Austrians had formed masses backed by artillery and Nansouty's troopers achieved little. Even more disappointing was the failure of the Guard heavy cavalry division commanded by General Walther, a veteran officer, 48 years old, with service dating back to the Revolutionary Wars. With Bessières out of action after he had impatiently ridden forward with Nansouty's cavalry and had been seriously wounded by a cannon ball, Walther, responding to Macdonald's call for assistance, replied that the 'Guard acted only on direct orders of the Emperor himself or from our chief Marshal Bessières'. As no direct orders from the emperor had been received and with Bessières incapacitated, the heavy division of the Guard halted in place. An angry Napoleon told his staff that his cavalry had never before let him down in this fashion. When he taxed Nansouty about the cavalry's poor performance, Nansouty first tried to explain and finally turned away muttering, 'After all, there is nothing Your Majesty can teach me about handling cavalry'. Despite their shortcomings on this occasion, both Nansouty and Walther would continue to serve as senior cavalry commanders.

By 2 p.m., then, Macdonald's advance had stalled but the emperor now had the augmented Bavarian division, over 5,000 men and equal in strength to some of the decimated French corps, at his disposal. When Wrede reported to Napoleon, he expected to be sent to support the extreme French left. Instead, however, Napoleon told him that 'You can see Macdonald's awkward position. March, relieve his corps, and attack the enemy, act [as] as you think best.' Wrede moved forward, his four 6-pounder batteries in front, infantry following and his cavalry brigade accompanied by its mounted battery on his right. Passing to the right of Macdonald's stalled column, he advanced to a line between Aderklaa and Süssenbrunn, his 6-pounders reinforcing the remnants of Macdonald's artillery. His infantry, however, did not see much action: the Austrians were already retiring in good order. During the artillery action Wrede was wounded lightly, grazed by a passing ball, but exclaimed to Macdonald, 'Tell the emperor that I die for him and recommend my wife and children to his care!' To this theatrical outburst, the French general replied that the Bavarian should tell this to the emperor in person and that, moreover, he could well make more children with his wife.[14]

With General Reille bringing up the battalions of the Young Guard, constrained by Napoleon's orders not to 'get involved in adventures because I have nothing left but two regiments of the Old Guard', the reinforced column resumed the advance. Supported by the Young Guard, the Bavarians captured Süssenbrunn. But now the troops were too exhausted to continue beyond their original object and so ended Macdonald's famous attack, with only the Bavarians, swinging north-west, continuing a slow pursuit. To relieve pressure on Macdonald, Napoleon had sent Pacthod's battered reserve division of the Army of Italy against Wagram, while Marmont's fresh 11 Corps marched to fill the gap created between Oudinot and the Army of Italy. Finally, to assist Masséna, who was ordered south to deal with Klenau, Durutte's division of the Army of Italy had seized Breitenlee.

For his leadership and courage in this action – Napoleon was heard to exclaim, 'What a brave man!' – Macdonald, much to the army's satisfaction, would be promoted to marshal. No doubt about his bravery, but a debate among historians continues as to whether the attack had been a glorious failure or whether it had achieved its objective. If, as some still maintain, its purpose was to bring the decision in the battle by breaking through the adversary's front, it failed. But if, as Macdonald described it, it was designed to fix the Austrians and prevent them from shifting major reinforcements to their left wing, it was a success. Even if there had been a breakthrough that might have made it possible to interfere with Archduke Charles's withdrawal to the north and north-west, the outcome was not certain. Giving the stubborn resistance offered by the Austrian rearguards and the heat exhaustion of the French and allied troops, leaving only a few formations, above all Marmont's corps and the Bavarians, capable of exploitation, it would most probably not have had major results.

THE FINAL GENERAL ATTACK

As soon as Davout had passed west of the tower at about 1 p.m., Oudinot's 2 Corps, which had exchanged artillery fire against Hohenlohe's II Corps all day, advanced to the Russbach and prepared to scale up the escarpment. Hohenlohe's corps still maintained its positions in and on both sides of Baumersdorf on the plateau, but was now coming under pressure from two sides, while the remaining elements of Rosenberg's IV Corps were retiring towards the Bockfluss where they remained under pressure by Friant and Morand. To avoid being outflanked, Hohenlohe had to refuse five battalions from his second line together with some batteries to confront the advancing French, who were also enfilading his line with batteries placed at Markgrafneusiedl. Perceiving the moment opportune, though he had not yet received direct orders, Oudinot, sword in hand and disregarding the heavy defensive fire, led his 2 Corps forward up the plateau. Wounded twice and having his horse shot beneath him, he evicted the stubborn Austrian defenders under MG Hardegg from Baumersdorf and then wheeled left, pressing Hohenlohe's corps back on Bellegarde's I Corps around Wagram. Seruzier pushed and dragged his horse guns across the Russbach then, joined by Colbert's divisional cavalry, deployed on the plateau to support the push on Wagram. Encountering staunch resistance, with attacks and counter-attacks, the French gradually advanced on Bellegarde. Most of the Russbach plateau was now in French hands. At around 2.30 p.m., Charles instructed his troops to disengage by corps and, with IV Corps already moving north, the remaining corps were to conduct a fighting retreat to the north-west. His instructions read: 'To the degree that GdK Bellegarde retreats, Prince Liechtenstein, FML d'Aspré, FZM Kolowrat and FML Klenau will conform.' The instruction continued that Bellegarde was to move towards Gerasdorf, Liechtenstein was to remain in the Gerasdorf plain and send patrols toward the Russbach, Kolowrat was to retire to the Stammersdorf heights, the grenadiers to Hagenbrunn and Klenau to take up positions between Gerasdorf and Leopoldsau. 'I shall establish my headquarters at Stammersdorf and each corps commander will send one officer there before nightfall to receive further orders.'[15]

Wagram and the adjoining heights, where Bellegarde left behind a strong rearguard, including one division of Hohenzollern's cavalry corps, to cover the retreat of the Austrian formations in the plain, was taken by Tharreau's division of Oudinot's corps and Pacthod's division of the Army of Italy. Pacthod's division, supported by elements of the Italian Royal Guard, took the village frontally, while Durutte's division stormed the adjoining heights.[16] The Austrians were not shaken and the assault was bitterly contested. An officer of the 52nd Line of Pacthod's division, Chef d'Batallion Bernard, described the action. 'At two in the afternoon the division moved out and the regiment followed the 1st brigade.' Crossing the muddy Russbach with some difficulty, he continued that '... where the enemy directed its fire ... the grape shot, shrapnel and cannonball fired by the pieces from an enemy redoubt, which was on our left, covered the ground. The regiment suffered considerable losses. Arriving on the plateau the regiment was met with a hail of canister and fire from the same pieces and five columns [masses] of Austrian infantry.' After exchanging a number of volleys the regiment crossed bayonets with the enemy and '... our pieces which came up to support routed the [Austrian] masses. But the 52nd had suffered heavy casualties, more than 1,000 men had been wounded.'[17]

In the centre III Corps, the Grenadier Corps and Liechtenstein's cavalry fell back according to orders with the cavalry and artillery, covering each other in turn as they took up new positions, shielding the retreat. The grenadiers retired to Hagenbrunn, III Corps to the heights of Stammersdorf. Overall, the Austrian phased retreat was well executed and the army remained combat capable as it withdrew in echelon with one formation retreating and the next covering it. Special credit should go to the Austrian artillery, directed by GM Smola, who managed to mass enough guns to enable an orderly retreat.

On the extreme right wing, Klenau found himself in a difficult position and had to guard against being cut off as he retreated from the river in the direction of Kagran and Leopoldsau to the heights of Stammersdorf. Masséna had responded to orders to attack. Legrand's division stormed Essling where the Austrians stubbornly defended the granary. When the 26th Light was repulsed, Masséna in his carriage placed himself in front of the 18th Line, shouting, 'Scoundrels, you get five sous a day and I am worth 600,000 francs a year and yet you make me go ahead of you!'[18] Spurred on by this strange encouragement the French infantry surged forward to capture the position. Meanwhile the remaining divisions, Saint-Cyr and Molitor on the right, swung north-west, while Boudet issued from the bridgehead to follow Klenau. Aspern fell without much resistance as Klenau disengaged and, apparently shaken by this sudden turn of events, reported at about 3 p.m. to Charles that he 'feared a disaster'.

None the less, Klenau's corps managed to retreat in good order. At Kagran, when pressed by Marulaz's light cavalry, two solid Austrian masses withstood their charges and the corps artillery had to be brought into action to blow the defenders away. At Leopoldsau, in the last great cavalry charge of the battle, Lasalle, charging ahead of the 8th Husssars accompanied by squadrons of the Saxon Prinz Klemens Chevaulegers, attacked the Austrian rearguard deployed behind a wide flood moat and supported by some 6-pounder guns. While trying to rally the troopers for a second charge, Lasalle, who had once pronounced that 'any hussar who is not dead at 30 is gold-bricking', was killed. He was 33 years old, the best-known light cavalry leader in the army. Marulaz now tried to avenge him, taking command of the 8th Hussars, but their charges, too, were repelled several times, their colonel shot dead. Persisting, Marulaz received a serious wound in his arm and a cannon ball killed his horse under him. Soon thereafter, at around 5 p.m., Klenau managed to disengage his corps and join the general retreat, during the night leading his trains through the narrow defile at Langen–Enzersdorf to elude his French pursuers.

After marching and fighting for forty hours, suffering from the heat, a cold night, little water and scanty rations, the exhausted French pursued slowly but were unable to impede seriously the retreating Austrian army, which remained combat capable. French exhaustion, physical and nervous, is illustrated by incidents in the centre and the right rear of the army. At about 4 p.m., there was a brief panic when there was some firing around Wagram with some dozens of French infantry scampering down the escarpment. The Old Guard hastily formed up in square to protect Napoleon's headquarters, but it soon became clear that some foragers had encountered enemy cavalry and panicked.[19] About an hour later, advance patrols of John's cavalry appeared near Glinzendorf. Again, this caused the Imperial Guard to stand to arms and some French troops to fall into formation, while to the south a crowd of wagoners, stragglers and such made for the bridges and were turned back with canister fire by General Reynier. But John, informed by courier that the battle was over, halted and then withdrew hastily.

At about 8 p.m. on 6 July the guns fell silent and, widely distributed across the plain and the plateau, the French lit their campfires. In the distance were the sounds of the retreating Austrian army. Napoleon held the field. Except for some formations attempting to follow the Austrians, generally held off by efficient rearguards, his troops were too fatigued to commence an immediate pursuit. Perhaps there was no need. Although Wagram was unlike the smashing victories of the past, it can none the less be called a decisive victory. It deprived the enemy of the will to continue fighting and convinced Archduke Charles, who always held that the army should be preserved at all costs, not to hazard another battle and to press for peace.

CHAPTER NINE

Wagram, Znaim and the end of the war

THE AUSTRIAN RETREAT

Wagram was Napoleon's last decisive victory. It compelled Austria to make peace, but it was no Austerlitz, Auerstädt or Jena where the enemy's armies had been destroyed. Archduke Charles managed to disengage the greater part of his army in good order and Napoleon came away with new respect for the Austrians. On more than one occasion he reprimanded those who belittled it stating, 'It is obvious that you were not at Wagram'.[1] Charles had already discussed the general direction for the line of retreat in early June, when there had been plans for an offensive across the Danube at Pressburg, and the subject came up again as Charles waited for the French attack on the Marchfeld. Properly cautious, the archduke had certainly been prepared for the contingency of defeat and had planned the outlines for an orderly retirement when he made his deployments during the first days of July. This alone can be the explanation for the archduke leaving V Corps, only a few miles from the battlefield, out of the action, and for detaching a battery and one of Kolowrat's brigades to take up positions behind Stammersdorf.

And finally, when early on the second day Prince Liechtenstein asked for permission to send additional units of the Cavalry Corps to Mark-grafneusiedl, permission was denied because, as the archduke explained, in case of retreat the cavalry would be required in the plain around Süssenbrunn.[2]

By the afternoon of 6 July, Charles had relocated his command post to Stammersdorf on the lower slops of the Bisamberg, an indication of the proposed line of retreat north-west. Passing the lower Bisamberg slopes, he intended to make a phased retreat with his main force, that is the right wing and centre – V Corps, I, II, and III Corps, the Cavalry Reserve and the Grenadiers – towards the Stockerau–Hollabrunn road. Leading eventually to Znaim and Brünn in Moravia, this was a good choice. Protected by V Corps, it passed over the western slope of the Bisamberg where there were a number of good defensive positions, through the narrow defile at Langen-Enzersdorf and then opened up into a plain around Korneuburg, a small walled town. The much smaller force on the left wing, Rosenberg's IV Corps joined by elements of Hohenzollern's II Corps, was already disengaging from the edge of the Russbach plateau north in the direction of Bockfluss-Schrick-Gaunersdorf and eventually to Brünn.

There have been suggestions that a retreat into northern Bohemia might have been a better strategic option for Charles. From there he might have threatened Napoleon's line of communications and would also have found substantial resources at Prague and Eger and in the fortresses of Königgrätz, Theresienstadt and Josephstadt.[3] But this, of course, would have sacrificed the southern part of the Habsburg Monarchy, especially Hungary where there was little war *matériel* available but where the Emperor Francis was shifting to establish his new headquarters at Komorn. Contact would also be lost with Archduke John's Army of Inner Austria and the *insurrectio* troops promised by the Palatine Archduke Joseph. Finally, Napoleon had been mustering a Westphalian X Corps. Commanded by King Jerome, this was a poor and undisciplined body of conscripts and volunteers, about 7,500 strong, operating in Saxony supported by a division from the Kingdom of Holland under GD Gratin, while also collecting a Reserve Corps under old Marshal Kellermann of Valmy fame at Frankfurt. Neither of these formations had high combat potential, but their position in the rear of an army retreating into northern Bohemia could not be ignored. The last option, a retreat straight north up the line of the river March had become precarious because of the Russian advance on Cracow. Most importantly, however, the archduke was not repositioning himself to continue the campaign. On the contrary. Almost from the outset of the war he had desired peace and his main objective was to reassemble his forces in Moravia to retain an army in being as a military asset for the negotiations he now considered as absolutely necessary for the survival of the Habsburg dynasty.

His immediate orders were for his left wing, II and IV Corps to retire in the direction of Seyring. The Austrians retreated in two columns. Hohenzollern's II Corps, with Brigade Hardegg still attempting to hold on to Baumersdorf, extricated itself without too much French interference and marched north-west, crossing the Russbach at Helmadorf. Meanwhile, Rosenberg's IV Corps was to retreat to Bockfluss some 6 miles further north. Oudinot followed Hohenlohe slowly, while Rosenberg extricated most of his IV Corps north, keeping Radetzky with the Erzherzog Ferdinand Hussars, elements of the Hessen-Homburg and Primatial Hussars and some light troops as a flank guard. Rosenberg outdistanced Morand's and Friant's infantry and halted at the Wendliger Hof to facilitate Hohenzollern's II Corps to cross the Russbach at about 4 p.m. in good order at Helmadorf. Across the river Hohenzollern took up positions around Gross-Engersdorf to the north, his infantry and artillery repelling a number of minor probing attacks. Late in the afternoon, on receipt of orders, II Corps moved north-west through Seyring to Enzesdorf, regaining control of its units that had joined IV Corps, and reached the road to Znaim by nightfall. Further east, in a vain effort to outflank IV Corps, Morand's light cavalry, the 12th *Chasseurs à cheval*, had managed to push to the

Bockfluss before Rosenberg's column reached it. But volleys from the formed masses of infantry, and a countercharge by two squadrons of Erzherzog Ferdinand Hussars repelled the French cavalry. At this point Davout ceased further pursuit action. The heat was still oppressive, his troops were fatigued and thirsty and his horses blown. In addition, he was still concerned that Archduke John might yet arrive on his right flank though, to be sure, Napoleon had ordered strong cavalry formations to screen his right wing against such an eventuality.

It was more difficult to extricate the Austrian centre right and right wings from their engagement around Wagram and Aderklaa. According to orders, Bellegarde's I Corps was to fall back on Gerasdorf in the plain, its movement covered by Liechtenstein's cavalry drawn up in front of Gerasdorf. Infantry of I Corps occupied the village, supported by the reserve brigade that Kolowrat had left behind in the morning and by guns on the Stammersdorf heights. Meanwhile Kolowrat's III Corps was to pull back to Stammersdorf and the Grenadier Corps was to return to Hagenbrunn. Both formations were to make contact with I Corps, Kolowrat to his left and the grenadiers to their right. Beyond Kolowrat's right was V Corps, now marching towards the Stockerau road to assume its original mission to cover a retreat. Finally, along the Danube and then up the road to the Stammersdorf heights, Klenau's VI Corps was being pursued by Masséna.

The degree of French pressure against the various Austrian formations on the right wing varied. Marmont, the Bavarians and the Young Guard division exerted but light pressure against I Corps. The retreat of III Corps was also relatively untroubled until dusk when it was attacked by French cavalry, including squadrons from Nansouty's heavy horse, the Guard Cavalry and the cavalry component of the Army of Italy. Liechtenstein countercharged with GM Kroyherr brigade, Cuirassier Regiments 1 Kaiser and 6 Moritz Liechtenstein and GM Teimern light brigade, the 1st Knesevich Dragoons and the 6th Rosenberg Chevaulegers. They managed to hit the French flank and drove it off. Still, by this time, around 8 p.m., Archduke Charles considered

III Corps' position around Gerasdorf too exposed and ordered a further withdrawal up the Bisamberg slopes towards Stammersdorf, where it took up positions across the Brünn road towards Hagenbrunn, roughly aligned with Klenau's VI Corps retreating up from the Danube.[4]

In fact, VI Corps and the Grenadier Corps faced the most difficult time withdrawing from their forward positions. The grenadiers had held a position in the plain south-west of Aderklaa and at about 3 p.m. began to retreat through the burning village, taking substantial losses from artillery fire. Among the casualties was their divisional commander, FML d'Aspré, another French emigré, who was killed by an artillery round shot. Once through the village, the grenadiers were attacked by French horse and had to form square, making another convenient target for artillery, until the approach of Liechtenstein's cavalry deterred further attacks and allowed the grenadiers to continue their march north to Hagenbrunn. Finally, on the extreme left of the Austrian line Klenau's VI Corps was facing Masséna, who pursued slowly but on a broad front with a strong column including most of his cavalry. After clearing the bank of the Danube beyond Aspern, he followed Klenau's line of retreat to the Stammersdorf heights. He hoped to outflank Klenau, who by then was passing through Leopoldsau. Aware of his exposed position, Klenau had already begun to withdraw shortly before 2.30 p.m., with the Splenyi brigade, still defending Aspern and Essling, gaining him time to form up for an orderly retreat and fight a number of rearguard actions. Retiring back to the Stammersdorf heights, the 4th *Landwehr* battalion unter dem Manhartsberg was placed to defend Stadlau, another block position, two battalions from IR 39 Duka were placed at Kagran, and a third positioned at Leopoldsau.

The isolated *Landwehr* battalion at Stadlau was forced to surrender after suffering heavy casualties while the two battalions of the Duka regiment were expelled from Kagran. The battalion at Leopoldsau, defending itself behind some stone walls, held out for some time, but attacked by infantry from the front and by Lasalle's light cavalry on its flank – an attack in which the gallant Lasalle was killed – it had to withdraw. BG Marulaz, the commander of the corps' light cavalry, took over command. Swinging north-west, Masséna again tried to attack Klenau beyond Leopoldsau before he reached the critical Lang Enzersdorf defile but was delayed by Austrian detachments, among them the combined Vienna *Landwehr* battalions under Major Waldstein. Finally, attempts to cut VI Corps off at Strebersdorf were blocked when III Corps sent some help, two battalions of IR 7 Karl Schroeder reinforced by four companies from IR 29 Lindenau joined later by a battery from V Corps. During the fighting here Marulaz was wounded and had to turn over command of the two divisions of light cavalry to GB Bruyère. The various setbacks and losses incurred during these actions induced Masséna to halt his pursuit and assemble his tired troops near Leopoldsau, with his advance elements near Gross Jedlersdorf skirmishing with Klenau's rearguards under GM Wallmoden. The Saxons, who had also advanced in the afternoon but had seen no action, their spirit shattered and their ranks depleted, also camped at Leopoldsau.

As night fell, Archduke Charles had managed to reestablish a fairly cohesive if irregular front. With army headquarters at Enzesfeld, I Corps was between Stammersdorf and Hagenbrunn, II Corps at Seyring, III Corps in front of Posthaus Rendezvous, IV Corps north of Wolkersdorf and Bockfluss and still moving towards Nikolsburg, V Corps on the Bisamberg and VI Corps at Jedlersdore, though with some elements still near Stammersdorf. The Grenadier Corps was rallying at Hagenbrunn while the Cavalry Corps was covering the area between Seyring and Hagenbrunn. The archduke wisely used the hours of darkness to concentrate his troops further. At about midnight III Corps moved across the Bisamberg to Korneuburg, a small walled town in the plain beyond the Lang Enzersdorf defile, to be joined some hours later by I Corps, the Grenadier and the Cavalry Corps. During the morning of 7 July, Archduke Charles established his headquarters at Göllersdorf north of Korneuburg on the road to Znaim.

The French army consolidated itself with Masséna at Leopoldsau and the Army of Italy at Gerasdorf. Oudinot spent the night at Seyring with Wrede's Bavarians resting to his south. Davout remained with his headquarters in Wagram, with Gudin's, Puthod's and Friant's divisions bivouacking between Wolkersdorf and Bockfluss, and Morand's just across that river. His cavalry divisions, Montbrun, Arrighi and Grouchy, camped further east, toward Auersthal. The emperor, deadly tired, tented in the midst of his Old Guard infantry between Aderklaa and Raasdorf. No further orders for action were issued that night and in fact, though Napoleon rose early the next day, 7 July, he only issued orders to begin an active large-scale pursuit at 2 that afternoon.[5]

NAPOLEON PURSUES ARCHDUKE CHARLES

Victory had been gained at a very high cost. As always, the worst fate was that of the severely wounded. Dead and dying men covered the battle-field, sometimes in rows where they had been struck down. Though some of the wounded tried to drag themselves to field hospitals, many died where they lay, their suffering increased by the heat and lack of water. Local civilians offered some succour, but their capabilities were limited. Napoleon placed no great emphasis on medical services and did not regard them as part of the line. For the 1809 campaign, Larrey had been able to hastily organize a number of flying ambulance detachments, one for each corps, but these never reached full strength and the heaviest burden of caring for the wounded had to be carried by the often poorly qualified regimental surgeons and their assistants. Only the Imperial Guard, whose medical officers were paid three times as much as regular surgeons, had a proper casualty clearing service, ambulances and hospitals. Larrey's men helped out where they could, but facilities remained totally inadequate.

Even his unwounded troops, all them exhausted, many of them dead drunk, having broken into the wine cellars that abounded in the region, were beyond further combat. A day of rest and reorganization was clearly indicated. Also, ammunition had to be replenished. With the French artillery having fired an estimated 90,000 to 100,000 rounds during the battle, caissons and divisional ammunition wagons were empty and had to be restocked. Finally, riderless horses, cavalry as well as draft animals, had to be corralled. An immediate pursuit was not possible.

Moreover, Napoleon had remained uncertain whether the archduke intended to renew the battle the next morning. Not until he rode forward in the early morning to survey the situation personally and to receive reports from his outposts was he convinced that the Austrian army was indeed in retreat, though he remained unsure about its exact direction. He commended commanders and troops he encountered, telling the Army of Italy: 'You are brave soldiers; you have covered yourself with glory.'[6] He ordered Macdonald to report and embraced him, exclaiming, 'On the battlefield of glory where I owe you so large a part of yesterday's success, I make you a Marshal of France.'[7] Macdonald was the only Napoleonic marshal created on the battlefield. The emperor was quite annoyed with Oudinot for his impetuous and unauthorized attack against the Russbach the previous day, telling him he should have been shot, and he still was angry about Marmont's delay in moving to the Lobau before the battle. Still, both men received the coveted marshal's baton. Finally, the emperor ordered investigations into Boudet's actions in defence of the bridgehead, specifically the loss of his artillery, and into the causes of the rout of Saint-Cyr's division and the Saxons at Aderklaa.

Napoleon had his headquarters shifted to Wolkersdorf, from where the Emperor Francis had observed the battle. Here, but only at about noon, he received reliable reports indicating the direction of the Austrian retreat, though he still remained somewhat uncertain about the exact direction of the two Austrian columns – the left one under Charles and the right one reduced now to Rosenberg's IV Corps. Therefore he ordered Marmont's relatively fresh corps, which had suffered only some 500 casualties, augmented by the Bavarians and three brigades of Montbrun's light cavalry division, to push forward on the Nikolsburg–Brünn road following Rosenberg. The next day, 8 July, Napoleon ordered Davout, accompanied by Grouchy's dragoons and

Arrighi's cuirassiers, to follow Marmont. Augmented by Bruyères' light cavalry, Masséna, with orders to catch and then maintain touch with the enemy, was dispatched to take the road to Znaim following the main Austrian column. Macdonald's small remnant brought up the rear. To provide support if needed for either of these two pursuit columns, Napoleon, with the Imperial Guard, Oudinot and Nansouty's heavy cavalry division, marched between the two highways. Curiously cautious, Napoleon remained concerned about a threat to his rear by John, now reinforced by the remnants of Chasteler's and Gyulai's divisions, a force whose potential he greatly overestimated. To keep an eye on John he shifted Vandamme east along the Danube closer to Vienna and told Masséna to remain in touch with the Vienna garrison. Moreover, he formed a new task force, assigning the Württembergers and Saxons to the Army of Italy to shield his army against Archduke John's, who still was maintaining a foothold on the Marchfeld and pushing various ambitious scheme to operate against the rear of the main army. Between 9 and 12 July, in some minor actions, Eugène pushed John back into Hungary.[8]

On 7 July, Charles, making good use of a series of night marches, had managed to assemble the main bulk of his forces, including V Corps, which joined the retreat at Korneuburg, on the Prague road towards Znaim. Only Rosenberg's IV Corps, separated during the last phase of the fighting on the Russbach heights, was still moving towards Brünn, an objective it managed to reach successfully. Masséna was in contact with the main force, but he remained at a fair distance, with fighting limited to some mounted *vedettes* exchanging a few shots. Even so, aware that the enemy would catch up, on 7 July Charles again informed Francis that peace was imperative if the dynasty were to survive. Meanwhile, with his cavalry and Legrand's division as lead elements, Masséna pushed on towards Znaim, fighting a number of small actions. On 8 July there was an encounter between Legrand's division and the Austrian rearguard under Klenau at Stockerau, and the following day there was a major engagement at Hollabrunn. While neither of these actions was decisive, they revealed the Austrians as still combat capable. In fact, at Hollabrunn, Masséna had to break off the combat to wait for the arrival of his three remaining divisions. But these encounters finally clarified the location and direction of the main Austrian body. Masséna could report to Napoleon that he was on the right track, Charles was retiring across the river Laa, a tributary of the Thaya. On the 10th, the bulk of the Austrian army took up defensive positions around Jetzeldorf on the river Pulka, but evacuated these when Charles was informed by a courier from the Emperor Francis, who was about to leave for Hungary, that a major column was approaching Znaim from the east.

The column in fact was Marmont, who had abandoned his march north towards Nikolsburg when his cavalry reconnaissance informed him that Charles was now attempting to reach Znaim. Correctly anticipating the archduke's intentions, Marmont drove his troops to the west, left the road north and instead marched his corps east along the Laa. He took a risk here, but Napoleon's orders had granted him certain operational latitude, and in any case he assumed that Davout would continue north to Nikolburg. Marching through fine wine country, his veterans' discipline weakened and, breaking into wine cellars, many became drunk and committed excesses against the civilian population. Drastic measures were needed and on the morning of 9 July an incensed Marmont had several looters shot to restore order. The same day, he continued his approach to Znaim, the open terrain and a good road along the left bank of the Thaya enabling 11 Corps to advance in combat formation. A Bavarian division, led by GM von Minucci, who had replaced Wrede, marched on the left, General Clauzel in the centre and Montbrun on his right flank with Dupas's division, now detached from the Saxon Corps, but only six battalions strong, following as support. Having been reprimanded repeatedly by Napoleon for his slow operational style, Marmont now pushed his corps to gain the bridges over the Thaya, and occupy the heights before Charles arrived. From the south-west, Masséna speeded up in pursuit of V Corps.

THE BATTLE OF ZNAIM, 10–11 JULY

But Charles had already left the Jetzeldorf position on the evening of 9 July and, force marching his troops through the night, arrived at Znaim at about 4 a.m. on 10 July just ahead of Marmont's advance guard. He immediately set about occupying the hills around the town, especially the dominating heights to the east around the village of Tesswitz. Marmont realized that his 10,000 men would not be able to defeat the Austrians, roughly 60,000 men from the Reserve Corps, II, VI and V Corps, the last, forming the rearguard, already under pressure from Masséna. But following the long-established Napoleonic precedent that the first corps of the army encountering the enemy was to engage at once in the hope of fixing him until the bulk of the French army came up, Marmont attacked. Pending the arrival of reinforcements, Marmont sent forward skirmishers supported by several formed companies of the 6th Bavarian Infantry to drive the Austrians from the heights around Tesswitz. After this was accomplished, some two hours after noon, Marmont ordered Generals Minucci and Clauzel to break through the Austrian centre, but Charles had plenty of reinforcements available, mainly units of I Corps, and in bitter fighting the village changed hands at least four times before night fell. The Bavarian division suffered 900 casualties, its heaviest loss during the 1809 campaign.[9]

Marmont's position was less than brilliant, but Masséna was hurrying to the battle, and at 10 o'clock that night Napoleon arrived with the infantry and the horse batteries of the Imperial Guard. Moreover Nansouty's heavy cavalry division reached Znaim by early morning on 11 August and by 10 a.m. Masséna's advance division, Legrand's, attacked Schalersdorf, a suburb of Znaim defended by V Corps, while Marmont attacked Zuckerhandl, a village to the north-east. Davout and Oudinot were not yet present but were expected to arrive the next day, by which point Napoleon would dispose a total of nearly 84,000 men against, at best, 60,000 Austrians. In the afternoon the French broke into Znaim where after several hours of sharp fighting in the streets, with Austrian losses totalling some 6,200, Archduke Charles decided to sign an armistice on his own responsibility. 'My army,' he explained to Emperor Francis, 'had not been able to cook for several days and was much fatigued and further retreat in the face of the enemy [was] risky, while an attack against his strong positions was even more dangerous. Under these circumstances I sought an armistice.'[10]

Although Berthier and other senior commanders recommended the battle be pressed the next day after Davout's and Oudinot's arrival and that Austria's main army be destroyed and its monarchy – 'the cause of so many wars' – demolished, Napoleon agreed to the archduke's proposal. He considered his army too exhausted; furthermore, for the moment he did not have enough troops to defeat the archduke's six corps around Znaim, though this would change once French reinforcements arrived the next morning. Meanwhile, he wanted to prevent the Austrians from slipping away north on the road to Iglau. 'Enough blood has been spilled', he declared. Around 7 p.m. on 11 July the fighting died down after a provisional ceasefire was arranged; a formal armistice, which only concerned military matters and was initially limited to one month, was signed early the following morning. This ended the active phase of the Wagram campaign. The same day Napoleon elevated both Marmont and Oudinot to the marshalate. He added, however, in a personal letter to Marmont that 'between ourselves, you have not yet done enough to entirely justify my choice'.[11]

ARCHDUKE CHARLES RESIGNS

Charles had sought to preserve his army in being and to prevent the breakup of the monarchy when he entered negotiations with Napoleon. In fact, undercutting the archduke's authority again, Francis had already appointed his own emissary, Prince Liechtenstein, one of Charles's corps commanders, to seek out Napoleon and arrange for an end to hostilities, an attempt which came to nothing when Napoleon dismissed Liechtenstein out of hand. None the less, Francis reacted furiously to Charles's initiative, though the armistice, negotiated by Wimpffen, had been limited to purely military matters, and, given the situation on the ground, was quite generous. But in Francis's view Charles, not for the first time, had interfered in matters beyond the scope of his authority and, by concluding an armistice on his own, had strayed across the boundary dividing military matters and politics, exactly what the emperor had always feared and resisted. In every campaign since 1796 the archduke had tried to play a political role, usually attempting to persuade the emperor to make peace. But in 1809 he had finally gone too far and his removal from supreme command was now just a matter of time.

Imperial disapproval was expressed in a series of letters. Charles tried to explain his reasons for wishing to end hostilities to his brother, while Francis answered that obviously control of the entire military establishment was too much for one general. He now reduced the archduke's authority, demoting him from his position as generalissimus, leaving him in command only of the troops under his immediate control, and demanding the removal of Grünne who was widely disliked at court. In a letter that reached Charles's headquarters on 18 July the emperor, now again totally under the influence of the war party, added that hostilities would continue in the near future after he had assembled a 60,000-strong army in Hungary. With the existence of the monarchy threatened, Francis continued, he intended to assume the supreme command personally.[12] This was the last straw. On 23 July the weary archduke resigned his command. 'A commander who has aroused Your Majesty's displeasure to such a degree can no longer have your confidence and therefore can no longer hold command of the army. These considerations lead me to lay command of the army at the feet of Your Majesty.'[13] The emperor accepted the resignation and placed Liechtenstein in command of the main army. Charles left the army on 30 July and retired until November to the estate of Duke Albert at Teschen. By this time many high ranking-officers had lost confidence in Charles and were no longer willing to serve under him.

NAPOLEON AND ARCHDUKE CHARLES COMPARED

It has been widely asserted that by 1809 Napoleon's military genius was in decline. Napoleon himself observed that ten years of war would burn out any commander. Even so, in 1809 and at Wagram in particular, he was clearly the better of the two supreme commanders. He practised a personal, highly centralized style of command aiming always to fight on the offensive. Even after a reverse such as at Aspern–Essling, he remained determined to seek victory and, with rare exceptions, he did not blame his senior subordinates after a setback, but immediately prepared for a new battle. A charismatic commander and a great battle captain, he imposed his genius and personality on his army and inspired his troops, veterans or recruits, Frenchmen or foreigners alike, with fierce pride, loyalty and devotion. Not just Frenchmen but Saxons, Bavarians, Württembergers and Italians cheered him wherever he appeared. Even the severely wounded would shout 'Vive l'Empereur!' when he came close. Another reason for high morale in the French ranks was the willingness of senior officers to share the risks of battle itself to a much higher degree than their Austrian counterparts.

One of the advantages of the Napoleonic method of waging war, sometimes considered a drawback, was that one individual, Napoleon himself, devised his own strategic, operational and, sometimes, tactical plans. Further, he was prepared to attend not only to great affairs but to the smallest details. For all practical purposes he was his own operations officer. The major drawback was that even a commander of his talents, energy and ability could not do everything. This centralization of authority had other adverse consequences. His senior subordinates were capable, often admirable, generals when operating under his supervision, but were rarely allowed to exercise independent command. He did not encourage independent initiative among his marshals, was often unfairly critical and tended to play off one against another. As his wars became multi-frontal, and with none among his often-quarrelling chief subordinates able to replace him, the result was, as one noted historian observed, that 'wherever Napoleon was, success was assured; but wherever he was not, it was disaster'.[14] But this unfortunate development emerged in full force only later, especially in Spain, Russia and, in 1813, in Germany. At Wagram, however, he still was able to command and order his subordinate commanders directly. In Berthier he was supported by an outstanding chief-of-staff, though he did not participate in planning but was the interpreter and executor of Napoleon's plans. None the less, even if it was only in accordance with the orders given by Napoleon, it was Berthier's detailed arrangements that enabled the army to cross the Danube to the Marchfeld on the night and early morning of 4–5 July, by any measure a most substantial achievement.

Napoleon's marshals, other than Bernadotte, who at Wagram failed him not for the first time, were all capable and competent battle captains, superior to their Austrian counterparts. On an extensive battlefield like Wagram they showed themselves capable of a considerable and surprising degree of initiative and judgment when needed. Masséna and Davout should be singled out for praise and were duly rewarded. Davout was named Prince of Eckmühl and Masséna Prince of Essling. For his contributions to organizing the assault crossings, Berthier became Prince of Wagram. Three senior generals received their marshal's batons. Their promotions were described by a popular ditty chanted by the ranks that showed the troops' perceptions: 'Macdonald is France's choice; Oudinot is the army's choice; Marmont is friendship's choice.' The ditty was at least partially wrong. None of the three had strategic talents. Macdonald was a fine tactician and he was the only marshal to receive his baton on the battlefield. Oudinot was brave but had angered the emperor by attacking without waiting for orders on the afternoon of the second day. Marmont, who received his baton only after Znaim, had often been harshly criticized by Napoleon for his slow movements – 'a turtle', the emperor had called him – and, in fact, he was surprised by his elevation.

Napoleon's marshals, if not a devoted band of brothers, though their rivalry and quarrels have been exaggerated, usually cooperated well enough when Napoleon was present. However, the case of

Bernadotte was singular. He was the least able and reliable of the marshals and, though a good tactician, had an inflated opinion of his capabilities. Married to Désirée Clary, one of Napoleon's old flames, he was allegedly involved in several plots to overthrow the first consul and, later, emperor. His relations with Napoleon were always tense and often hostile. Even so, he was among the first eighteen marshals, fourteen active and four honorary, made in 1804. A fair field commander, he had served with distinction in 1805, but the following year nearly ruined his career by failing to employ his corps at either Jena or Auerstädt. At Wagram he mishandled his 9 Saxon Corps during the night attack and the next morning he evacuated the key village of Aderklaa without orders. He had already criticized Napoleon's battle handling the night before and, after being relieved from command, he issued a proclamation to his Saxons in which he made the most inflated claims for their conduct during the battle. Harshly rebuked, with his corps broken up, he remained in charge of the brigade-strength remnant until the final battle and was only then removed from the army. He returned to Paris in semi-disgrace, but was saved by the belated British landings in Walcheren in August when he was given a temporary appointment to command a hastily collected army to contain the British, though even now his boastful conduct led to further friction with the emperor. It was a relief for both sides when in 1810 he was elected Crown Prince of Sweden and the two men parted with insincere flattery.

Overall Napoleon was lavish in distributing awards, favours and promotions: he awarded over 1,000 medals of the Légion d'Honneur after Wagram. Recognizing the important, perhaps decisive, role of artillery, he presented the medal to all surviving non-commissioned officers of the artillery of the Guard and promoted Drouot to colonel. He praised the conduct of his troops, giving credit above all to the French units though perhaps neglecting the German contribution; distributed substantial amounts of money; and made many of his spot promotions on the recommendations of unit commanders.

By contrast, Archduke Charles had to contend with the distrust of, and constant interference by, his brother, the Emperor Francis, as well as by government ministers and a court clique. Though personally brave, he did not enjoy the kind of devotion from his officers and men Napoleon aroused. Charles's victory at Aspern–Essling is usually regarded as the high point of his military career, and over time he achieved near-iconic stature in Habsburg historical literature, entering the pantheon of great Habsburg military commanders. Yet Aspern–Essling remained a tactical victory only. Indeed Charles's planning and conduct of the war of 1809 was faulty from the very outset though, of course, he was always subjected to interference from Vienna. Still, always overawed by Napoleon, and never more so than after his defeats in Bavaria, the arch-duke looked on the coming battles with trepidation, no longer longing for victory but willing to make peace at almost any price. Of course, he lacked the authority of his opponent and was burdened with the mistrust of his imperial brother and his entourage. Some of the blame for his defeat at Wagram must also be attributed to the cumbersome and slow Austrian system of command and control. But then, always concerned with asserting his position as a member of the dynasty, relations with his commanders remained formal and he never took them into his confidence. There were no conferences before battle and he did not reveal his battle plans to his commanders. Wagram exposed these shortcomings. Having left the Advance Guard and VI Corps exposed for too long on the first day, and with orders issued too late during the night of 5 July, the next day his commanders could only act according to his standing instructions that left them little flexibility or initiative. Handling a major battle with a frontage of over 12 miles according to a rigid eighteenth-century command system was at best slow and at worst led to hesitation, lack of coordination and missed opportunities.

Ever since, there has been debate as to who was responsible for the defeat. Charles, as is only right, has not escaped criticism. He was blamed for not keeping a battle reserve (V Corps was left in reserve to cover an eventual retreat, not as a battle reserve proper). In the weeks between Aspern–Essling and Wagram he inexplicably failed to fortify his main line of resistance on the Russbach plateau. Also, as repeatedly noted, he was wrong in leaving too many troops, the Advance Guard and VI Corps, along the river line and for not permitting them to retreat earlier and thus cutting their losses. Finally, his dispositions for the general attack on the morning of 6 July, perhaps an attempted double envelopment, though Charles later maintained that he had merely planned a general attack, were clearly faulty. He should have brought VI and III Corps and the Grenadier Reserve closer to the battle area. The crucial discrepancy in the timing of the attacks due to the delayed issue of orders during the night has been blamed on Grünne and Wimpffen, with Charles allegedly too exhausted to speed up the cumbersome process. However, because these two were the archduke's immediate subordinates, their shortcomings have not attracted much attention.

Archduke John, whose advance patrols only reached the battle area after 4 p.m., when it already was too late, has become a favourite scapegoat. On 7 July Charles sent an angry note to John, declaring that 'I am sorry to have to note that your appearance a few hours earlier and even with a few thousand men would have been decisive for the outcome of the battle'.[15] But this remains speculation. Up until almost the last minute Napoleon retained the ability to disengage Marmont's corps for action on the right wing and there always remained the infantry of the Old Guard. Even when, in the afternoon, Napoleon had committed almost all his reserves, it is doubtful that the appearance of some second-rate Austrian forces on the right French wing would have changed the situation in the centre. But this, too, is speculation. What is clear, however, is that John had been dilatory in executing his orders. After a long delay before marching out, he had moved with slow deliberation. He had heard the sound of the guns but failed to hurry and arrived eleven hours too late.

Of course, if John had arrived on the first day, the Austrian left wing would have been strengthened, though again whether this would have altered the ultimate outcome remains doubtful. As it was, the archduke's ire concentrated on Rosenberg, whom he blamed for losing the battle by his poor handling of troops. All the other corps commanders – Bellegarde, Kolowrat, Hohenzollern, Klenau and Liechtenstein – were promoted or decorated, though none had shown extraordinary combat leadership and certainly no initiative. Klenau had managed to conduct a competent retreat on the first day and, offsetting his hesitation to attack in the morning of the second day, that afternoon he again managed his retreat with great skill. Finally, Nordmann, the commander of the Advance Guard, has been unjustly criticized for allegedly having been totally surprised by the French river crossing; it has even been suggested that had he not been killed on 6 July at Markgrafneusiedl he would have been court-martialled.

Rather ungenerously, an exasperated Charles felt that some regimental officers and troops had let him down. In a message to his corps commanders, he complained that 'the troops on the left wing have failed to achieve their assigned mission, one which considering their numbers, their position and the importance of the day I had every right to expect being carried out. These troops are responsible for the unhappy outcome of the battle.' There had been confusion and disorder during the advance on the first day and the withdrawal on the second day had been too rapid. 'In general,' the archduke continued, 'with some exceptions I am not satisfied with the conduct of the infantry.' The regimental officers had not done their best to keep order and 'shouting was so general that commanders could not be heard'. In the future, the colonels should either keep their regiments quiet or they would be cashiered, the officers dismissed and the rank and file decimated, with the remainder assigned to other regiments. Finally GM Riese, who had been conspicuously absent during the desperate fighting on the plateau at Markgrafneusiedl, was dismissed from the service.[16] The message, to say the least, revealed Charles at his worst and hurt troop morale. It blamed IV Corps when his own belated orders had failed to bring his right wing into combat at the appointed time and heaped scorn on the troops. Yet the troops had more than done their duty and fought well despite a steadily deteriorating situation.

THE CASUALTY TOLL

Wagram was the largest battle fought in Europe up to this time. Over 300,000 men had fought for two days along an extended front with very heavy losses, largely inflicted by an unprecedented concentration of artillery. While the estimates for losses suffered by both sides vary greatly, some 72,000 casualties – that is, killed, wounded, prisoners and missing – divided almost evenly between the two sides, seems the most likely number, the highest for any Napoleonic battle thus far.

Details are difficult to determine because many of the Austrian casualty returns include not just the great battle on 5–6 July and subsequent retreat but the final battle at Znaim on 10–11 July and there were a great number of stragglers. For instance, the return from Hohenzollern's II Corps for 5–6 July shows about one fourth of its line infantry 'missing', while the 8th *Jäger* Battalion that had defended Baumersdorf was noted as 'destroyed'.[17] However, a careful reckoning results in an approximate total of 37,000 casualties, amounting to roughly 26 per cent of the Austrians' total strength. They included 4 general officers, 120 officers and 5,507 men killed; and 13 generals, 616 officers and 17,490 men wounded. The Austrians also had 18,000 men taken prisoner. In addition, according to the morning reports of 11 July there was a difference of 51,626 officers and men compared with the strength available on 5 July, which even when casualties must be considered, would for the most part appear to have gone missing during the fighting retreat.

At Wagram itself there were considerable differences in casualty rates between the corps. The exposed Advance Guard lost around 50 per cent, by far the heaviest proportion, while Kolowrat's rather timorously led III Corps suffered but 11 per cent casualties. The heaviest losses occurred in defence of the Russbach line where I, II, and IV Corps each lost 30 per cent. Mainly fighting in the plain, the Cavalry Reserve lost 21 per cent of its strength, while Klenau's VI Corps and the Grenadiers suffered losses of 16 per cent. In short, the corps taking the offensive on their flanks had fewer casualties than those standing on the defence.

Napoleon's casualty reports are notoriously unreliable but the French losses were certainly higher than the grossly understated '1,500 killed and 3,000 or 4,000 wounded' claimed in Napoleon's official bulletin. One tabulation shows French and allied losses at about 27,500, including 5 generals, 238 officers and 17,490 other ranks killed and 37 generals, 883 officers and 25,847 other ranks wounded. It gives the number of French prisoners as 4,000. Included in this are the severe losses incurred by the Army of Italy. Of its 20,300 troops, most of them French, it had 6,350 casualties at Wagram. Casualties among the other corps varied: Bernadotte's Saxons lost 590 killed, 2,189 wounded and 1,356 captured; 2, 3 and 4 Corps together lost about 12,000 killed or wounded; while Marmont's 11 Corps, which only saw action briefly on 6 July, lost under 500 men to cannon fire. Finally, the losses among the cavalry divisions varied. Arrighi's cuirassiers suffered the heaviest in officers and men, almost 500, including 29 officers, the result of the failed charge up the plateau ordered by Davout. Unusually for a battle that left one side in possession of the battlefield, the defeated Austrians actually carried away more trophies than the victor, claiming 12 standards or eagles and 21 guns. The French claimed to have captured 10 flags and 20 guns, though the Austrians conceded the loss of only one, clearly omitting the losses suffered the first day, the regimental flag of IR 35 Argenteau, as well as 18,000 prisoners, with most of them wounded.

A NEW STYLE OF WAR

It has become a commonplace among historians to assign the limited but still decisive victory achieved at Wagram to a decline in Napoleon's genius and the alleged inferior quality of infantry unable to execute complex evolutions and therefore having to be deployed in columns. This, however, cannot be accepted. Napoleon was the attacker and columns were normally used in assaults against defended positions. Then, too, Wagram was a new style of battle, requiring new tactics. Many analysts regard Wagram as a success won by sheer bludgeoning carried out by a combination of massed manpower and artillery, fore-shadowing the battles of the American Civil War, Verdun and the Somme. It is true that Wagram was the first great artillery battle. Each side fired well over 90,000 rounds and artillery inflicted the most casualties. By the same token, skirmishers had become less important and the cavalry's role more restricted. But more decisive, however, as the historian Robert Epstein suggested some years ago, was the adoption of new tactical and operational formations by the Austrians, the corps system that changed the dynamics of combat. Although poorly understood and not fully exploited by the Austrian commanders, as well as indifferently executed, the introduction of the corps system made it much more difficult to achieve the complete overthrow and destruction of an opposing army.[18] In the past, Napoleon had faced old-fashioned unitary armies, with at best divisional formations, and by employing his corps system had been able to manoeuvre across a broad front, concentrating his forces for a decisive battle at a decisive point. So long as his opponents did not adopt a similar system, this provided a decisive advantage. But in 1809 he faced an army that in its organizational structure, if not its system of command and control, mirrored that of his own. While imperfect, with a commander who had despaired of victory and an ineffective and cumbersome staff system, it was still enough to change the nature of the enemy army and with it the dynamics of warfare. Army corps, formations combining several divisions with their own artillery and a small cavalry component, were not only powerful but more resilient in battle. After Wagram, where casualties were about even and the defeated army actually took more trophies than the victor, Napoleon is supposed to have exclaimed that 'War was never like this, neither prisoners, nor guns. This day will have no results.' Actually, the emperor was wrong. Admittedly, though it was not an Austerlitz or a Jena, Wagram must be considered a Napoleonic victory. It broke Austria's will and capabilities to resist and so, for all practical purposes, it ended the war of 1809.

THE SLOW END TO THE WAR OF 1809

Various factions continued to sway the Emperor Francis, who with his entourage was making his way to Hungary, first establishing his headquarters at Komorn fortress and then at the nearby manor house at Totis. Almost all his civilian advisors favoured continuing the war and the various factions competed to promote schemes to reverse the verdict of Wagram or, at the very least, obtain more favourable terms from Napoleon. Archduke John talked about great schemes to assemble an army of 60,000 at Oedenburg to attack Napoleon's rear in the Marchfeld and, with the Tyroleans still fighting on, raising a popular revolt spreading from the Tyrol into Upper Austria. Metternich, Austria's envoy to Paris and now released from internment in France, who had replaced Stadion as foreign minister and chancellor, maintained that Austria still had 250,000 effectives and that the people were willing to support and continue the war. He did, however, propose that this strength should be used to obtain the best possible peace terms. Most of this talk was quite unrealistic. Charles had left behind a plan to resume along the left bank of the Danube west of Vienna, but Liechtenstein rejected this as totally impractical.[19] On 15 August, Wimpffen submitted a sober assessment to the emperor. Without discussing the issue of war or peace he pointed out that troop morale was shaken and discipline deteriorating. There was neither transport nor ammunition for major offensive operations and little had been done to prepare fortified positions for defensive operations.[20]

Under these circumstances, despite all the posturing at imperial headquarters, the provisions of the armistice were accepted. The line of demarcation between the armies was the border between Bohemia and Upper Austria including the Znaim and Brünn districts in Moravia. To the south the line went to Pressburg, then along the Danube to Raab and the Styrian border and along Carniola and Istria to the Adriatic at Fiume. A large part of this area was either already occupied by French troops or soon would be. The Austrian main army went into cantonments at Budwitz on the road to Vienna. The final disposition of territory was left to the final peace negotiations. Napoleon meanwhile returned to take up residence in Schönbrunn Palace outside Vienna.

French occupation was harsh on occasion and imposed burdens on the civilians, but other than the Tyroleans, who, despite his solemn promises, the Emperor Francis abandoned, the Austrian population was tired of war and accepted the new order. The Hungarians, of course, had been lukewarm from the outset. It was against this resigned background that on 11 August, and after much delay, Britain finally made its move, landing troops in Holland, rather than Germany as agreed, on the island of Walcheren. It was much too late to bring relief to the Austrians. The operation soon turned into a fiasco. After capturing Flushing, the British failed to advance on lightly held Antwerp. Once French troops under Bernadotte, a large proportion of them National Guards, were deployed, so the British were contained on the unhealthy island. On 30 September, the British evacuated their fever-ridden troops. If initially Benjamin Bathurst, the newly arrived British emissary in Komorn, had reported to London that, 'the landing of His Majesty's forces in the North of Germany ... has infused animation in the Austrian councils', the evacuation changed the situation. He now informed his superiors that 'from what I can learn the Emperor appears to have peace constantly on his mind'.[21]

THE TREATY OF SCHÖNBRUNN

Delaying ratification of the peace treaty could only be pushed so far and in the end Emperor Francis was compelled, once again, to sign a harsh peace. The Treaty of Schönbrunn was signed on 14 October 1809. Austria was compelled to make territorial concessions to the Grand Duchy of Warsaw and surrendered parts of Carinthia, Carniolia, a large portion of the Military Border, the Hungarian littoral and Croatia south of the Sava river to France, which added them to its empire as the Illyrian Provinces. In addition Austria had to pay a heavy indemnity and to limit its army to no more than 150,000 men. None the less, in Vienna news of the humiliating treaty was cheered in the streets and when, on 27 November Archduke Charles returned unaccompanied to Vienna, dressed in the uniform of a colonel of hussars and riding in a simple coach, there was no official reception. The Emperor Francis, the government, the military and even the people were only too willing to ignore him. He never again held active command.

From 1 November, most French troops were withdrawn from Austrian territory, though some remained to take control of the ceded provinces. As usual, additional territory served to augment Napoleon's manpower. The newly created Illyrian Provinces included the regimental districts of the six Karlstadt and Banal *Grenz* regiments. Though Prince Eugène was titular head of the Illyrian Provinces, actual administration was confided to Marmont, who was named governor general and commander of all military forces. In November the Austrian administration withdrew and on 1 December 1809 the advance guard of Marmont's corps clattered across the old wooden bridge over the Kupa into Karlstadt.

The much-repeated story about the undying loyalty and devotion of the *Grenzer* and their grief at the passing of Habsburg rule must be considered a patriotic legend. While the civilian districts of Croatia were apprehensive about their future under the French, in the *Grenzer* regiments the French were well received. Though its senior officers left the country, the regimental officers remained at their posts. In effect, the *Grenzer* passed from Austrian to French rule without any real change in their circumstances. After some deliberations, Napoleon decided to follow Marmont's recommendations and he retained the regiments as a self-supporting military institution, a bulwark against the Turks and a potential springboard for expansion into the Balkans. From 1811 on, the six *Grenzer* regiments were assimilated to the light infantry in the imperial service with French replacing German as the official language of command. Initially used as garrison troops, when in 1811 the emperor began to assemble his Grande Armée to invade Russia, they were included as provisional regiments, armed, equipped and organized on the French pattern.[22]

The year after Wagram, Napoleon still looked unbeatable, but Wagram was his last decisive victory, the last to break the enemy's political will to resist. To compound the humiliation, Napoleon, intent on founding a legitimate dynasty, demanded the hand of his defeated enemy Francis's 19-year-old daughter, the Archduchess Marie-Louise. The marriage took place the following year. None the less, Wagram was the high-water mark. The war in Spain continued, demanding more and more troops, relations with the Tsar deteriorated and within two years Napoleon was to assemble his largest army ever, over 600,000, men for his ill-fated invasion of Russia in 1812.[23] The Russian debacle encouraged first Prussia and then a reluctant Austria, both supplied with British funds and arms, to join in a final great alliance against Napoleon. Defeated in Saxony in October 1813, his satellites defected, and the following year the victorious allies invaded France. Napoleon, with his marshals unwilling to fight any longer, was forced to abdicate.

Selected short biographies

Albert Kasimir, Herzog von Sachsen-Teschen (1738–1823)
Governor of the Austrian Netherlands 1780–92, adoptive father and confidant to Archduke Charles.

Beauharnais, Viceroy Eugène de (1781–1824)
Napoleon's stepson, viceroy of Italy in 1805, who in command of the Army of Italy proved a competent commander. He distinguished himself at Wagram and later during the Russian campaign.

Bellegarde, Heinrich Graf von, General der Cavallerie (1756–1845)
Originally a cavalry officer, he served as an advisor to Archduke Charles in the 1796 campaign on the Lower Rhine. An associate of Chancellor Thugut, he received command of a reserve army. In 1800 he was promoted to General of Cavalry and in 1805 commanded in Italy before being replaced by Archduke Charles. Supported the war faction in 1808 and commanded I Corps in Bavaria, Aspern–Essling, Wagram and Znaim in 1809.

Bernadotte, Marshal Jean-Baptiste Jules,
prince de Ponto Corvo (1763–1844)

Sergeant major in the Royal Army, commissioned in 1791, he became général de division by 1794. In 1797 he served under Napoleon in Italy and, after holding a number of military and civilian appointments, was among the first eighteen generals elevated to marshal in 1804. As corps commander in the war against Prussia in 1806 he failed to commit his corps at either Jena or Auerstädt, infuriating Napoleon. Appointed to command the Saxon army, the 9 Corps, in March 1809, he mishandled his command at Wagram. He was returned to France in semi-disgrace, but when the British landed at Walcheren in August, the Council of Ministers appointed him to contain the British. His relations with Napoleon deteriorated further when he made a bombastic declaration against him in September. On 21 October, however, he was elected Crown Prince of Sweden and later became king.

Berthier, Marshal Louis-Alexandre,
prince de Neuchâtel et de Wagram (1753–1815)

Served as a staff officer in the Royal Army. He was promoted to général de brigade in 1795 and to général de division in the same year. He became Napoleon's chief-of-staff in March 1792 and, with only few interruptions, served him until 1814. Elevated to marshal in 1804, he became chief-of-staff to the Grande Armée in 1805 and served Napoleon in all his major campaigns. He was created Prince de Neuchâtel in 1806 and in recognition of his staff work at Wagram received the title of Prince de Wagram. He was left behind in 1812 when, during the retreat from Moscow, Napoleon departed for Paris. He was Napoleon's chief-of-staff in 1813–14, but committed suicide in Bamberg on 1 June 1815.

Bertrand, Général Henri-Gratien, comte (1773–1844)

A distinguished engineer officer serving with Napoleon in Italy, Egypt, Syria. Promoted to général de brigade in 1800, Inspector General of Engineers in 1804, and général de division in 1807. He was made a count in 1807. In 1809 he built the bridges across the Danube at Aspern–Essling and at Wagram.

Bessières, Marshal Jean-Baptiste, duc d'Istrie (1768–1813)

A distinguished cavalry commander, he served with Napoleon in Italy and Egypt and became a général de division in 1802. He was made a marshal in 1805. He commanded the cavalry of the Imperial Guard in the famous charge at Austerlitz, and fought at Jena, Eylau and Friedland. He fought in Spain, and he commanded the Reserve Cavalry at Aspern–Essling and Wagram. A cavalry commander in 1812, he was killed by a cannonball during the German campaign of 1813.

Bonaparte, Jerome, King of Westphalia (1784–1860)

Napoleon's youngest brother, Jerome began his career in the navy. His marriage to an American heiress caused a rift between the brothers, who were reconciled only in 1806. He became King of Westphalia in 1807. He served as commander of 10 Corps in 1809, but was not a distinguished commander.

Davout, Marshal Louis-Nicholas, duc de Auerstädt, prince de Eckmühl (1770–1822)

Nicknamed the 'Iron Marshal', Davout was appointed Marshal of the Empire in 1804. His usual command, 3 Corps, was always considered the best trained and disciplined in the army. A stern man and not a courtier, he was not liked by his peers, but his merits were indisputable. In 1806 his corps, seriously outnumbered and left unsupported by Bernadotte, defeated the main body of the Prussian Army at Auerstädt. In 1809 he again commanded 3 Corps in Bavaria and the right wing of the army at Wagram.

Drouot, Général Antoine, Baron, comte (1774–1847)

A competent artillery officer he held a series of staff and line appointments and in 1808 became director of the Imperial Guard artillery park in Spain. He played a major role in the formation of the Grand Battery at Wagram in 1809 and was wounded during the action.

Espagne, Général Jean Louis Brigitte, comte de (1769–1809)

An able cavalry commander who joined the Royal Army as a trooper, he rose to général de division in 1805 and was made a comte de l'Empire in 1808. In 1809 he commanded the 3rd Cuirassier division of Lannes's corps and was mortally wounded at Aspern–Essling.

Ferdinand d'Este, Archduke, Feldmarschall (1781–1835)

Archduke Charles's brother, able cavalry commander in 1805, he led VII Corps in Poland in 1809. Initially successful against Polish Army, he was forced to retreat when Russia became more active.

Francis I, Emperor of Austria (1768–1835)

A mediocre and reactionary ruler, whose relations with Archduke Charles were often strained, he succeeded Leopold II in 1792 as Emperor Francis of Germany, but dropped the title when Napoleon dissolved the Holy Roman Empire in 1806. He conducted a series of unsuccessful wars against France between 1792 and 1809, frequently mixing in military operations. In 1810 he married his daughter Marie-Louise to Napoleon.

Friant, Général Louis, comte (1758–1829)

After service in the French Guards and the National Guard of Paris he was elected lieutenant colonel, promoted to général de brigade, and served with Napoleon in Italy and Egypt. Général de division in Davout's corps, he commanded the 2nd division at Eckmühl, Ratisbon and Wagram.

Grouchy, Général de division Emmanuel, comte (1766–1847)

Capable cavalry commander, he commanded the dragoon division supporting Davout's corps at Wagram.

Grünne, General Phillip Ferdinand (1762–1851)

First adjutant to Archduke Charles, much disliked at court.

Gudin, de la Sablionnière, Général Charles Etienne, comte (1768–1812)

Fought with Army of the Rhine, promoted to général de division in 1800, thereafter commanded division in Davout's 3 Corps. Made count in 1808 and the following year fought in Bavaria and at Wagram.

Hiller, Feldmarschalleutnant, Johann Freiherr von (1754–1819)

In 1809 he commanded VI Corps in Bavaria, fought with distinction at Aspern–Essling, but, always on bad terms with Archduke Charles, resigned his command on the grounds of bad health just before Wagram.

Hofer, Andreas (1767–1810)

An innkeeper, he became one of the leaders of Tyrolean revolt against Bavarian rule in 1809. Repeatedly liberated large parts of country, but could not maintain himself against large Bavarian and French forces sent after Wagram. Captured after lengthy pursuit, condemned to death and executed at Mantua in 1810.

**Hohenzollern-Hechingen, Feldmarschalleutnant,
Franz Xavier Prince zu** (1757–1844)

Served with Charles in Italy in 1797, distinguished himself by his breakout from Ulm in 1805, and in 1809 commanded III Corps.

John, Archduke Baptist Joseph Sebastian von Habsburg (1782–1859)

The youngest brother of Francis I of Austria, he was badly defeated at Hohenlinden in Bavaria in 1800. Advocated formation of the *Landwehr*, he supported Tyrolean insurrection. In 1809 he led the Army of Inner

Austria and after initial success in Italy was defeated, retreated into Hungary, was again defeated at Raab, and failed to join Charles at Wagram.

Kienmayer, Feldmarschalleutnant Michael Freiherr von (1755–1828)

Commanded II Reserve Corps in 1809 at Aspern–Essling and then various detachments operating in Saxony.

Klenau von Janowitz, Feldmarschalleutnant Johann Graf (1758–1819)

Initially commanding Advance Guard, he took over VI Corps at very short notice when Hiller resigned, and commanded the Corps at Wagram and during the retreat to Znaim.

Kolowrat-Krakowsky, Feldzeugmeister Johann Nepomuk Karl (1748–1816)

Commanded III Corps in 1809 in Bavaria, Aspern–Essling, and Wagram and during the retreat to Znaim.

Lannes, Marshal Jean, duc de Montebello (1769–1809)

Named to the marshalate in 1804, he commanded 5 Corps at Jena, and the Advance Guard at Friedland. In 1808 he became duc de Montebello. In February 1809 he was recalled from Spain to join Napoleon in Bavaria. He commanded at Landshut and stormed Ratisbon. In command of 2 Corps, he fought at Aspern–Essling and was mortally wounded. Napoleon mourned him as a friend and as his best general.

Lasalle, Général Antoine Charles Louis, comte (1775–1809)

A daring leader of light cavalry, he served under Napoleon in Italy, Egypt, at Austerlitz and gained renown for his pursuit of the Prussians after Jena–Auerstädt. He was made comte de l'Empire in 1808. In 1809 he served under Bessières in Bavaria, fought at Essling and was killed during the pursuit after Wagram.

Lefebvre, Marshal François Joseph, duc de Danzig (1755–1820)

Rapidly rising to general, Lefebvre, a blunt soldier, supported Napoleon during Brumaire and in 1804 became one of the original eighteen marshals. He captured Danzig in 1807 and was elevated to duc de Danzig. After service in Spain, he was appointed commander of 7 (Bavarian) Corps and together with Davout managed to contain the Austrian offensive. After Ratisbon detached to put down Tyrolean insurrection.

Legrand, Général Claude Juste Alexandre, comte (1762–1815)

A former sergeant major in Royal Army, he fought on the Rhine front and by 1799 had reached the rank of général de division. Raised to comte in 1808, in 1809 he commanded the 1st Division of Masséna's corps at Aspern, Wagram and Znaim.

Liechtenstein, General der Cavallerie Johann Prinz von (1760–1836)

A cavalry commander and diplomat. He commanded Reserve Corps at Aspern–Essling and Wagram and negotiated the peace treaty in 1809. After Charles left the army in 1809, he became its commander-in-chief.

Ludwig, Archduke Joseph Anton, Feldmarschalleutnant (1784–1864)

Younger brother of Archduke Charles, he initially commanded V Corps in Bavaria, but laid down command at the end of the Bavarian campaign. Not a talented commander, he was an example of the nepotism pervading the Habsburg Army.

Macdonald, Marshal Jacques Etienne Joseph Alexandre, duc de Tarente (1765–1840)

After a rapid career, he was made a général de division in 1794, but fell from grace in 1804 when he defended Moreau's reputation. In 1809 he was sent to assist Eugène in handling the Army of Italy. At Wagram he led the great column against the Austrian centre, and for his bravery was appointed marshal, the only marshal appointed by Napoleon on the battlefield. In December 1809 he was created duc de Tarente and awarded a substantial annuity.

Maria Ludovica, Empress of Austria (1787–1816)

Third wife of Francis I and an influential member of the war faction at court.

Marmont, Marshal Auguste Frederic Louis Viesse de, duc de Raguse (1774–1852)

He accompanied Napoleon throughout the Italian campaign, Egypt, and after Marengo was promoted to général de division but not included in the first list of marshals. In 1806 he was appointed governor general of Dalmatia, and drove the Russians out of Ragusa. In command of 11 Corps in 1809 he served at Wagram and pinned the Austrians at Znaim, which earned him the marshal's baton.

Masséna, Marshal André, duc de Rivoli, Prince d'Essling (1758–1817)

One of the ablest and most rapacious commanders of the Revolution and the Empire, he gained the rank of général de division for his service at Toulon. Thereafter he served with distinction in Italy, Switzerland, and again in Italy. He was appointed a marshal in 1804 and in 1805 commanded the Army of Italy. In 1809 he assumed command of 4 Corps in Germany and fought with distinction in Bavaria and at Aspern–Essling, where he covered the retreat on to the Lobau island. Despite serious injury, he commanded 4 Corps at Wagram and at Znaim.

Metternich, Clemens Lothar Wenceslas, Graf (1773–1859)

Austrian ambassador to France from 1806 to 1809, he advocated war in 1809, but after Wagram he became Minister of Foreign Affairs and Chancellor and after arranging the peace treaty he hoped for a special relationship with Napoleon.

Morand, Général de division Charles Antoine Louis Alexandre, comte (1771–1835)

Fought on the Rhine, Italy, and Egypt. He distinguished himself at Austerlitz and was promoted to général de divison. In 1808 he was made comte de l'Empire. In 1809 he commanded a division in Davout's corps at Abensberg, Eckmühl, Ratisbon and Wagram.

Mouton, Général de division Georges, comte (1770–1838)

A senior aide-de-camp to Napoleon in 1809, he led the bayonet charge by the Young Guard recapturing Essling. Napoleon regarded him highly, and elevated him to comte de Lobau in May 1809, but never appointed him a marshal.

Oudinot, Marshal Nicolas Charles, duc de Reggio (1767–1847).

A former officer in the Royal Army he served with the Armies of the Rhine and Moselle. A 'follow me' combat leader, he was frequently wounded. Promoted to général de division in 1799, he served under Masséna and in 1805 led an elite unit of grenadiers in Lannes's corps. Wounded again, he led his division at Friedland. He was made a comte de l'Empire in 1808. Following the death of Lannes, he assumed command of 2 Corps which he fought at Wagram. On 12 July he was promoted to marshal and in April 1810 made duc de Reggio.

Poniatowski, Minister of War Prince Josef Anton (1763–1813)

Minister of War of the Grand Duchy of Warsaw from 1808, and in 1809 he successfully led Polish forces fighting Archduke Ferdinand, capturing Cracow in July.

Radetzky, Feldmarschalleutnant, Joseph Graf von Radetz (1766–1855)

With a fine reputation as a fighting soldier against the Turks and the French, he distinguished himself at Aspern–Essling and at Wagram and during the retreat to Znaim. After Liechtenstein took command of army, he appointed Radetzky as his chief-of-staff.

Rapp, Général de division, comte (1771–1821)

Much wounded senior aide-de-camp to Napoleon, promoted général de division after Austerlitz, count in 1809, and together with Mounton he led charge to rescue Boudet's division at Essling.

Rosenberg-Orsini, Feldmarschalleutnant Prinz Franz von (1761–1832)

A better than average Austrian commander, he and his IV Corps were unjustly blamed by Archduke Charles for the defeat at Wagram.

Saint-Cyr, Général de division Carra, comte (1760–1834)

After service in various posts, he rose to général de division in 1803 and in 1808 became a count. In 1809 he commanded a division in Masséna's 4 Corps at Aspern–Essling and Wagram.

Saint-Hilaire, Général Louis Vincent Joseph le Blond, comte (1766–1809)

Former officer in the Royal Army promoted to général de division in 1799. In 1808 became a comte de l'Empire. In 1809 he commanded a division in Lannes's 2 Corps at Eckmühl, Ratisbon, and Aspern–Essling, losing his foot in the last battle and dying of wounds on 5 June 1809 in Vienna.

Schill, Major Ferdinand von (1776–1809)

Prussian lieutenant who during the siege of Kolberg in 1807 commanded a mixed arms raiding force. Promoted to major in command 2nd Brandenburg Hussars. On 28 April 1809, in the hope of provoking a mass rising, he led his regiment out of Berlin to begin operations against the French. There was no rising, his regiment was driven into Stralsund where he was killed in street fighting, and eleven of his captured officers were sent to the galleys.

Stadion, Johann Philip Carl Josef Graf (1768–1824)

Austrian Foreign Minister in 1809 and prominent in war faction at court.

Wimpffen, Generalmajor Maximilian Graf (1770–1854)

Chief-of-staff to Archduke Charles in 1809. Advocate of a cautious strategy.

Wrede, Generalleutnant Carl Philipp Freiherr von (1767–1838)

In 1809 commanded 2nd Division of VII (Bavarian) Corps which participated on the second day of Wagram.

Suggestions for further reading

The literature on warfare on Napoleon and his times is immense, with new books added constantly. Therefore the suggestions for further reading are highly selective and concentrate on books in English, although specifically on the Battle of Wagram several works in French and German are indispensable. For a basic account and excellent maps see Vincent J. Esposito and John R. Elting, *A Military History and Atlas of the Napoleonic Wars* (New York, 1965) and later reprints. The discussion of Napoleonic strategy, tactics and campaigns in David G. Chandler's magisterial *The Campaigns of Napoleon* (New York, 1966) remains indispensable and can be supplemented by the author's edited, *Napoleon's Marshals* (New York, 1987). The nature of armies during this time, their officers and men, arms, tactics, strategy and supply can be found in Gunther E. Rothenberg, *The Art of Warfare in the Age of Napoleon* (London, 1977) and the same author's *Napoleon's Great Adversaries:The Archduke Charles and the Austrian Army 1792–1814* (London and Bloomington, 1982). An excellent study of the Archduke Charles's evolving combat doctrine and a commentary by historians on this is Lee W. Eysturlid, *The Formative Influences, Theories, and Campaigns of the Archduke Carl of Austria* (Westport, Conn., 2000).

The first English account of the 1809 campaign is by a lieutenant in the King's German Engineers, W. Müller, *Relation of the Operations and Battles of the Austrian and French Armies in the Year* 1809 (London, 1810) reprinted in Ken Trotman, *Military History* Monographs (No. 8 London, 1986). Perhaps the most utilized study despite its age is the fine if highly opinionated work by F. Loraine Petre, *Napoleon and the Archduke Charles: A history of the Franco-Austrian Campaign in the Valley of the Danube in 1809* (London, 1909: reprinted London, 1976). This is an excellent and detailed book based on the best Austrian and French literature with observations and commentary by a retired military officer thrown in. Even now it has remained a basic literary source. For the main battles in Bavaria and on the Marchfeld, there are two outstanding studies by the same author, Ian Castle. The first is *Eckmühl 1809*. No. 56 in the Osprey Campaign Series (Oxford, 1988) and the second is *Wagram & Aspern 1809* No. 33 in the Osprey Campaign Series (Oxford, 1995). Both contain well-written and clear accounts of the opposing forces, short biographies of major leaders, battle maps and other details. Also useful for details on the leaders, orders of battle, famous episodes and the like are two fine volumes by James Arnold covering the 1809 campaign. The first is *Crisis on the Danube: Napoleon's Austrian Campaign of 1809* (New York, 1990) and the second is *Napoleon conquers Vienna* (Westport, Conn., 1995), which in addition to the details mentioned above also provides observations of the wider compass of contemporary events in Europe. Finally, a most valuable compendium, especially regarding orders of battle and numerical details based on French and Austrian repositories, is the volume by Scotty Bowden and Charlie Tarbox, *Armies on the Danube 1809* (Arlington, 1980).

The campaign and the two major battles are placed in their operational context by Robert M. Epstein, *Napoleon's Last Victory and the Emergence of Modern War* (Lawrence, 1994). John H. Gill, *With Eagles to Glory: Napoleon and his German Allies in the 1809 Campaign* (London, 1992), deals with the often-neglected subject of the Confederation of the Rhine contingents in detail, while the Army of Italy is ably handled in Frederick C. Schneid, *Napoleon's Italian Campaigns 1805–1815* (Westport, Conn., 2002). A favourable look at the military career and evolution as a military commander of Viceroy Eugène is provided by Robert M. Epstein, *Prince Eugène at War* (Arlington, 1984).

In German there is the well-reputed and authoritative series issued by the Kriegsachiv, Wien, *Krieg 1809* (4 vols. Vienna, 1907–10) which curiously does not contain a volume on Wagram, though it has a volume on war preparations and another one on Aspern. Manfried Rauchensteiner, an archivist, extensively uses Austrian archival sources in his balanced studies *Die Schlacht von Aspern am 21. und 22. Mai 1809,* No. 11 of the *Militärhistorische Schriftenreihe* of the Militärhistorisches Institut (Vienna, 1969) and No. 36 in the same series his *Die Schlacht bei Deutsch-Wagram am 5. und. 6. Juli 1809* (Vienna, 1809). For a thoughtful biography of Archduke Charles, see H. Hertenberger and F. Wiltschek, *Erzherzog Karl. Der Sieger von Aspern* (Graz, 1983). Concentrating on military affairs there are Moritz v. Angeli, *Erzherzog Carl als Feldherr und Heeresorganisator* (5 vols. Vienna–Leipzig, 1896–97) and Oskar Criste, *Erzherzog Carl von Oesterreich* (3 vols. Vienna, 1912).

In French there are a number of works written by staff officers utilizing the Archive de la Guerre. Perhaps the best are Edouard Buat, *De Ratisbonne à Znaim* (2 vols. Paris, 1909) and Charles G. L. Saski, *Campagne de 1809 en Allemagne et Autriche* (3 vols. Paris–Nancy, 1895–1902). Of course, the *Correspondence de Napoleon I* (32 vols. Paris, 1858–62) is a treasure trove. The illustrated history of the 1809 campaign by J. Tranié and J.C. Carmigniani, *Napoleon et l'Autriche: La campagne de*

1809, not only provides a source for great illustrations and maps, but also a brief and sensible text. Finally, a most comprehensive and almost indispensable definitive bibliographic source, listing books as well as articles, organized by country and campaigns, is Donald D. Horward ed., *Napoleonic Military History. A Bibliography* (New York–London, 1986).

Orders of battle: Aspern–Essling

Troops engaged at Aspern–Essling 21–22 May 1809
Napoleon's Order of Battle

Supreme Commander: Napoleon I, Emperor of the French
Imperial Guard

Under immediate control of the Emperor Napoleon

		Bns/Sqdrs
1st (Young Guard) Division: General of Division Curial		
Brig. Gen. Rouget	Tirailleurs chasseurs	2
	Tirailleurs grenadiers	2
Brig. Gros	Fusiliers chasseurs	2
2nd (Old Guard) Division: General of Division Dorsenne		
	Chasseurs à pied	2
	Grenadiers à pied	2
3rd Cavalry Division: Brigadier General Arrighi		
Combined service squadrons of the Guard		
Brig. Gen. Guyot	Chasseurs à cheval	2
	Grenadiers à cheval	1
	Dragons de l'Impératrice	1
Brig. Gen. Krazinski	Chevaulegers polonais	3
	Gendarmerie d'élite	½

Guard Artillery: detachment of four 12-pdr. guns on Lobau and one 6-pdr. battery firing to support French right flank.
Summary: approximately 7,900 infantry, 1,300 cavalry and 8 guns

2 Corps: Marshal Lannes

1st Division: General of Division Tharreau

Brig. Gen. Conroux	6th, 24th, 25th, 9th, 16th Line, 27th Light, 4th Bn only (the 4th bn of cav. regt).
Brig. Albert	8th, 24th, 45th, 94th, 95th and 96th Line 4th Bn only
Brig. Gen. Jarry	4th, 18th, 54th, 63rd Line 4th Bn only

2nd Division: General of Division Claparède

Brig. Gen. Coehorn	17th, 21st, 26th, 28th Light from 4th Bn only	
	Tirailleurs du Po	1
	Tirailleurs corses	1
Brig. Gen. Lesuire	27th, 39th, 59th, 69th, 76th Line 4th Bn only	
Brig. Gen. Ficatier	40th, 88th, 64th, 100th, 103rd Line 4th Bn only	

3rd Division: General of Division Saint-Hilaire

Brig. Gen. Marion	10th Light	3
Brig. Gen. Lorencez	3rd Line	3
Brig. Destabenrath	72nd Line	3
	105th Line	3

Reserve Division: General of Division Demont

7th Light, 12th, 17th, 21st, 30th, 33rd, 61st, 111th Line. All units 4th bns.
This formation remained near the Mühlau bridge and did not participate in fighting and is not counted in corps totals.
Summary: approximately 25,650 infantry, 56 guns

4 Corps: Marshal Masséna

1st Division: General of Division Legrand

Brig. Gen. Ledru	26th Light	3
	18th Line	3

2nd Division: General of Division Carra Saint-Cyr

Brig. Gen. Cosson	24th Light	3
Brig. Gen. Dalesme	4th Line	3
	46th Line	3
Hesse Darmstadt	Leibgarde 1st and 2nd Bns	2
	Leibgarde Fusiliers, 1st and 2nd Bns	2

3rd Division: General of Division Molitor

Brig. Gen. Leguay	2nd Line	2
	16th Line	3
Brig. Gen. Viviez	37th Line	3
	67th Line	3

4th Division: General of Division Boudet

Brig. Gen. Fririon	3rd Light	2
Brig. Gen. Valory	93rd Line	3
	56th Line	3

4th Corps Cavalry: Brigadier General Marulaz

Brig. Gen. Marulaz	23rd, 3rd, 14th, 19th Chasseurs à cheval	11
	Baden Light Dragoons	4
	Hesse-Darmstadt Chevaulegers	3
	Württemberg Chevaulegers	2

Artillery 64 guns. Summary: approximately 27,300 infantry, 4,500 cavalry

Light Cavalry Division: General of Division Lasalle

(Attached to 4th Corps)

Brig. Gen. Piré	8th Hussars	4
	16th Chasseurs à cheval	4
Brig. Gen. Bruyère	13th Chasseurs à cheval	4
	24th Chasseurs à cheval	3
	Württemberg Chevaulegers	3

Reserve Cavalry: Marshal Bessières
1st Heavy Cavalry Division: General of Division Nansouty

Brig. Gen Defrance	1st Carabiniers	4
	2nd Carabiniers	4
Brig. Gen. Doumerc	2nd Cuirassiers	4
	9th Cuirassiers	4
Brig. Gen. Saint-Germain	3rd Cuirassiers	4
	12th Cuirassiers	4

2nd Heavy Cavalry Division: General of Division Saint-Sulpice

Brig. Gen. Lagrange	1st Cuirassiers	4
	5th Cuirassiers	4
Brig. Gen. Guiton	10th Cuirassiers	4
	11th Cuirassiers	4

3rd Heavy Cavalry Division: General of Division d'Espagne

Brig. Gen. Raynaud	4th Cuirassiers	4
	6th Cuirassiers	4
Brig. Gen. Fouler	7th Cuirassiers	4
	8th Cuirassiers	4

Artillery: 18 guns

(Numbers and units for the heavy cavalry and their support artillery engaged are not precise. These were approximately 8,400 troopers, of whom 5,450 crossed the Mühlau. Nansouty's division has been listed though Brig. Doumerc's brigade may not have crossed to the north bank. Not listed are batteries, types of guns, sappers and engineers. A likely estimate for Armée d'Allemagne troops engaged at Aspern–Essling is approximately 77,000: 67,000 infantry, 10,000 cavalry and 152 guns, excluding artillery and engineers.)

Order of battle K.K. Hauptarmee at Aspern–Essling 21–22 May 1809
Commander-in-Chief: Generalissimus Archduke Charles

1st Column (VI Corps) Feldmarschalleutnant Hiller

Advance Guard Major General Nordmann

	IR 60 Gyulay	2
	6th St Georg Grenzer	1
	7th Brod Grenzer	1
	1st and 2nd Vienna Vols.	2
	Liechtenstein Hussars	8

Division Feldmarschalleutnant Kottulinsky

	1st Erzherzog Johann Dragoons	8
Maj. Gen. Hohenfeld	IR 14 Klebek	2
	IR 59 Jordis	2
	4th Vienna Vols.	1

Division Feldmarschalleutnant Vincent

Maj. Gen. Mesko	8th Kienmayer Hussars	7
Col. Splényi	IR 31 Benjowsky	3
	IR 51 Splényi	
	3rd Moravian Vols.	1
Maj. Gen. Bianchi	IR 39 Duka	2
	3rd Vienna Vols.	1

Artillery 54 guns. Summary: approximately 10,500 infantry, 1,800 cavalry

2nd Column (I Corps): General der Cavallerie Bellegarde
Division Feldmarschalleutnant Fresnel

Maj. Gen. Vécsey	Vincent Chevauleger	8
	Klenau Chevauleger	8
Maj. Gen. Wintzingerode	2nd Jäger Bn	1
	IR 10 Anton Mittrowsky	2

Division Feldmarschalleutnant Vogelsang

Maj. Gen. Henneberg	IR 17 Reusz-Plauen	3
	IR 36 Kolowrat	3

Division Feldmarschalleutnant Ulm

| Maj. Gen. Wacquant | IR 11 Erzherzog Rainer | 3 |
| | IR 47 Vogelsang | 3 |

Division Nostitz

| Col. Schaeffer | IR 35 Argenteau | 3 |
| | IR 42 Erbach | 3 |

Artillery: guns 68. Summary: approximately 20,000 infantry, 1,500 cavalry

3rd Column (II Corps) Feldmarschalleutnant Hohenzollern

Advance Guard

Maj. Gen. Provenchères	3rd O'Reilly Chevaulegers	8
Maj. Gen. Mayer	7th and 8th Jäger Bns	2
	Legion Erzherzog Karl	2
	IR 50 Stain	2

Division Feldmarschalleutnant Brady

Maj. Gen. Buresch	IR 15 Zach	2
	IR 57 Josef Colloredo	2
Maj. Gen. Koller	IR 25 Zedwitz	2
	IR 54 Froon	2

Division Feldmarschalleutnant Weber

Maj. Gen. Wied-Runkel	IR 18 Stuart	3
	IR 21 Rohan	3
	IR 28 Frelich	3

Artillery: 62 guns. Summary: approximately 19,400 infantry, 670 cavalry

4th Column (Part IV Corps) Feldmarschalleutnant Rosenberg/Dedovich

Advance Guard Division: Feldmarschalleutnant Klenau

	1st Jäger Bn	1
	IR 3 Erzherzog Karl	3
Col. I. Hardegg	10th Stipsicz Hussars	8
	6th Rosenberg Chevaulegers	2
	10th Stipsicz Hussars	8
	Schwarzenberg-Uhlans	7

Division Feldmarschalleutnant Dedovich

Col. Gratze	Wallach-Illyrian Grenzer	1
	2nd Moravian Frei Bn	1
Maj. Gen. Grill	IR 8 Erzherzog Ludwig	3
	IR 22 Koburg	3

Maj. Gen. Neustädter	IR 9 Czatoryski	3
	IR 55 Reuss-Greitz	2
	6th Rosenberg Chevaulegers	4

Artillery 34 guns. Summary: approximately 11,000 infantry, 1,950 cavalry

5th Column (Part IV Corps) Feldmarschalleutnant Hohenlohe/Rosenberg

Advance Division: Feldmarschalleutnant Rohan

Maj. Gen. Carneville	Carneville Freikorps	1 mixed bn
	Wallach-Illyrian Grenzer	1
Maj. Gen. Stutterheim	3rd Erzherzog Ferdinand Hussars	8
	6th Rosenberg-Chevaulegers	4

Division Feldmarschalleutnant Hohenlohe

Maj. Gen. Riese	IR 46 Chasteler	3
	IR 44 Bellegarde	3
Maj. Gen. Reinhard	IR 2 Hiller	3
	IR 33 Sztárary	3

Summary: approximately 10,700 infantry, 2,000 cavalry, 34 guns

Reserve Corps: General der Cavallerie Liechtenstein
Reserve Cavalry

Maj. Gen. Wartensleben	6th Blankenstein Hussars	8
Maj. Gen. Kerekes	Primatial Hussars	6
	Neutra Hussars	

Division Feldmarschalleutnant Hessen-Homburg

Maj. Gen. Siegenthal	3rd Herzog Albert Cuirassiers	6
	2nd Erzherzog Franz Cuirassiers	6
Maj. Gen. Lederer	4th Kronprinz Ferdinand Cuirassiers	6
	8th Hohenzollern Cuirassiers	6

Division Feldmarschalleutnant Kienmayer

Maj. Gen. Kroyher	1st Kaiser Cuirassiers	6
	6th Liechtenstein Cuirassiers	6
Maj. Gen. Rottermund	6th Riesch Dragoons	6
Maj. Gen. Clary	3rd Knesevich Dragoons	6
	Kronprinz Ferdinand Cuirassiers	6

Summary: approximately 6,700 cavalry, 18 guns

Grenadier Reserve
Grenadier Division Feldmarschalleutnant Lindenau

| Maj. Gen. Murray | Grenadier Battalions: Leiningen, Portner, Georgy, Wienawsky, Demontant, Legraud, Hohnelohe, Hahn |

Grenadier Division Feldmarschalleutnant D'Aspré

Lt. Col. Scovaud Grenadier Battalions: Brzezinski, Puteany, Scovaud, Scharlach, Mayblümel, Oklopsia, Bissingen, Kirchenbetter

Summary: 11,240 infantry, 24 guns

Summary of K.K. Hauptarmee engaged at Aspern–Essling

Total: approximately 99,000, including 84,000 infantry, 14,250 cavalry, 288 guns
Numbers exclude gun crews, engineers and teamsters.

Orders of battle: Wagram

Napoleon's Order of Battle at Wagram 5–6 July 1809

Supreme Commander: Napoleon I, Emperor of the French

Imperial Guard

Under immediate control of the Emperor Napoleon

		Bns/Sqdrs
1st (Young Guard) Division: General of Division Curial		
Brig. Gen. Roguet	Tirailleurs chasseurs	2
	Tirailleurs grenadiers	2
Brig. Gen. Frederich	Fusilier chausseurs	2
	Fusilier grenadiers	2
2nd (Old Guard) Division: General of Division Dorsenne		
Brig. Gen. Gros	Chasseurs à pied	2
Brig. Gen. Michel	Grenadiers à pied	2
3rd (Cavalry) Division: General of Division Walther		
Brig. Gen. Guyot	Grenadiers à cheval	4
Brig. Gen. Thiry	Grenadiers à cheval	4
Brig. Gen. Krazinski	Chevaulegers polonais	4
Brig. Gen. Letort	Dragoons de l'Impératrice	4
Brig. Gen. Savary	Gendarmerie élite	2

Guard Artillery: 60

Summary: 12 battalions, 18 squadrons. Approximately 7,350 infantry, 3,350 cavalry

2 Corps: *General of Division Oudinot*

1st Division: General of Division Tharreau

Brig. Gen. Conroux	6th Light	1
	24th Light	1
	25th Light	1
	9th Light	1
	27th Light	1
	Tirailleurs corses	1
Brig. Gen. Albert	8th Line	1
	24th Line	1
	45th Line	1
	95th Line	1
	96th Line	1
Brig. Gen. Jarry	4th Line	1
	18th Line	1
	54th Line	1
	63rd Line	1

2nd Division: General of Division Frère

Brig. Gen. Coehorn	7th Light	1
	21st Light	1
	28th Light	1
	16th Light	1
	26th Light	1
	Tirailleurs du Po	1
Brig. Gen. Razout	27th Line	1
	39th Line	1
	59th Line	1
	69th Line	1
	76th Line	1
Brig. Gen. Ficatier	40th Light	1
	88th Line	1
	64th Line	1
	100th Line	1
	103rd Line	1

3rd Division: General of Division Grandjean

Brig. Gen. Marion	10th Light	3
Brig. Gen. Lorencez	3rd Line	3
	57th Line	3
Brig. Gen. Brun	72nd Line	3
	105th Line	3

Portuguese Legion

Brig. Gen. Carcomelego	13th Elite Demi-brigade	2
	Chasseurs à cheval	2

Corps Light Cavalry Brigade

Brig. Gen. Colbert	9th Hussars	3
	7th Chasseurs à cheval	3
	20th Chasseurs à cheval	3

Artillery 48 guns, 34 regimental pieces. Summary: approximately 26,000 infantry, 1,650 cavalry (46 battalions, 11 squadrons)

3 Corps: Marshal Davout

1st Division: General of Division Morand

Brig. Gen. Lacour	13th Light	3
	17th Line	3
Brig. Gen. L'Huillier	30th Line	3
	61st Line	3

2nd Division: General of Division Friant

Brig. Gen. Gilly	15th Light	3
	33rd Line	3
Brig. Gen. Barbanègre	48th Line	3
Brig. Gen. Grandeau	111th Line	3
	108th Line	3

3rd Division: General of Division Gudin

Brig. Gen. Boyer	12th Line	3
	21st Line	3
Brig. Gen. Duppelin	25th Line	3
	85th Line	3
Brig. Gen. Leclerc	7th Light	4

4th Division: General of Division Puthod

Brig. Gen. Girard (vieux)	17th Light	1
	30th Line	1
	61st Line	1
	65th Line	1
	33rd Line	1
Brig. Gen. Desailly	111th Line	1
	7th Light	1
	12th Line	1
	25th Line	1
	85th Line	1

Light Cavalry Division: General of Division Montbrun

Brig. Gen. Pajol	5th Hussars	3
	7th Hussars	3
	11th Chasseurs à cheval	3
Brig. Gen. Jacqinot	1st Chasseurs à cheval	3
	2nd Chasseurs à cheval	3

Summary: 31,530 infantry, 6,200 cavalry, 60 guns (including 30 regimental and 8 horse battery guns)

Cavalry Divisions attached to Marshal Davout's Corps
Dragoon Division: General of Division Pully

	23rd Dragoons	4
	28th Dragoons	3
	29th Dragoons	4

Dragoon Division: General of Division Grouchy

	7th Dragoons	4
	30th Dragoons	4
	Attached (Italian) Dragoni Regina	4
	1st Cacciatore a Cavallo	1

4 Corps: Marshal Masséna

1st Division : General of Division Legrand

Brig. Gen. Ledru	26th Light	4
	18th Line	4
Baden Brigade:	Leibregiment	2
Col. v. Neuenstein	Erbgrossherzog	2
	Jäger	1
	Hochberg	1

2nd Division: General of Division Carra Saint-Cyr

Brig. Gen. Cosson	24th Light	4
Brig. Gen. Stabenrath	4th Line	4
	46th Line	3
Hessian Brigade:	Leibbrigade	3
Brig. Gen. v. Schinner	Leib Fusilier	1
Brig. Gen. Cozpe	2nd Musketeers	1
	Fusiliers	1

3rd Division: General of Division Molitor

Brig. Gen. Leguay	2nd Line	3
	16th Line	3
Brig. Gen. Viviez	37th Line	3
	67th Line	2

4th Division: General of Division Boudet

Brig. Gen. Grillot	3rd Line	2
Brig. Gen. Valory	56th Line	3
	93rd Line	2

Light Cavalry Brigade: Brigadier General Marulaz

Brig. Gen. Marulaz	3rd Chasseurs à cheval	3
	19th Chasseurs à cheval	3
	23rd Chasseurs à cheval	3
	14th Chasseurs à cheval	3
	Baden Light Dragoons	3
	Hesse Garde Chevaulegers	4

Attached to 4 Corps
Light Cavalry Division: General of Division Lasalle

Brig. Gen. Bruyère	13th Chasseurs à cheval	3
	24th Chasseurs à cheval	3
Brig. Gen. Piré	8th Hussars	4
	16th Chasseurs à cheval	4

Artillery: 66 guns (including 18 from German contingents), 24 regimental guns
Summary: 49 battalions, 31 squadrons, 90 guns

9 Corps (Saxons): Marshal Bernadotte

Advance Guard: General Major v. Gutschmidt

	Prinz Klemens Chevaulegers	4
	Hussars	3
	Herzog Albrecht Chevaulegers	1

1st Division: General Leutnant Zezschwitz

Maj. Gen. v. Hartitzsch	Leibgrenadiergarde	1
	2nd Bose Grenadier Bn	1
	2nd Schützen Bn	1
Maj. Gen. v. Zeschau	Regiment König Bn	2
	Niesemeuschel Bn	1
	Comb. IR Dyherrn and Obschelwitz	1

Cavalry Brigade: General Major Gutschmidt

	Gardes du Corps	2
	Carabiniers	2
	Prince Klemens Chevaulegers	4
	Herzog Albrecht Chevaulegers	1
	Hussar	3

2nd Division: General Leutnant v. Polenz

Maj. Gen. Lecoq	Prinz Klemens Bn	1
	Prinz Anton Bn	1
	Prinz Maximilian Bn	1
	IR Loew	1
	IR Cerrini	1
Col. v. Steindel	IR Prinz Friedrich August	1
	IR Prinz Anton	1
	IR Prinz Maximilian	1
	Schützen Bn Egidy	1

Cavalry Brigade General Major v. Feilitzsch

	Prinz Johann Chevaulegers	4
	Leib Cuirassier Garde	4
Artillery: 26 guns		

Attached French Division: General of Division Dupas

Brig. Gen. Gency	5th Light	2
Brig. Gen. Veaux	19th Line	3
Artillery: 16 guns		

Summary: 24 battalions, 20 squadrons, 42 guns. Approximately 15,600 infantry, 2,500 cavalry
In mid June Napoleon ordered three Saxon Schützeon battalions – v. Metzsch, v. Radeloff and v. Winkelmann – to be attached to the Dupas division.

Army of Italy
Commander: Viceroy Prince Eugène de Beauharnais

5 Corps: *General of Division Macdonald*

1st Division: General of Division Lamarque

Brig. Gen. Almeyras	18th Light	2
	13th Line	3
	92nd Line	2
Brig. Gen. Huart	23rd Line	2
	29th Line	4

2nd Division: General of Division Broussier

Brig. Gen. Quétard	9th Line	3
	84th Line	3
Brig. Gen. Desaix	92nd Line	4

6 Corps: *General of Division Grenier*

1st Division: General of Division Serras

Brig. Gen. Moreau	35th Line	1
	53rd Line	4
Brig. Gen. Roussel	42nd Line	1
	106th Line	3

2nd Division: General of Division Durutte

Brig. Gen. Valentin	23rd Light	4
	60th Line	2
Brig. Gen. Bruch	62nd Line	3
	102nd Line	3

3rd Division: General of Division Pacthod

Brig. Gen. Testé	8th Light	2
	1st Line	4
Brig. Gen. Abbé	52nd Line	4

Light Cavalry Division: General of Division Sahuc

	6th Chasseurs à cheval	4
	8th Chasseurs à cheval	4
	9th Chasseurs à cheval	3

Guardia Reale

Guard Division: General of Division Fontanelli

Brig. Gen. Guerin	Guardia del onore	1
	Dragoni	2
Brig. Gen. Lecchi	Granatieri	1
	Cacciatori	1
	Veliti	1

Note: The Army of Italy was reorganized on 6 July to reflect the new tactical situation.
Summary: 58 battalions, 15 squadrons, 44 guns. Approximately 19,600 infantry, 1,800 cavalry

Army of Dalmatia (11 Corps): General of Division Marmont

1st Division: General of Division Claparède

Brig. Gen. Bertrand	18th Light	2
	5th Line	2
Brig. Gen. Delzons	79th Line	2
	81st Line	2

2nd Division: General of Division Clauzel

Brig. Gen. Soyez	8th Light	2
	23rd Line	2
Brig. Gen. Bachelu	11th Line	3
	24th Chasseurs à cheval	1

Summary: 17 battalions, 1 squadrons, 28 guns. Approximately 9,800 infantry, 270 cavalry

2nd Bavarian Division (7 Corps): General Leutnant. Wrede

Maj. Gen. v. Minucci	6th Light Bn	1
	3rd IR Prinz Karl	2
	6th IR Herzog Wilhelm	2
Maj. Gen. v. Beckers	13th IR	2
	7th IR Löwenstein	2

Cavalry Brigade General Major Preysing

	3rd Chevaulegers Leininngen	4
	2nd Chevauleger König	4

Summary: 9 battalions, 8 squadrons, with 2 batteries augmented from 1st Bavarian Division
36 guns. Approximately 5,500 infantry, 1,100 cavalry

Reserve Cavalry: Marshal Bessiérès
Heavy Cavalry Division: General of Division Nansouty

Brig. Gen. Defrance	1st Carabiniers	4
	2nd Carabiniers	4
Brig. Gen. Doumerc	2nd Cuirassiers	4
	9th Cuirassiers	4
Brig. Gen. Berckheim	3rd Cuirassiers	4

Heavy Cavalry Division: General of Division Saint-Germain

Brig. Gen. Fiteau	1st Cuirassiers	4
	5th Cuirassiers	4
Brig. Gen. Guiton	10th Cuirassiers	4
	11th Cuirassiers	4

Heavy Cavalry Division: General of Division Arrighi

Brig. Gen. Raynaud	4th Cuirassiers	4
	6th Cuirassiers	4
Brig. Gen. Bordesoult	7th Cuirassiers	4
	8th Cuirassiers	4

Note: Arrighi was detached on the morning of 6 July to Davout.

Summary of French and Allied troops engaged at Wagram

	Bns	Sqdrs	Guns
Imperial Guard	12	18	60
2 Corps	46	11	82
3 Corps	52	43	98
4 Corps	49	31	90
9 Corps	21	20	42
Army of Italy	58	15	100
Army of Dalmatia	15		12
Bavarian Division	9	8	36
Reserve Cavalry		56	24
Grand total			
not counting Lobau garrison:	262	202	544

Lobau garrison was approximately 8,500 infantry, 129 guns

In the vicinity of battlefield but not engaged

VIII (Württemberg) Corps: General of Division Vandamme

12 battalions, 12 squadrons, 22 guns along the Danube to Melk; Nassau Regt. of Division Rouyer, 2 battalions in Vienna.

Brig.Thiery: 1 Provisional Regt Chasseurs à cheval and the Württemberg Heinrich Chevaulegers at Bruck on the Leitha.

Division Severoli and the attached 25th Chasseurs à cheval before Pressburg and in Raab.
6th Hussars from the Divison Sahuc in Wiener-Neustadt.

Order of battle K.K. Hauptarmee at Wagram 5–6 July 1809
Commander-in-Chief: Generalissimus Archduke Charles

Advance Guard: Feldmarschalleutnant Nordman

Maj. Gen. Vecsey	Primatial Hussars	6
	IR 58 Beaulieu	2
	3rd Landwehr Manharts Berg.	1
	1st Jäger Bn	1
Maj. Gen. Fröhlich	Stipszicz Hussars	8
	Wallach-Illyr. Grenzer	2
	7th Jäger Bn	1
Maj. Gen. Riese	IR 44 Bellegarde	3
	2nd Lower Vienna Woods Landwehr	1
	IR 46 Chasteler	3
	1st Lower Vienna Woods Landwehr	1

Maj. Gen. Mayer	IR 4 Hoch und Deutschmeister	3
	IR 49 Kerpen	3
	5th Lower Vienna Woods Landwehr	1
Maj. Gen. Schneller	4th Hessen-Homburg Hussars	8

(24 battalions, 22 squadrons, 48 guns). Approximately 11,500 infantry, 2,500 cavalry, 48 guns

I Corps: General der Cavallerie Bellegarde

Division Feldmarschalleutnant Dedovich

Maj. Gen. Henneberg	IR 17 Reuss-Plauen	3
	IR Kolowrat	3
Maj. Gen. Wacquant	IR 11 Erzherzog Rainer	3
	IR 47 Vogelsang	3

Division Feldmarschalleutnant Fresnel

Maj. Gen. Clary	IR 10 Anton Mittrowsky	2
	IR 42 Erbach	2
	1st Hradisch Landwehr	1
Maj. Gen. Motzen	IR 35 Argenteau	1
	4th Bn Erzherzog Karl Legion	1
Maj. Gen. Stutterheim	5th Klenau Chevauleger	8
	2nd Jäger Bn	1

Summary: 22 battalions, 8 squadrons, 68 guns. Approximately 21,000 infantry, 800 cavalry

II Corps: Feldmarschalleutnant Hohenzollern-Hechingen

Maj. Gen. Hardegg	Vincent Chevauxlegers	6
	8 Jäger Bn	1
	2nd Bn Legion Erzherzog Karl	1

Division Feldmarschalleutnant Brady

Maj. Gen. Paar	IR 54 Froon	3
	3rd Bn Hradisch Landwehr	1
	IR 25 Zedwitz	1
	2nd Bn Znaim Landwehr	1
Maj. Gen. Buresch	IR 57 Joseph Colloredo	3
	1st Bn Brünn Landwehr	1
	3rd Bn Brünn Landwehr	1
	IR 15 Zach	2

Division Feldmarschalleutnant Siegenthal

Maj. Gen. Altstern	IR 21 Rohan	3
Maj. Gen. Wied-Runkel	IR 18 d'Aspre	3
	IR 28 Frelich	3

Summary: 26 battalions, 6 squadrons, 68 guns. Approximately 24,500 infantry, 520 cavalry

III Corps: Feldzeugmeister Kolowrat

| Col. Schmuttermayer | Schwarzenberg Uhlans | 6 |
| | Lobkowitz Jäger | 1 |

Division Feldmarschalleutnant St. Julien

Maj. Gen. Lilienberg	IR 1 Kaiser	2
	IR 23 Würzburg	2
	IR 43 Manfredini	3
Maj. Gen. Bieber	IR 20 Kaunitz	3
	IR 38 Württemberg	2

Division Feldmarschalleutnant Vukassovich

Maj. Gen. Grill	IR 56 Colloredo	3
	IR 7 Carl Schröder	3
Col. Wratislaw	1st/2nd Comb. Prague Landwehr	1
	1st/2nd Berauner Landwehr	2

Summary: 22 battalions, 6 squadrons, 58 guns. Approximately 15,900 infantry, 670 cavalry

IV Corps: Feldmarschalleutnant Rosenberg

Division Feldmarschalleutnant Radetzky

Maj. Gen. Provenchères	Erzherzog Ferdinand Hussars	8
	Watrich Jäger	
	(1st Bn Legion Erzherzog Carl)	1
	2nd Moravian Freibn	2
	Carneville Freikorps ⅓	½
Maj. Gen. Weiss	IR 3 Erzherzog Carl	3
	IR 50 Stain	3
	4th Lower Vienna Woods Landwehr	1
	4th Landwehr O. Manharts Bn	1

Division Feldmarschalleutnant Hohenlohe-Bartenstein

| Maj. Gen. Hessen-Homburg | IR 3 Hiller | 3 |
| | IR 33 Szátary | 3 |

Division Feldmarschalleutnant Rohan

Maj. Gen. Swinburn	IR 8 Erzherzog Ludwig	3
	IR 22 Koburg	3
	Comb. Iglau and Znaim Landwehr	2

Summary: 24⅓ battalions, 8½ squadrons, 60 guns. Approximately 17,300 infantry, 670 cavalry

VI Corps: *Feldmarschalleutnant Klenau*

Division Feldmarschalleutnant Vincent

Maj. Gen. Wallmoden	Kienmayer Hussars	8
	Liechtenstein Hussars	8
Maj. Gen. Mariássy	1st Vienna Volunteer Bn	1
	2nd Vienna Volunteer Bn	1
	4th Landwehr Lower Manharts Bn	1
Maj. Gen. August Vecsey	St Georg Grenzer	1
	Brod Grenzer	½

Division Feldmarschalleutnant Hohenfeld

Maj. Gen. Adler	3rd Bn Legion Erzherzog Carl	1
	1st Bn Upper Vienna Woods	1
	IR 14 Klebek	2
	IR 59 Jordis	2
	Upper Austria Landwehr	1
Maj. Gen. Hoffmeister	IR 60 Gyulai	3
	IR 39 Duka	3

Division Feldmarschalleutnant Kottulinsky

Maj. Gen. Splényi	3rd Vienna Volunteers	1
	4th Vienna Volunteers	1
	IR 51 Splényi	3
.	IR 31 Benjowsky	2
	Comb. Moravian Landwehr	1

Summary: 25½ battalions, 16 squadrons, 64 guns. Approximately 17,300 infantry, 840 cavalry

Reserve Corps: *General der Cavallerie Prince Liechtenstein*

Grenadier Reserve Division Feldmarschalleutnant d'Aspre

Maj. Gen. Merville	Grenzer Bn Scharlach, Grenzer Bn Brzeczinski, Grenzer Bn Scovaud, Grenzer Bn Jambline.
Maj. Gen. Hammer	Grenzer Bn Kirchenbetter, Grenzer Bn Bissingen, Grenzer Bn Oklopsia, Grenzer Bn Locher
	1st Landwehr U. Manharts Bn 1

Division Feldmarschallleutnant Prochaska

GM Murray	Grenzer Bn Frisch, Grenzer Bn Georgy, Grenzer Bn Portner, Grenzer Bn Leiningen
GM Steyrer	Grenzer Bn Hahn, Grenzer Bn Hromada Grenzer Bn Legrand, Grenzer Bn Demontant Grenzer Bn Berger

Cavalry Reserve

Division Feldmarschalleutnant Hessen-Homburg

GM Roussel	Herzog Albert Cuirassiers	6
	Erzherzog Franz Cuirassiers	6
GM Lederer	Kronprinz Ferdinand Cuirassiers	6
	Hohenzollern Cuirassiers	6
GM Kroyher	Kaiser Cuirassiers	4
	Moritz Liechtenstein Cuirassiers	6

Division Feldmarschalleutnant Schwarzenberg

GM Teimern	Rosenberg Chevaulegers	8
	Knesevich Dragoons	6
GM Kerékes	Neutra Hussars	6

Division Feldmarschalleutnant Nostitz

GM Rothkirch	Erzherzog Johann Dragoons	6
	Riesch Dragoons	6
GM Wartensleben	Blankenstein Hussars	10
	O'Reilly Chevaulegers	8

Summary: 18 battalions, 84 squadrons, 48 guns. Approximately 9,900 infantry, 8,000 cavalry

Summary of Austrian troops engaged at Wagram

	Bns	Sqdrs	Guns
Advance Guard	23	22	48
I Corps	22	8	68
II Corps	26	6	68
III Corps	22	6	58
IV Corps	22 ⅓	8 ½	60
VI Corps	25 ⅓	16	64
Reserve Corps	18	84	48
Grand total:	163 ⅔	150 ½	414

Approximately 121,500 infantry, 14,700 cavalry

In the vicinity of the battlefield but not engaged

V Corps: Feldzeugmeister Reuss

Division Feldmarschallleutnant Weissenwolf

Maj. Gen. Neustädter	IR 55 Reuss Greitz	3
	IR 9 Czatorisky	3
	3rd Perauer Landwehr	1
	4th Brünn Landwehr	1

Maj. Gen. Pfluger	IR 29 Lindenau	2
	5th Vienna Volunteers	1
Maj. Gen. Klebelberg	3rd Jäger Bn	1
	4th Jäger Bn	1
	Erzherzog Karl Hussars	8

Summary: 15 battalions, 8 squadrons, 32 guns. Approximately 8,300 infantry, 700 cavalry

Army of Inner Austria: General der Cavallerie Archduke John

Division Feldmarschalleutnant Frimont

Col. Besan	Ott Hussars	8
	Erzherzog Josef Hussars	8
	Hohenlohe Dragoons	5
Maj. Gen. Lutz	Grenzer Bn Chimani	1
	Grenzer Bn Welsperg	1
	Grenzer Bn Gersanich	1
	Grenzer Bn Zetlar	1

Division Feldmarschalleutnant Colloredo

| Maj. Gen. Devaux | IR 19 Alvinczy | 3 |
| | IR 61 St Julien | 3 |

Division Feldmarschalleutnant Jellacic

Maj. Gen. Eckhardt	IR 32 Esterhàzy	3
	Warasdin-Kreutz Grenzer	3
Maj. Gen. de Best	IR 62 Franz Jellacic	3
	1st Banat Grenzer	1

Summary: 20 battalions, 21 squadrons, 50 guns. Approximately 10,800 infantry, 1,420 cavalry

Notes

CHAPTER 1

1 For an account of the Austrian Army during the French Revolution and Napoleonic Wars see Gunther E. Rothenberg, *Napoleon's Great Adversaries: The Archduke Charles and the Austrian Army 1792–1814* (London, 1982).

2 Peter Paret, *Yorck and the Era of Prussian Reform, 1807–1815* (Princeton N.J., 1966), 73–4.

3 Carl to Francis, 24 March 1797, Rothenberg, 62.

4 General von Clausewitz, *Hinterlassene Werke über Krieg und Kriegsführung,* cited in Rothenberg, 74.

5 An excellent account of the tense relations between the Emperor Francis and the Archduke Charles, based on archival sources in the Vienna and Budapest archives, is provided in Manfried Rauchensteiner, *Kaiser Franz und Erzherzog Carl* (Munich–Vienna, 1972).

6 Oskar Christe, *Erzherzog Carl von Oesterreich* (3 vols. Vienna, 1912), 2, 71–2.

7 Eduard Wertheimer, 'Erzherzog Karl und die zweite Coalition bis zum Frieden von Lunéville 1798–1801,' *Archiv für Oesterreichische Geschichte,* 67 (1882), 211.

8 Rothenberg, 80.

9 Kriegsarchiv Wien [hereafter KA]. MNKF B 473/55. The first reform period is discussed in some detail in Rothenberg, 86–104.

10 The second reform period is discussed in ibid., 134–58.

11 KA, FA (CA) F 11/16. Printed in Criste, 2, 252–7.

12 Moritz von Angeli, *Erzherzog Carl als Feldherr und Heeresorganisator* (5 vols. Vienna, 1896–8), 4, 10.

13 Rothenberg, 160–69.

CHAPTER 2

1 Oskar Criste, *Erzherzog Carl von Oesterreich* (3 vols. Vienna, 1912), 2, 385–7.

2 *Grundsätze der höheren Kriegs-Kunst für die Generäle der österreichischen Armee* (Vienna, 1806). The archduke's strategic and tactical theories are discussed by Lee W. Eysturlid, *The Formative Influences, Theories, and Campaigns of Archduke Carl of Austria* (Westport, Conn., 2000), 39–65.

3 Carl Erzherzog von Oesterreich, *Ausgewählte Schriften* (ed. Franz X. Malcher, 6 vols. Vienna, 1893–4), 6, 356.

4 Helmut Hertenberger and Franz Wiltschek, *Erzherzog Karl. Der Sieger von Aspern* (Vienna, 1983), 187–8.

5 Carl, 'Denkschrift über die militärischen-politischen Verhältnisse in Oesterreich von 1801–1809' in *Ausgewählte Schriften,* 6, 356–7.

6 Hans Delbrück, 'Erzherzog Carl' in *Erinnerungen, Aufsätze, und Reden* (Berlin, 1902), 605.

7 Karl, *Ausgewählte Schriften*, 5, 153.

8 Ibid., 357.

9 *Dienst-Reglement für die kaiserlich-königliche Infanterie* (2 parts. Vienna, 1807–8), I, 1–2, and 2, para. 5.

10 Ibid., 19–21.

11 For more detail on the following sections see Gunther E. Rothenberg, *The Art of Warfare in the Age of Napoleon* (London, 1978), 126–56.

12 Henry Lachouque, *Napoleon's Battles. A History of His Campaigns* (London, 1966), 223–6.

13 By far the best book on the Rheinbund troops in 1809 is John H. Gill, *With Eagles to Glory: Napoleon and his German Allies in the 1809 Campaign* (London, 1992).

14 The problem is ably discussed in Robert M. Epstein's operational study, *Napoleon's Last Victory and the Emergence of Modern War* (Lawrence, 1994), 40–41.

15 Col. H. Hess, 'Gedrängte Darstellung des Feldzuges in Bayern,' KA, FA 1809, Hauptarmee, F 13 402.

16 Lachouque, 224.

17 See for example David Chandler's comprehensive *The Campaigns of Napoleon* (New York, 1966), 673–80.

CHAPTER 3

1 KA, *Krieg 1809*, 1, 222.

2 Col. H. Hess, 'Gedrängte Darstellung des Feldzuges in Bayern,' KA, FA 1809, Hauptarmee, F 13–402.

3 Eysturlid, 90–92.

4 *La Correspondance de Napoleon Ier* (32 vols. Paris, 1858–70), 18, Nr. 15087.

5 F. Loraine Petre, *Napoleon and the Archduke Charles: A history of the Franco-Austrian Campaign in the Valley of the Danube in 1809* (London, 1909), 29.

6 Epstein, 62–3.

7 Lachouque, 245.

8 Ibid., 248–9.

9 KA, *Krieg 1809*, 1, 578, 581–2.

10 The letter in its entirety printed in Edouard Gachot, *1809. Napoleon en Allemagne* (Paris, 1913), Appendix J, 429.

11 Rothenberg, *Napoleon's Great Adversaries*, 177.

12 A detailed account of this engagement in Rudolf W. Litschel, *Das Gefecht bei Ebelsberg am 3. Mai 1809* (Vienna, 1968).

13 KA, Kartensammlung Inland Envelope C-1.

14 O'Reilly's report on the capitulation, 13 May 1809, KA FA, Hauptarmee, F 5, 264.

15 L. F. Lejeune, *Souvenirs d'un officier sous l'Empire* (3 vols. Paris, n.d.), 1, 300–301.

16 Eduard Wertheimer, 'Zur Geschichte Wiens im Jahre 1809,' *Archiv für österreichische Geschichte*, 74 (1889), 164–94.

17 *Correspondance*, 18, 15431 of 24 June 1809.

18 KA, Krieg 1809, 1, 596–8.

19 Criste, 3, 108.

CHAPTER 4

1 Excerpts and commentary of these instructions in Robert M. Epstein, *Prince Eugène at War* (Arlington, Texas, 1984), 20–29.

2 Epstein, ibid., 35–8.

3 André du Casse ed., *Mémoires et Correspondence Politique et Militaire du Prince Eugène* (10 vols. Paris, 1858–60), 4, 397. Hereafter cited as DCC.

4 Frederick C. Schneid, *Napoleon's Italian Campaigns 1805–1815* (Westport, Conn., 2002), 66–7.

5 DCC, 4, 440–41.

6 Ibid., 5, 134–6.

7 Ibid., 157–60.

8 Epstein, *Prince Eugène*, 77–99, provides a most detailed account of the Battle on the Piave.

9 Extensive details in KA, *Krieg 1809*, 2, 474–6.

10 Orders of 6 June 1809 in Napoleon I, *Correspondance*, 19, 76–8.

11 Ibid., 28 June 1809, 186–7.

12 Charles J. Esdaile, *The Wars of Napoleon* (London–New York, 1995), 135.

13 Gill, 321–84 provides orders of battle and tactical details of the revolts.

14 Marcus Junkelmann, *Napoleon und Bayern* (Regensburg, 1985), 264–8.

15 Carl von Clausewitz, *On War* (ed. and transl. by M. Howard and P. Paret, Princeton, 1976), 424.

16 Gill, 411–64 provides an excellent detailed account of these small matters.

17 KA, Memoires III/135, 'Feldzug in Dalmatien 1809'.

18 Adolf von Horsetzky, *Kriegsgeschichtliche Ubersicht von den wichtigsten Feldzüge in Europa seit 1792* (Vienna, 1905), 216–20, provides a short view of this confusing campaign.

CHAPTER 5

1 Ministre de la Guerre, *Correspondance militare de Napoleon I* (Paris, 1895), 6.

2 Rothenberg, *Napoleon's Great Adversaries,* 188.

3 The memorandum in KA, FA Hauptarmee F, 13–17.

4 Sources vary on the exact numbers available to Charles but a most detailed summary of various sources is provided by Harold T. Parker, *Three Napoleonic Battles* (Durham, 1983), 48–9.

5 Arthur J. Butler trans., *The Memoirs of Baron de Marbot* (London, 1894) 332–3.

6 *Correspondance,* 15189.

7 James R. Arnold, *Napoleon Conquers Austria: The 1809 Campaign for Vienna* (Westport, Conn., 1995), 46–8.

8 The description derived from Manfried Rauchensteiner, *Die Schlacht von Aspern am 21. Und 22. Mai 1809* (No. 11 of Militärhistorische Schriftenreihe, Vienna), 1969, 4–5.

9 See the very critical observations by A. Menge, *Die Schlacht von Aspern am 21. und 22. Mai 1809* (Berlin, 1900), 160–64.

10 Gill, 228–32.

11 The incident is told in detail by Marbot, 337–40.

12 General A.J.M.R. Savary, *Memoirs of the Duke of Rovigo* (3 vols. London, 1828) 2, 84.

13 Criste, 3, 143–44.

14 Ministry of War, *Correspondance militaire, 191.*

15 Manfried Rauchensteiner ed., 'Das sechste österreichische Armeekorps im Kriege gegen Frankreich 1809' *Mitteilungen des österreichischen Staatsarchivs,* 15–16 (1964–65), 187.

16 E. Buat, *De Ratisbonne à Znaim. Vol. 2 D'Essling à Wagram et à Znaim* (Paris, 1909); Hertenberger and Wiltschek, 253.

17 Rauchensteiner, 'Das sechste österreichische Armeekorps', 187–8.

CHAPTER 6

1 Manfried Rauchensteiner, *Dynastie und Heerwesen in Oesterreich 1796–1809* (Vienna, 1972), 100.

2 Jules A. Paulin, *Les Souvenirs du Général Bon Paulin* (Paris, 1895), 193.

3 Buat, 2, 121–2.

4 Arnold, 117.

5 A detailed description of the transport and emplacement of the Lobau and adjoining islands is given in Buat, 2, 129–33.

6 Ministre de la Guerre, *Correspondance Militaire, 194–96.*

7 See ibid., 254–55 and, one week later, on 28 June, Napoleon,*Correspondance,* 15453.

8 As often the exact number is disputed. Chandler, 709, gives Napoleon 160,000 with more on the way and no fewer than 500 guns, Petre also says 180,000 and 554 guns, while General Sir James Marshall-Cornwall, *Napoleon as a Military Commander* (London, 1967), says 175,000. What is not in dispute is that Napoleon disposed of a substantial numerical advantage.

9 Both letters in Criste, 3, 163–4, 176.

10 Rothenberg, *Napoleon's Great Adversary,* 207.

11 KA, FA 1809 Hauptarmee 13/28.

12 Christian v. Binder-Kriegelstein, *Der Krieg Napoleons gegen Oesterreich 1809* (2 vols. Berlin, 1906), 1, 293.

13 KA, FA 1809, Hauptarmee, F 7 103/1.

14 KA, FA 1809, Hauptarmee, F 7–98 1/3.

CHAPTER 7

1 *Correspondance,* 19, 217.

2 Manfried Rauchensteiner, *Die Schlacht bei Deutsch Wagram am 5 und 6 Juli 1809,* No. 36 of *Militärhistorische Schriftenreihe* (Vienna, 1977), 9, 17.

3 For the Italians at Deutsch Wagram see Frederick C. Schneid, *Napoleon's Italian Campaigns,* 94–6.

4 The best and most up-to-date treatment on Bernadotte and the Saxons during the night of 5/6 July 1809 is John H. Gill, *With Eagles to Glory.* 299–302.

5 Jean Thiry, *Wagram* (Paris, 1966), 175.

CHAPTER 8

1 Hertenberger and Wiltschek, 271–2.

2 KA, FA Hauptarmee 1809, Operationsjournal.

3 Rauchensteiner, *Wagram*, 23–5.

4 Général Lejeune, *De Valmy à Wagram* (Paris, 1896), 387.

5 Arnold, 147, places this incident later in the morning.

6 Marbot, 386–7.

7 Vividly described in Arnold, 143–5.

8 KA, FA 1809, Hauptarmee, VI Corps Operations journal.

9 The shortcomings of the Austrian battle command system are discussed in Rauchensteiner, *Wagram*, 25–6.

10 Schneid, 96–7.

11 Anon. 'La Grande batterie de la Garde à Wagram,' *Revue d'Artillerie* (1895), 437–48.

12 Henri Lachouque and Ann Brown, *Anatomy of Glory* (London, 1971), 163.

13 Friedrich A. Heller v. Hellwald, *Der k.k.österreichische Feldmarshall Graf Radetzky* (Stuttgart-Augsburg, 1858), 203.

14 Jacques Etienne Jospeh Alexandre Macdonald, *Souvenirs* (Paris, 1892), 160.

15 'Disposition zum Rückzug', 2.30 p.m. 6, July, KA, FA 1809 VI Corps, 7/76.

16 Schneid, 135.

17 Chef de battalion Bernard, cited in ibid., 98.

18 John R. Elting, *Swords around a Throne: Napoleons Grande Armée* (New York, 1988), 154.

19 Lejeune, 394.

CHAPTER 9

1 Quoted in Louis Madelin, *Histoire du consulat et de l' Empire* (Vol. 8, Paris, 1945), 238.

2 Max R. v. Hoen, *Wagram* , Vol 8 of *Das Kriegsjahr 1809 in Einzeldarstellungen* (Vienna–Leipzig, 1909), 79.

3 Arnold, 173–4.

4 Ibid., 98–105.

5 Petre, 377–8; Buat, 278–9.

6 Cited in Arnold, 173.

7 Etienne Macdonald, *Marshal Macdonald's Recollections* (London, 1892), 346.

8 Gill, 306–9.

9 Ibid., 114–16.

10 Criste, 3, 276–7; KA, FA 1809, Hauptarmee F 7 153.

11 John L. Pimlott, 'Marmont: Friendship's Choice', in David G. Chandler, *Napoleon's Marshals* (New York, 1987), 260.

12 Hertenberg and Wiltschek, 286–9.

13 Cited in Rothenberg, *Napoleon's Great Adversary*, 216.

14 J. F. C. Fuller, *Decisive Battles* (New York, 1940), 642.

15 H.v. Zwiedeneck-Südenhorst, *Erzherzog Johann von Oesterreich im Feldzug von 1809* (Graz, 1892), 148–49.

16 Cited in Rothenberg, *Napoleon's Great Adversary*, 215–16.

17 KA, FA 1809, II AK VII–3.

18 Epstein, *Napoleon's Last Victory*, 176–7 and passim.

19 H. Rössler, *Oesterreich's Kampf um Deutschlands Befreiung* (Hamburg, 1940), 71–73.

20 Criste, 3, 502–7.

21 Bathurst to Canning, PRO London, Foreign Office, 7 50 and 7 80.

22 P. Boppe, *La Croatie Militaire 1809–1813* (Paris, 1900), passim.

Index